International Dimensions
of the Western Sahara Conflict

International Dimensions
of the Western Sahara Conflict

Edited by
Yahia H. Zoubir
and Daniel Volman

Foreword by Mervyn M. Dymally

Westport, Connecticut
London

Library of Congress Cataloging-in-Publication Data

International dimensions of the Western Sahara conflict / edited by
    Yahia H. Zoubir and Daniel Volman ; foreword by Mervyn M. Dymally.
        p.   cm.
    Includes bibliographical references and index.
    ISBN 0-275-93821-2 (alk. paper)
    1. Western Sahara—International status.   2. Western Sahara—
Foreign relations.   3. International relations.   4. Western Sahara—
History—1975-   I. Zoubir, Yahia H.   II. Volman, Daniel.
JX4084.S7I35   1993
341.2'9'09648—dc20   90-23212

British Library Cataloguing in Publication Data is available.

Library of Congress Catalog Card Number: 90-23212
ISBN: 0-275-93821-2

First published in 1993

Praeger Publishers, 88 Post Road West, Westport, CT 06881
An imprint of Greenwood Publishing Group, Inc.

Printed in the United States of America

The paper used in this book complies with the
Permanent Paper Standard issued by the National
Information Standards Organization (Z39.48-1984).

10 9 8 7 6 5 4 3 2 1

To my father and in Memory of my dear mother

Y.H.Z.

To all People with AIDS and in Memory of
John Herlin

D.H.V.

Contents

Foreword

Representative Mervyn M. Dymally

As Chairman of the House Foreign Affairs Subcommittee on Africa, I am heartened by the scholarly endeavors contained in the *International Dimensions of the Western Sahara Conflict*, edited by Daniel Volman and Yahia H. Zoubir. I have attempted during my tenure on the subcommittee to heighten public awareness of this problem by sponsoring legislation on the Western Sahara, holding hearings, and generating joint letters from Members of Congress to U.S. and United Nations officials.

The Polisario Front has been fighting against Morocco for the independence of the Western Sahara since 1975. For over ninety years, the Western Sahara was a Spanish colony. When the Spanish were driven out, the Moroccans crossed the border and occupied the territory which was formerly the Spanish Sahara.

Despite the United Nations' adopting a peace plan calling for a free and fair referendum of self-determination in the Western Sahara on April 19, 1991, resulting in a cease-fire currently in effect, the referendum of self-determination for the Western Sahara is in jeopardy. The Polisario Front continues its protracted battle on behalf of the Sahrawi people in the face of huge obstacles.

Many Americans have never heard of the Sahrawi people, African Arabs who speak Spanish and have survived over sixteen years of exile in the Algerian desert and throughout Europe. They are struggling for the right to vote on their future, as to whether they will have their own country or be a part of Morocco. The international community, through the United Nations, has granted them the right to choose, but whether or not they are able to exercise that right depends on the support they are able to amass throughout the world.

The contributors and editors of this text provide an excellent opportunity to educate readers about a complicated and compelling subject--the century-old struggle of the Sahrawi people to determine their destiny. Having travelled both to Morocco and to the refugee camps in Tindouf, Algeria, I have become deeply involved in attempting to remedy this dispute. Hopefully, through studying this subject thoroughly, the leaders of the future will gain more insights into how best to end this seemingly endless conflict.

I congratulate all those who collaborated on this very worthwhile effort.

Acknowledgments

This book grew out of the Conference on the Superpowers in North Africa that was held at The American University in Washington, D.C., on March 4 - 5, 1988. We would like to express our thanks to the Kennedy Political Union, the Washington College of Law, and the Washington Semester and Capitals of the World Programs of The American University for sponsoring the conference.

Yahia H. Zoubir would like to thank his students for their help during the conference, especially Tracy Rhodes, Christiana Birkeland, Kamel Husseini, Beth Payne, Fadi Mudares, and Nizar Ayoobi. Their help and dedication were most valuable. He would like to express his thanks to Dr. David C. Brown, dean of the Washington Semester Program, Dr. Samih Farsoun of the Department of Sociology, and Dr. Shaik Ismail, director of study abroad, for their constant support and encouragement. He is grateful to the scholars, diplomats, and journalists who participated in the conference, particularly his colleagues Nicholas Onuf, Fantu Cheru, Gary Weaver, and F. Jackson Piotrow of the School of International Service for chairing the panels. He would also like to acknowledge his eternal gratitude to Gert H. Müeller and Steven I. Levine, two great scholars, for their impact on his academic career. And he would like to thank his friends Abdelkader Zerougui and Salem.

Special thanks are due to Alicia S. Merritt. Major Carlos Wilson's participation in the conference and inspirational support for the book deserve special acknowledgment. And last, but certainly not least, both editors are indebted to Dr. Robert A. Mortimer, whose contribution, advice, and encouragement are inestimable.

Professor Zoubir would like to acknowledge that neither the

conference nor the book would have been possible without the loving support and sacrifice of his wife, Cynthia, and his children, Nadia and Jamel, who tolerated his interminable hours. Without their understanding and patience, this book would never have seen the light of day.

Daniel Volman would like to acknowledge the constant love and encouragement of his parents, David and Ruth. Their support has sustained him in everything he has done. He would also like to express his appreciation to Michael Klare for his affection and counsel.

Introduction

The war in the Western Sahara is now completing its seventeenth year. Although progress toward peace has been made since August 1988, when Morocco and the Polisario Front agreed to the United Nations (UN) peace plan for the territory, concrete steps to a final resolution have not yet been taken. This has had serious political, social, economic, and military consequences for the countries in the region. And even though the end of the Cold War has made it easier to resolve regional conflicts in Afghanistan, Namibia, and Central America, neither the United States nor Russia has had any effective impact on a resolution of the conflict in the Western Sahara.

Despite the significance of the issue, very few scholarly works have dealt with the regional and international dimensions of the conflict. In particular, little attention has been paid to the role of the superpowers and of the UN in the region and other related issues that are the focus of this book.

Thus, the Western Sahara conflict has raised serious questions about the role of international law and of the UN in achieving the decolonization of former colonial territories and resolving regional conflicts. As Beth A. Payne, an international lawyer, demonstrates convincingly in her chapter, the occupation of the Western Sahara by Morocco is in clear violation of UN resolutions on decolonization and on the right to self-determination. She also shows that Morocco's actions are a violation of international legal principles that were upheld in the 1975 ruling by the International Court of Justice (World Court) on Morocco's territorial claims over the Spanish Sahara. Furthermore, she argues that by providing military equipment for Moroccan troops in the

Western Sahara, the United States not only violates its own domestic laws, but it also fails to abide by its obligations under international law and relevant UN resolutions.

Anthony G. Pazzanita, also an expert in international law, corroborates Payne's analysis in his work on the decolonization of the Western Sahara. His study describes in detail the UN proposal for a referendum for self-determination that would decide the future of the territory and its inhabitants, which has been the subject of intensive action by UN Secretary-General Javier Pérez de Cuéllar over the past two years. He also discusses the obstacles to the implementation of the UN proposal.

Another important issue relates to the role outside powers have played in the conflict. As demonstrated by a number of contributors, the United States, the Soviet Union, Spain, and France have been deeply involved in the conflict, either directly or indirectly.

Phillip C. Naylor's study offers a historical analysis of Spain's and France's objectives in the region and of how their national interests were affected by developments within the region. Naylor also highlights Spain's continuing responsibility as the former colonial power and France's impact in the area as a major economic and military power.

Two contributors have provided their perspectives on U.S. objectives in the region and how these have determined America's position on the conflict. Richard B. Parker, former U.S. ambassador to Algeria and Morocco and an eminent expert on the region, argues that the United States has historically been overcommitted to Morocco at the expense of its important economic relations with Algeria. He perceives that there has been a noticeable change in policy toward Algeria in recent years, but he also argues that this more even-handed policy has not given the United States greater leverage in resolving the conflict.

Stephen Zunes, a leading academic expert on U.S. foreign policy, takes a more critical view of U.S. involvement in the region. In his view, U.S. policy toward the war in the Western Sahara has been determined less by the United States' regional interests than by Morocco's strategic role as an American proxy. Therefore, the United States has given its tacit military backing to King Hassan of Morocco as a trade-off for Morocco's actions on behalf of Western interests in Africa and the Middle East.

Unlike the United States' pronounced tilt in favor of Morocco in the conflict, Yahia H. Zoubir, an academic specialist on Soviet policy in the Maghreb (the area usually defined as Algeria, Morocco,

Mauritania, and Tunisia; Libya is also sometimes considered to be part of the Maghreb), argues that the Soviet Union has kept a surprisingly consistent neutrality in the conflict. Because of its multifaceted interests in both Morocco and Algeria, and despite its relatively close political and military relationship with the latter, Moscow has found it more expedient to avoid taking any actions that would antagonize either country. Hence, the Soviet Union has persistently supported a peaceful resolution of the conflict under the auspices of the United Nations.

In his chapter, Daniel Volman, an expert on African military affairs, gives a detailed analysis of the impact of military assistance provided by the United States, the Soviet Union, and France to Morocco and Algeria. He demonstrates that this foreign military assistance has prolonged the war and increased its destructiveness, thus creating a military stalemate. At the same time, however, Volman suggests that neither of the two superpowers has found it in its interests to elevate the conflict to a direct East-West confrontation.

According to Robert A. Mortimer, a leading expert in North African studies, just as the superpowers have recognized the limits of their ability to control the course of the conflict, Maghrebi states have shown an ability to define and promote their own national interests within a regional context, thus reducing outside interference.   The Maghrebi states have also sought to solve regional problems through a process of integration.   The failure of previous attempts to unite politically and ideologically has led to a new pragmatic emphasis on regional economic integration.

Taken together, the work of these scholars, diplomats, and experts in international law contributes significantly to our understanding of the role of outside powers in the origins and evolution of the war in the Western Sahara. Their work also casts new light on the efforts of the Maghrebi states to overcome regional divisions by themselves and on the continuing attempts by the United Nations to resolve the conflict in the Western Sahara and restore respect for international law.

International Dimensions
of the Western Sahara Conflict

1

Origins and Development of the Conflict in the Western Sahara

Yahia H. Zoubir

For more than seventeen years a war has been raging for control over the Western Sahara, a mineral-rich territory on the Atlantic coast of northwest Africa bordered by Morocco, Algeria, and Mauritania. This conflict has its origins in the transfer of sovereignty over the land from Spanish colonial rule.[1]

From the mid-1960s onward, the United Nations urged Spain to hold a referendum on self-determination in the territory known as the Spanish Sahara, which it had been occupying since 1884. In fact, two UN resolutions passed in 1972 and 1973 clearly affirmed the rights of the people of the Spanish Sahara (the Sahrawis) to be independent.[2] Within the Spanish Sahara, Sahrawi nationalists created an anticolonial organization, the Frente Popular para la Liberación de Saguia el-Hamra y Río do Oro--Polisario Front--in May 1973, which began guerrilla attacks on Spanish garrisons. As a result of growing international pressure, along with effective Polisario military assaults, Spain finally agreed to hold a referendum on self-determination for the Spanish Sahara under UN auspices in early 1975.

But the Sahrawi nationalists were not alone in desiring control over the Spanish Sahara. In December 1974, Morocco convinced Spain, through the United Nations, to delay holding such a referendum until after the International Court of Justice (ICJ) rendered its opinion on Morocco's historic claims to the territory. King Hassan II asserted that the Spanish Sahara had historically been part of "Greater Morocco," a territory that includes portions of southwest Algeria, all of Mauritania, and parts of Mali and Senegal.

In October 1975, the ICJ ruled that the referendum should proceed, because it found no

> indications of the existence, at the relevant period [i.e., before colonization by Spain], of any legal tie of territorial sovereignty between Western Sahara and the Moroccan state. At the same time, they [the Judges] are in accord in providing indications of a legal tie of allegiance between the Sultan and some, though only some, of the tribes of the territory, and in providing indications of some display of the Sultan's authority or influence with respect to those tribes.[3]

Nonetheless, King Hassan interpreted this ruling as an affirmation of Morocco's own claims.

Despite the ICJ's ruling, Spain did not fulfill its promise to hold the referendum because of its internal political weakness (due to the transition period following General Francisco Franco's fatal illness) and its fear of a confrontation with Morocco at a time of domestic instability. Furthermore, due to its globalist concerns, the United States also put pressure on Spain to compromise with Morocco. The United States was anxious that another state not be added to the list of socialist countries aligned with the USSR. Specifically, Secretary of State Henry Kissinger declared that "the United States will not allow another Angola on the east flank of the Atlantic Ocean."[4] Therefore, in view of the increasing Moroccan pressures on Spain, especially following the November 1975 Green March, when 350,000 Moroccan civilians followed Moroccan troops into the Western Sahara, the Spanish government ceded the territory to Morocco and Mauritania on February 26, 1976, under the terms of the Madrid Accords.[5]

The occupation of the Western Sahara by Moroccan and Mauritanian troops in November 1975 not only created tension in the region but complicated the prospects of a peaceful settlement.[6] Polisario shifted its guerrilla war to Moroccan and Mauritanian occupying forces. The day after Spain formally withdrew from the Western Sahara on February 26, 1976, the Polisario Front proclaimed the Western Sahara an independent state, known as the Sahrawi Arab Democratic Republic (SADR). The Algerian recognition of the new state on March 6, 1976, led the Kingdom of Morocco to break off diplomatic relations with its eastern neighbor the following day. After the Spanish army and administration began to withdraw in November 1975, Moroccan and Mauritanian troops started their occupation of the territory. Moroccan bombardments of the refugee camps set up outside the major Sahrawi cities, created a new wave of forced migration. Thousands of Sahrawi refugees now found refuge in the southwestern part of Algeria, where camps were set up and administered by Polisario. Moreover, persistent Algerian support for Polisario--motivated by Algeria's traditional commitment to movements of national liberation, but also by concern about the regional consequences of Morocco's expansionism--led to Moroccan threats of "hot pursuit" against Sahrawis living in Tindouf, Algeria, in retaliation for Polisario attacks against Moroccan positions in the Western Sahara. A direct military confrontation between Algeria (Polisario's main supporter) and Morocco seemed imminent. But, although a few isolated border clashes erupted between Algerian and Moroccan troops, they never resulted in an all-out war. Nonetheless, a diplomatic war began between the two countries that has only recently cooled; diplomatic ties were reestablished in May 1988, but the Western Sahara situation remains a sensitive issue.

Encouraged by French and U.S. military assistance, Morocco proceeded to consolidate its position in the occupied territory. In order to strengthen the occupation it began in 1975, Morocco started to make considerable investments,[7] to encourage its citizens to settle in the Western Sahara, and to almost double the size of its armed forces.

Convinced of Morocco's claims to the territory, King Hassan viewed Sahrawi nationalists as Moroccan secessionists sponsored by the Algerian government. Hence, he refused to accept the question of the Western Sahara as a decolonization issue or to agree to direct talks with Polisario.

Despite their numerical superiority, Moroccan troops suffered serious military defeats. Therefore, in 1981, Morocco began to build costly but effective defensive walls that were relatively difficult for Polisario to penetrate. Six walls, or berms, surround the major Moroccan-held settlements in the occupied territory. The berms constitute a highly fortified defensive system with a double barrier of sand and stone bunkers where artillery and infantry units are sheltered. The system is protected by mines and electronic devices provided by Western companies. Undoubtedly, these walls have strengthened Morocco's military position in the Western Sahara. Nevertheless, diplomatically and politically, the Kingdom of Morocco became increasingly isolated. This is probably why the king eventually accepted the principle of holding a "confirmatory" referendum in the Western Sahara. It appears, however, that he never contemplated the possibility of an independent Sahrawi state, and he was slow to make any concrete move to carry out his promise to hold such a referendum. He also vehemently refused (until December 1988) to have any talks with Polisario, claiming that the conflict was between his kingdom and Algeria.

MOROCCAN DOMESTIC POLITICS

The question of the Western Sahara was elevated to a national debate in Morocco when internal problems had reached a dangerous threshold. Two failed military coups were orchestrated against the monarchy in 1971 and 1972, which led to tenuous relations between the military and the royal palace. The suspension of Parliament, the absence of elections, and the repression of opposition parties and other mass organizations (students, unions, etc.) created an unstable political situation. The king skillfully used the Sahara issue as a way out of the political crisis by making it a test of patriotism and of "national" resolve. The opposition parties had no choice but to rally around the palace on what was now defined as a national question. In fact, Moroccan parties across the political spectrum supported the king on the occupation of the Western Sahara.

The king also hoped that the kingdom's economic problems could be alleviated as a result of the sharp rise in phosphate prices in 1974. Moroccans believed that the integration of the Western Sahara, a territory extremely rich in phosphates and other minerals, would bring Morocco considerably more income. However, Moroccan expectations never materialized; the prices of phosphates fell sharply in 1975-76 and again in 1981-82.[8] One way to alleviate such a problem was to borrow money in the international financial market. The obvious result was an increasingly higher foreign debt. The war with the Polisario absorbed most of the country's financial resources. The financial assistance coming from the United States, France, and the conservative Arab states did little to solve the kingdom's financial difficulties. Austerity programs were greatly resented by the population, leading to serious food riots in 1981 and 1984 in which hundreds were killed by the Moroccan army.

The cost of the war, coupled with the high expenditures on settlement colonization in the Western Sahara (material incentives for settlers, civilian construction, and new administrative organizations) added much to the country's economic problems.[9] By 1984, the military and construction efforts of the fortification walls in the Western

Sahara cost Morocco approximately 40 percent to 50 percent of the national budget.[10] War spending has been estimated at one billion dollars a year.[11] The construction of the defensive walls alone, which were finished in 1987, cost about $2 million per day.[12] The number of Moroccan troops in the Western Sahara continually increased, reaching about 150,000 in 1988.[13]

The burden of the war fell mainly upon the Moroccan population. In order to comply with measures advocated by the World Bank and the International Monetary Fund (IMF), the king attempted to reduce the cost of food subsidies (flour, sugar, cooking oil, etc.). Each time such policies were carried out food riots took place.[14] Morocco's inclusion in the 1985 Baker Plan[15] did little to improve the economic situation. Neither the increased liberalization of the economy nor the rescheduling of the enormous debt have produced tangible results yet. Moreover, despite all these sacrifices, Morocco was unable to win the war militarily, nor was it able to win it diplomatically.

ALGERIAN-MOROCCAN BILATERAL RELATIONS

Algerian leaders, on the other hand, insisted that they had no territorial claims over the Western Sahara, nor did they have any conflict with Morocco. They defined their legal position as one of a "concerned" (or "interested") party. In reality, Algeria's position was largely determined by its geopolitical fear of Morocco's traditional covetousness for parts of its territory, as illustrated by the Fall 1963 border war when Moroccan troops occupied southwestern portions of Algerian territory. Although it only lasted for a few months and Moroccan forces withdrew from the zones they claimed, the conflict aggravated the animosity between the Moroccan monarchy and the revolutionary regime in Algeria.

Despite the absence of diplomatic relations and the continued tension that had existed between them, Algeria and the Kingdom of Morocco never ceased to communicate either directly, albeit secretly, or through intermediaries. Twice, in 1983 and 1987, Algeria's President Chadli Bendjedid and King Hassan met publicly. However, these two meetings did not produce tangible results because both sides maintained their respective positions. The king insisted on Moroccan sovereignty over the Western Sahara, while Algeria defended the notion of a referendum for self-determination, based on Organization of African Unity (OAU) and UN resolutions, and advocated direct negotiations between Morocco and Polisario. Apparently, the king even refused to accept Algeria's 1985 proposition to grant the Western Sahara internal autonomy as an alternative to the full independence demanded by the Polisario.[16]

Although discussions have often taken place between Polisario and Moroccan officials through UN and OAU officials (e.g., in Bamako in 1978, in Algiers in 1983, in Lisbon in 1985, and in New York in 1986), Moroccans have continued to oppose the UN resolution passed in December 1985, which emphasized the necessity of direct negotiations between Polisario and the Kingdom of Morocco. The January 1989 meeting, as discussed below, was the only public reconsideration of this policy.

MOROCCO AND MAGHREBI UNITY

In the mid-1980s, the Maghrebi states (Algeria, Morocco, Mauritania, Tunisia, and Libya) attempted to resolve their bilateral problems as well as the conflict in the Western Sahara through a process of integration. In Fall 1986, Algeria in particular, continued to lay the foundations of the Greater Maghreb. High-level official visits between Tripoli, Libya, Tunis, Tunisia, and Algiers, Algeria became more frequent. One of their objectives was to help improve diplomatic relations between Tunisia and Libya. Algeria blamed Morocco for being an impediment to faster Maghrebi integration because of its policy concerning the Western Sahara.[17]

In late 1986 and Spring 1987, Morocco was busy finishing the last defensive wall. The expansion and completion on April 16, 1987, of the sixth wall troubled Algeria, because it came so close to Mauritania's border, suggesting expansionist motives.[18] Preoccupied with tension between Morocco and Algeria, coupled with events in the Near East and the Persian Gulf, King Fahd of Saudi Arabia arranged for a second meeting between Bendjedid and Hassan. The meeting took place in the presence of King Fahd on May 4, 1987, in the Algerian-Moroccan border town Akid Lotfi.[19] Although the meeting eased tension between the two countries, both sides remained apart as far as conflict in the Western Sahara was concerned. Nonetheless, because of the king's interest in emerging from his diplomatic isolation and integrating his kingdom into the Greater Maghreb, diplomatic probes continued throughout the year. Saudi influence was instrumental in persuading

Hassan to seek a negotiated settlement of the conflict. There was increasing evidence that the Saudis would use their financial leverage to bring the king around to their point of view.[20]

In 1987, the theme of Maghreb unity dominated relations in the region. In the summer, Algerian relations with Libya progressed at a rapid pace. Moreover, under Algeria's pressure, the Libyan regime made giant steps in solving all contentious issues with Tunisia.[21] The Libyans were also more forthcoming in resolving their problems with Chad in order to improve their image at the OAU. High-level meetings between Moroccans and Algerians continued despite the failure of the Akid Lotfi meeting. The "locust crisis" in the region created the necessary climate for cooperation between the two countries.

Moroccan diplomacy, which had hitherto turned to Western Europe and the United States, began to readjust to the regional realities. The rejection of Morocco's daring application to the European Community (EC) in Summer 1987 reminded the king, and the other Maghrebi states, for that matter, of the difficult times the Maghreb would face in the 1990s with EC 1992.

One of the king's major concessions that summer was his statement that conflict in the Western Sahara was between Morocco and Polisario, not with Algeria, as he had hitherto claimed.[22] This recognition did indeed mark a departure from his earlier position that blamed Algeria for the war and defined the Sahrawis as "mercenaries" supported by the eastern neighbor.

The continuous dialogue, coupled with Algeria's desire to produce a successful Arab Summit scheduled for June 1988, led to the reestablishment of diplomatic relations between Algeria and Morocco on May 16, 1988.

THE WESTERN SAHARA CONFLICT SINCE THE RENEWAL OF DIPLOMATIC RELATIONS BETWEEN ALGERIA AND MOROCCO

Diplomatic relations between Algeria and Morocco were renewed on May 16, 1988. Opinions were divided as to what effect this would have on the conflict in the Western Sahara. Undoubtedly, Polisario leaders were initially nervous. Their attitude changed once they realized that renewed diplomatic relations between Algeria and Morocco might compel King Hassan to seek a political solution,[23] because one of the conditions set forth for the renewal of diplomatic ties was a political settlement in the Western Sahara. The joint Algerian-Moroccan communiqué stated the following:

> Eager to promote the success of international efforts undertaken to hasten the process of good offices for a just and definitive solution to the Western Sahara conflict through a free and regular referendum for self-determination held without any constraints whatsoever and with utmost sincerity . . . [the two countries] have decided to reestablish diplomatic relations.[24]

The new era of détente in the Maghreb received a positive reaction worldwide. In the United States, in particular, the reestablishment of ties between Algeria and Morocco was welcomed, in part because of a belief that such a rapprochement would doom the Sahrawi cause.[25] In Summer 1988, the conflict attracted much diplomatic attention. From July 12 to July 22 secret discussions were held in Taëf, Saudi Arabia, between Sahrawis and Moroccans. Even though the talks did not produce any concrete results they did create an atmosphere for continued dialogue.[26]

On August 11, 1988, UN Secretary-General Javier Pérez de Cuéllar proposed a peace plan to Morocco and the Polisario Front that offered, among other things, suggestions for a cease-fire and a referendum for self-determination. On August 30, the two parties accepted, albeit with reservations, the secretary-general's peace proposal.

Despite much optimism, the new commitment to peace did not mean the end of the war. On September 16, the Polisario Front launched a heavy offensive against the Royal Moroccan Armed Forces (FAR) in Oum Dreiga, inflicting serious losses, including that of an experienced army colonel.

In October the United Nations Fourth Committee (Committee on Decolonization) overwhelmingly passed a resolution that called for direct negotiations between Polisario and Morocco, with 87 affirmative votes, 53 abstentions, and no opposition.[27] Morocco, however, saw a contradiction between the call for direct negotiations and the secretary-general's efforts to mediate between the two parties.[28]

Meanwhile, there was increased pressure on Morocco from the international community to hold direct negotiations with Polisario in order to begin a cease-fire that would allow a referendum on self-determination. On November 20, 1988, the UN General Assembly voted overwhelmingly for a similar resolution on the need for direct negotiations 86 to 0, with 53 abstentions. Although Morocco's reluctance to negotiate directly with Polisario was as strong as ever, growing international pressure finally led to a change in policy. In December 1988, the king announced to the French press that he would agree to meet Sahrawi nationalists, including representatives of the Polisario Front.[29] Although the king insisted that his meetings with Polisario on January 4 and 5, 1989, would consist of "discussions," *not* "negotiations," the change in attitude was indeed a major breakthrough.

Despite Moroccan insistence that the meetings consisted of talks, the substance of the discussions could well be described as quasi-negotiations, because not only were the details of the referendum raised, but truce arrangements and the exchange of prisoners were also at the center of these talks.[30]

Although the full content of the talks has been kept secret, they inspired optimism, because many countries and observers believe that direct talks represent the best avenue for reaching an agreement concerning the conditions for holding a referendum. There is no evidence, however, that the Polisario agreed to autonomy under Moroccan sovereignty.[31]

Morocco's position, however, has remained ambiguous. One reporter, for example, stated that "the talks . . . focused on the situation prevailing in *our southern Saharan provinces* in the perspective of the referendum decided upon."[32] Undoubtedly, the opposition parties that have adopted an uncompromising position on the Western Sahara could not but be suspicious about the king's meetings with Polisario leaders. In a meeting with leaders of the main political parties, Hassan reassured them that Morocco "will not give up one inch of its territory."[33] He denied that he had met Sahrawi nationalists. Instead, he argued, "It is Moroccans who had gone astray that I met in the hope that they would be put back on the right path. Never were they received as members of so-called Polisario."[34] This statement contradicted his earlier declaration to the French magazine, *Le Point*, that he would receive Sahrawis as representatives of Polisario.[35]

In late January, Polisario announced that it would unilaterally cease all its military operations against Moroccan troops during the month of February, hoping that new meetings would take place as promised by King Hassan.[36]

King Hassan acknowledged, in an interview to *Le Nouvel Observateur*, that he should have met with Sahrawi nationalists much earlier. However, other statements in the same interview raised serious questions about his policy. First, Hassan insisted that the Western Sahara *is* a Moroccan territory. Second, he argued that the referendum would be bothersome even to Polisario (the implication being that Morocco would win it) and that he agreed to hold it only to avoid having Morocco put on the defensive and accused of expansionism. Third, Hassan admitted that he was convinced by some foreign leaders, particularly François Mitterrand, that "only the concerned populations could give the proof of their willingness to belong to Morocco." Fourth, he praised President Bendjedid for his genuine desire to find a way to "rid the region of this problem which is poison for Algeria, Morocco, and Mauritania." Finally, he promised the Sahrawi nationalists that "once they have reintegrated their homeland [i.e., Morocco], they would benefit, like the other Moroccan provinces, from the regionalization plan which has been envisaged."[37]

It is not yet clear why King Hassan did not renew talks with Polisario. Polisario eventually decided to end its unilateral cease-fire. In the meantime, a new regional association, the Arab Maghreb Union (UMA) was founded in mid-February without the SADR's participation.[38]

King Hassan has capitalized on renewed relations with Algeria and Maghrebi integration. He has apparently been able to repair his ties with the eastern neighbor without making substantial concessions on the Western Sahara. Moreover, in May 1989, Morocco ratified the 1972 Treaty of Ifrane, which delineates the borders with Algeria, ending a long dispute over the precise tracing of the frontier.

Although some observers suggested that Polisario had been sacrificed by Algeria for the sake of better relations with Morocco, the Algerian government continued to assert its support for Polisario.[39] Algeria also continued to press Morocco to resume direct negotiations with Polisario and, on September 1, 1989, King Hassan promised President Bendjedid that he would meet again with Polisario before his trip to Spain. But King Hassan changed his policy again on September 21, when he declared that there was no reason to meet with Polisario since "there is nothing to negotiate because the Western Sahara is Moroccan territory."[40] In response, Polisario fulfilled its promise to renew military operations unless direct negotiations with Morocco took place, and launched a major new offensive against Moroccan positions in the occupied territory on September 24. Algerian government approval for Polisario's decision to resume fighting was demonstrated by an October

2 editorial in the semi-official newspaper, *El-Moudjahid*, which stated that since "Morocco is not yet mature for peace . . . [it] still dreams of a 'Great Morocco' and has returned to an obsolete language [of calling Sahrawis Moroccans], Sahrawi leaders have consequently drawn the conclusion [that] one can no longer accommodate a regime . . . which only understands the language of force."[41]

Moroccan officials repeatedly denied that they had ever promised to resume direct negotiations with Polisario, but after the fighting began again they declared that the new offensive made it impossible for them to hold the "planned meeting."[42] Polisario continued its offensive, launching an attack on Guelta Zammour on October 7, an attack on the Hawza sector of the earthen wall on October 11, and an attack on the central Amgala sector of the wall on November 7, followed by another attack on the Amgala sector on November 16, all of which resulted in heavy human and material losses for the Moroccans. Although the attacks showed that Polisario remained a credible military force, on November 6, King Hassan praised the Royal Moroccan Armed Forces for their military successes.[43] In Algeria, the government's growing frustration with King Hassan's policy shifts resulted in public criticism of Morocco in the press and a reaffirmation of support for Polisario.[44] By Spring 1990, consequently, relations between Morocco and Algeria returned to the cooler conditions that had prevailed before the reestablishment of diplomatic relations in May 1988. Progress toward regional economic integration through the UMA had been brought to a halt.

The United Nations has shown greater interest than ever before in resolving what has become the last decolonization issue in Africa (after Namibia's independence in March 1990). In June 1990, UN Secretary-General Pérez de Cuéllar asked Polisario and the Moroccans to bring representatives of Sahrawi tribes from the occupied territory and the refugee camps in Algeria to Geneva in order to discuss with UN officials the options for organizing a referendum in the Western Sahara.[45] Despite some controversy regarding the legitimacy of the Sahrawi chieftains, the meeting did take place in Geneva that month.

In the summer of 1990, the firm commitment of the United Nations Security Council to accelerate the process of resolving the conflict in the Western Sahara revived hope. In June, the UN Security Council called upon the Polisario Front and the Kingdom of Morocco "to cooperate fully with the Secretary-General of the United Nations and the current Chairman of the Organization of African Unity in their efforts aimed at an early settlement of the question of the Western Sahara.[46] A UN technical team was scheduled to leave for the area in mid-July in order to determine the logistical needs for the organization of the referendum.[47]

A direct meeting between Polisario representatives and Moroccan officials was scheduled to take place in the presence of Pérez de Cuéllar. The secretary-general declared that "we shall see at the end of this meeting whether we can be more hopeful and if the political will is confirmed as to a lasting resolution of the conflict in the Western Sahara."[48] Despite this optimism, however, no direct talks were held, because Morocco refused to meet with Polisario. Instead, the secretary-general had to shuttle between the two delegations at the UN headquarters in Geneva.[49] In April 1991, the secretary-general's plan to organize a referendum in the Western Sahara over a nine-month period was approved by the UN General Assembly.[50]

Algeria expressed its disappointment with Morocco's refusal to hold direct talks. Less than two weeks before the UMA meeting scheduled in Algiers on July 22, 1990, the Algerian foreign minister, Sid Ahmed Ghozali, declared that "the potential for economic and political cooperation in the Greater Maghreb is extraordinary; however, there still remains one major problem; the conflict in Western Sahara."[51] The situation has been complicated by the process of political democratization in Algeria, but all Algerian parties and associations have extended their support to the Sahrawi cause.[52] Thus, Morocco's assertion that the Sahrawi issue was Algerian President Houari Boumedienne's creation has lost all credibility. Speculation that Algeria has abandoned support for Polisario and wants to strengthen its ties with Morocco is not supported with concrete evidence.[53] Regardless of circumstantial optimism, the situation remains unchanged.

Thus, neither the efforts of Morocco, nor of Algeria, nor of Polisario, nor of the UMA, nor of the United Nations have so far produced a definitive breakthrough in this long and costly conflict. As the following chapters demonstrate, the prolonged dispute over this little-known desert territory has had wide repercussions and diplomatic consequences for the Maghreb, for the foreign powers involved in the region, and for the regional and international organizations that have sought to resolve the conflict. Self-determination is always a controversial and contentious political process, and it is a process that has not yet run its course in the Western Sahara. Perhaps, the experience of the Gulf War in January and February 1991 will have positive repercussions on the stalemated situation in the Western Sahara. An implementation of UN resolutions will certainly lead to a final solution.

NOTES

1. For a detailed account and analysis of the historical background of the conflict, see Tony Hodges, *Western Sahara: The Roots of a Desert War* (Westport, Connecticut: Lawrence Hill, 1983); and John Damis, *Conflict in Northwest Africa: The Western Sahara Dispute* (Stanford, Calif.: Hoover Institution Press, 1983).

2. Tony Hodges, "The Origins of Sahrawi Nationalism," in Richard Lawless and Laila Monahan, eds., *War and Refugees: The Western Sahara Conflict* (London and New York: Pinter Publishers, 1987), 44.

3. International Court of Justice, *Western Sahara: Advisory Opinion of 16 October 1975* (The Hague: ICJ, 1975), 56-57.

4. Quoted in Leo Kamil, *Fueling the Fire: U.S. Policy and the Western Sahara Conflict* (Trenton, New Jersey: Red Sea Press, 1987), 44.

5. See Phillip Naylor, "Spain and France and the Decolonization of Western Sahara: Parity and Paradox, 1975-1987," *Africa Today* 34, no. 3 (Fall 1987): 7-16.

6. The numerous Polisario attacks on Mauritania had a serious impact on the country's domestic situation. This resulted in a military coup that overthrew President Mokhtar Ould Daddah in July 1978. Eventually, the country reached an agreement with Polisario on August 5, 1979, whereby Mauritania dropped all territorial claims over the Western Sahara. However, Morocco annexed the portion of the territory that Mauritania had hitherto occupied and administered.

7. See Moroccan political advertisements in *The New York Times*, October 18, 1989; *Time*, November 13, 1989 (international edition); and *Time*, December 4, 1989; see also *The New York Times*, November 2, 1988; *The Middle East*, September 1989; and *West Africa*, November 20-26, 1989.

8. *Middle East Economic Digest* (hereafter *MEED*) 29, March 1, 1985, 12. For a more detailed analysis of the economic situation, see Werner Ruf, "The Role of World Powers: Colonialist Transformations and King Hassan's Rule," in Lawless and Monahan, eds., *War and Refugees*, 75-81.

9. See Mark Tessler, *Explaining the "Surprises" of King Hassan II: The Linkage Between Domestic and Foreign Policy in Morocco, Part I: Tensions in North Africa in the Mid-1980s*, Universities Field Staff Reports, no. 38 (1986): 6.

10. Tessler, *Explaining, Part II: "The Arab-African Union Between Morocco and Libya*, Universities Field Staff Reports, no. 39 (1986): 2.

11. *The Economist*, July 4, 1987.

12. *In These Times*, April 20-26, 1988.

13. Ibid.; see also Toby Shelly, "Slow Steps Towards Peace," *West Africa*, September 12-18, 1988, 1668.

14. Remy Leveau, "Stabilité du Pouvoir Monarchique et Financement de la Dette," *Maghreb-Machrek*, no. 118 (October-December 1987): 6.

15. The Baker Plan called for austerity measures and economic reforms as outlined by major lending institutions (privatization, reduction of subsidies on foodstuffs, cuts in public spending, etc.).

16. See *MEED* 29, March 1, 1985, 42.

17. Speech of President Bendjedid, Algiers, December 16, 1986, reproduced in *Revue Algérienne des Relations Internationales* (Algiers), no. 5 (1st Quarter 1987): 172.

18. France also expressed her concern about this issue during President Mitterrand's visit to Morocco in April 1987. See *Jeune Afrique*, no. 1374, May 6, 1987, 17-18.

19. See *Jeune Afrique*, no. 1375, May 13, 1987; *Jeune Afrique*, no. 1376, May 20, 1987.

20. The Saudis until 1988 provided about one billion dollars a year to help the king wage his war against the Sahrawis. See David J. Dean, *The Air Force Role in Low Intensity Conflict* (Maxwell Air Force Base, Ala.: Air University Press, 1986), 40; and *The Guardian*, September 28, 1988.

21. Diplomatic relations between Tunisia and Libya, broken in 1985, were reestablished in December 1987.

22. *Financial Times*, July 14, 1987; *Jeune Afrique*, no. 1386, July 29, 1987.

23. *Africa News*, May 30, 1988; *The Guardian*, September 28, 1988.

24. *El Moudjahid*, May 17, 1988; *The New York Times*, May 17, 1988.

25. *Africa News*, May 30, 1988.

26. On the meeting see *Jeune Afrique*, no. 1452, November 2, 1988.

27. *The Middle East*, December 1988, 16.

28. *Maghreb Arab Press (MAP)*, Rabat, October 22, 1988, reprinted in *Arab Press Bulletin* 5, Issue 81, October 28, 1988.

29. *Le Point*, no. 847, December 12, 1988; see also *Le Monde*, December 25-26, 1988; *Le Monde*, December 27, 1988; *The New York Times*, December 28, 1988; *El-Moudjahid*, December 25, 1988.

30. Algiers Domestic Service in Arabic, January 4, 1989, reprinted in *Foreign Bulletin Information Service/Near East and South Asia* (hereafter FBIS/NES) 89-003, 18.

31. *The Washington Times*, January 13, 1989, for instance, reported one "source" as saying that "Polisario is talking about something that is not full integration into Morocco and not full independence."

32. *MAP* in English, January 6, 1989, reprinted in *FBIS/NES* 89-005, January 9, 1989, 26. (emphasis added).

33. *Agence France Press (AFP)*, January 16, 1989.

34. Ibid.; See also *Jeune Afrique*, no. 1464, January 25, 1989.

35. *Le Point*, no. 847, December 12, 1988.

36. *Algérie Press Service (APS)*, January 28, 1989.

37. *Le Nouvel Observateur*, January 12-18, 1989. The reference is to a program of regionalization modeled on the German federal states that Hassan has put forward on several occasions.

38. For details on this development, see Robert A. Mortimer, "Maghreb Matters," *Foreign Policy* 76 (Fall 1989): 160-75.

39. The secretary-general of the FLN, Abdelhamid Mehri, attended the Polisario Seventh Party Congress in April 1989. In his speech he reaffirmed Algeria's support for the movement. *AFP*, April 29, 1989.

40. *ABC* (Spain), September 24, 1989; *West Africa*, October 2-8, 1989, 1666.

41. *El-Moudjahid*, October 2, 1989. A week earlier, the Algerian foreign minister, Sid Ahmed Ghozali, stated that Algeria favored a negotiated settlement through a fair and regular referendum; see *El-Moudjahid*, September 27, 1989. He later declared that Algeria was still trying to arrange for a meeting between King Hassan and Polisario; see *APS*, October 2, 1989.

42. *Al Sharq al Awsat*, October 10, 1989; *Middle East International*, October 20, 1989, *The Middle East*, November 1989.

43. *MAP*, November 7, 1989; reprinted in *FBIS/NES*, November 16, 1989, 24.

44. See, for instance, *El-Moudjahid*, November 10, 1989; and *Algérie-Actualité*, November 30-December 6, 1989. In the latter, Morocco is stated to be using the UMA as a framework within which it hoped to induce Algeria to abandon the Sahrawi cause. The author of the article made it clear that this was a miscalculation on the part of the king.

45. *AFP*, June 5, 1990.

46. United Nations Security Council, Forty-Third Session, Official Records, Resolution 658 (XXXXIII), S/Res/658, 1990.

47. *Christian Sciencer Monitor*, July 3, 1990.

48. *APS* (Geneva), July 5, 1990.

49. *The Economist*, July 14, 1990, 41.

50. *The New York Times*, April 23, 1991.

51. *Al Sharq al Awsat* (Arabic), July 10, 1990.

52. *West Africa*, July 9-15, 1990, 2067.

53. For a detailed analysis of this issue, see Yahia Zoubir, "The Western Sahara Conflict: Regional and International Dimensions," *The Journal of Modern African Studies* 28, no. 2 (June 1990): 225-43.

2

Spain, France, and the Western Sahara: A Historical Narrative and Study of National Transformation

Phillip C. Naylor

INTRODUCTION

This article surveys the historical involvement of Spain and France in the Western Sahara (formerly the Spanish Sahara). It studies the "levels of events" that include not only a surface narrative, but also a description of how policies toward the Western Sahara relate to underlying discourses and transformations of national power and identity.[1]

For over a century, Spain and France have been closely connected to the history of the Western Sahara. While Madrid's intimate association is obvious, given its colonial administration of its Spanish Sahara, Paris, too, has been linked directly and indirectly to the territory, especially since the "scramble" for Africa. As shall be seen, neither country's involvement and interest ended with the Tripartite (Madrid) Accords of November 1975. Indeed, during the subsequent postcolonial period, their policies have disclosed continuities alongside discontinuities.

THE COLONIAL PERIOD

The Western Sahara received repeated attention during the Age of Exploration as the Portuguese and Spanish traded and raided along the coast.[2] The region became another area of intra-Iberian contention that was partially resolved by the Tordesillas Treaty of 1494, which allowed a Spanish sphere of influence to stretch from Cape Bojador to Messa. Though both powers violated this agreement, it became clear that Spain especially viewed the African littoral across from the Canary Islands (secured by Spain during the fifteenth century) as having strategic importance. Although Spaniards made contact with Sahrawi tribes (especially Berbers), Madrid's colonial ambitions were deflected by the astonishing discoveries in the New World.[3] The establishment of a great colonial empire had a profound effect upon the development of an imperial discourse and Spain's power and identity.

For the next 350 years, Spain was content to leave the inhospitable Saharan region alone. It viewed occasional Moroccan Saadian and Alawite military campaigns into the Saharan *bilad al-siba* (land of dissidence) as representing little threat to its interests, although these incursions would contribute to Moroccan sovereignty rationales later. During the mid-nineteenth century, however, Spain renewed its interest in the region.

A brief conflict between Spain and Morocco, precipitated by Madrid's apprehension of increasing British influence in Morocco and tribal attacks on Ceuta, resulted in a Spanish success, which inspired imperial ambitions. The Tetouan Treaty of 1860 allowed Spain to enlarge its coastal enclaves of Ceuta and Melilla. The treaty also stipulated the reestablishment of Santa Crus de Ma Pequeña, a former Spanish outpost located along the Sahara coast opposite the Canaries.[4]

Spain's anxieties concerning colonial rivals in the region intensified due to the establishment of a British presence in Tarfaya (southern Morocco) and a French interest in the rich offshore fishing grounds.[5] From its point of view, Spain saw that not only were its interests in the area threatened, but that its imperial identity was also at stake.

For centuries, Spanish discourse was conditioned by its acquisition of a vast empire. Spain's loss of control over its American colonies greatly reduced its prestige and led to a redefinition of its power. The success of Spain in getting Morocco to concede territory in 1860 rekindled an "imperial vocation," the *Hispanidad* (a Pan-Iberian movement with both political and cultural dimensions), and a sense of mission in Africa. The power of this imperial discourse was disclosed as Madrid sought to acquire territories in Africa, including the Western Sahara.[6]

The formation of several colonial organizations underscored this regenerated imperial impetus. One of them, the Sociedad Española de Africanistas y Colonistas, secured Sahrawi treaties in January 1884, and by the end of the year Villa Cisneros (Dakhla), Angra da Cintra, and La Guera were founded. Spain applied the principle of the Act of Berlin and proclaimed a protectorate named Río de Oro, a claim recognized by the European powers. Until subsequent treaties with the French demarcating borders, the Spanish presence was limited to the coast.

France's imperial involvement in the Western Sahara was impelled by several reasons: (1) the chauvinistic urge to assert French power especially after her defeat in the Franco-Prussian war of 1870-71; (2) European rivalries such as Spain's irritating ambitions in Morocco and the Western Sahara and the ominous specter of German ambitions in the Maghreb; (3) indigenous anticolonial resistance that could only be contained by a French military response; and (4) the eventual competition between French officers and colonial bureaucrats championing respective French interests in Morocco and Algeria.[7]

These variables often operated simultaneously and synergetically. They also reflected a renovated imperial discourse similar to Spain's (e.g., compensation for lost territory [Alsace-Lorraine]; military and political prestige [after the Prussian Debacle]). For example, this was shown, especially during the 1890s, by the particularist chauvinism of soldiers and settlers in Algeria (even disclosed by the progressive Governor-General Jules Cambon), who lobbied acquisitive Third Republic governments to assert authority in the Western Sahara.[8]

The French also showed increasing interest in a transsaharan railway from Algeria to Timbuktu. Efforts to construct a Dakar-to-Djibouti line were frustrated by the British at Fashoda, but the French received subsequent British support for Saharan expansion. Paris aimed at what one historian called a "delicate expansion" and a "peaceful penetration" of the region.[9] Negotiations with Madrid, concluded in 1900, producing the first of several conventions concerning colonial borders.[10] Germany's political intentions in the regions heightened French (and world) anxieties, which lead to the Algeciras Act in 1906 invalidating Moroccan sovereignty, and finally resulting in the Treaty of Fez (March 30, 1912), which established the protectorate. Concurrently, indigenous resistance was suppressed through French military campaigns.

Acting as an Alawite representative (*khalifa*) the Mauritanian-born Ma al-Ainin spearheaded local opposition to the French and, to a lesser degree, the Spanish.[11] This dynamic figure attempted to unite and mobilize Sahrawi resistance, built Smara as a Sahrawi political and religious center, and threatened the French position in Mauritania. Furthermore, Ma al-Ainin secured arms from the Woermann Company of Hamburg and even Torres of Barcelona. Madrid often intrigued against Paris, despite Spain's dependence upon France's regional expansion for its own, and permitted Spanish firms to supply the Sahrawi's with arms. But as the Sultanate lost its authority, Ma al-Ainin also found his own power and influence declining. He was finally decisively defeated in June 1910 and died several months later.

Ahmad al-Hiba, Ma al-Ainin's son, continued resistance against the French. During World War I, Germany attempted to provide him assistance. His death in 1919 did not end Sahrawi hostilities.

Muhammad al-Mamun, a nephew of Ma al-Ainin and an Islamic intellectual, organized Sahrawi resistance in Mauritania after participating in the Rif War with Abd al-Krim. Though conducting remarkable long-distance raids, the attacks were sporadic and Sahrawi operations were often uncoordinated. The establishment of the *Confins Algéro-Marocains* (CAM) in 1930 created a unified Algerian-Moroccan command that ended dissidence in southern Morocco and eventually extended its authority into northern Mauritania. Contentions between French colonialists in Morocco and Algeria over borders and respective jurisdiction were left unresolved, however, and this proved to have profound postcolonial consequences.[12] By the end of 1934, the region was relatively secure even though Sahrawis continued to pursue their nomadic way of life. French pacification of Morocco and Mauritania expedited Spanish expansion into Río de Oro's interior. Smara and Daoura were reached in 1934.

Spain's modest Maghrebi colonial territories had profound political importance. They symbolized a glorious historical legacy that was embraced by a politicized military that, from its perspective, was unappreciated by the Republican government. Francisco Franco organized and mobilized his Nationalist rebellion against the Republic from bases in Spanish Morocco. And, as the victorious Generalissimo stated in 1939, "Without Africa, I wouldn't have been able to begin to understand myself."[13] The imperial discourse deeply influenced Franco's policies. Indeed, during World War II the Falangist government even entertained the idea of African expansion at the expense of defeated France.[14]

After World War II, economic and political developments decisively changed the entire Western Saharan situation and affected colonial discourses. Spanish geologists discovered phosphates in the late 1940s in the Sahara. In 1962, the *Empress Nacional Minera del Sáhara* SA (ENMISA) was organized and an "ultra-modern mine" began extraction in 1972.[15] The idea of Spanish Sahara enriching the metropolitan state reinforced the imperial discourse.

Reflecting France's parallel interests, in 1952 a French-controlled consortium called *Mines de Fer de Mauritania* (MIFERMA) began extracting Mauritania iron ore that had been found near Fort Gouraud (Zouerate) before the war. Large iron ore deposits discovered in 1953 at Gara Djebilet, south of Tindouf, Algeria, again attracted attention to the disputed border zone. In January 1957, France created the *Organisation Commune de Régions Sahariennes* (OCRS), designed to share mineral resources (e.g., Mauritanian iron and Algerian petroleum [discovered in 1956]) among the peoples of the Sahara. The idea that the Sahara was "the new Siberia of the French economy" reinvigorated France's imperial discourse despite the rapid approach of decolonization.[16]

Politically, the radicalization of Moroccan and Algerian nationalism during the 1950s, characterized by the Moroccan *Istiqlal* (independence) party and the Algerian National Liberation Front (FLN), threatened colonial presumptions and power in the region. As shall be seen, both independence movements would have a profound effect upon the evolution of nationalism in the Sahara.

The French deposition of the nationalist Sultan Muhammad V in 1953 incited the formation of an irregular "Army of Liberation" that received support from Sahrawi tribes in the South.[17] Though France reversed its decision and allowed the sultan to return to Morocco in November 1955, the leaders of the army met in Madrid (disclosing Spain's proclivity toward embarrassing France) in January 1956 and planned operations.

France preempted the potential of another major revolt, like the one that began in Algeria in November 1954, by proclaiming Moroccan independence in March 1956. Efforts to incorporate Liberation soldiers into the newly formed Royal Moroccan Armed Forces (FAR) failed; the army remained intact and determined to liberate the rest of the Maghreb.

In June 1956, the Army of Liberation launched attacks in Algeria; combat commenced in Mauritania in February 1957. Three months later the Spanish found themselves hard-pressed in Ifni as a result of Madrid's reluctance to transfer South Morocco (Tarfaya) and the Spanish Sahara to Rabat (Morocco's capital).[18]

Eventually, French and Spanish military commands collaborated and coordinated a successful counteroffensive called *Opération Ouragon* in February 1958. The army disintegrated as many joined the FAR while others left for the desolate Spanish Sahara. These irregulars did, however, reinforce the appeal of aggressive Moroccan nationalists such as the *Istaqlal's* leader, Allal el-Fassi, who desired an end of Spanish colonialism coupled with an extension of Morocco's borders.[19]

Sensitive to the border issue and anxious to secure Moroccan support during the liberation struggle, Ferhat Abbas, the president of the Algerian nationalist provisional government, signed an agreement with King Hassan on July 6, 1961, which stipulated that Morocco and Algeria would settle the frontier dispute after the War of Independence.[20] Ironically, during the Evian negotiations (1961-62) with France, the nationalists defended the colonial position maintaining the permanence of Algerian borders.[21]

After Algeria attained its independence (July 1962), FAR units crossed the border, anticipating the implementation of the July 1961 agreement. During this time, Algeria suffered multiple dislocations caused by colonialism, the War of Independence, the flight of *pieds-noirs* (European settlers) and management cadres, and, in particular, the postindependence elite fratricide. Algerian nationalist leader Ahmed Ben Bella's efforts to consolidate power delayed negotiations with the impatient Moroccan king, who had ordered the FAR to withdraw but who still urged a settlement of the frontier question.[22] The Kabyle (or Berber) Revolt in Fall 1963 against President Ben Bella's government provided King Hassan with an opportunity to resolve the issue through a direct military confrontation with Algeria.

The brief "War of the Sands" demonstrated Morocco's military superiority. However, diplomatic pressure from the new Organization of African Unity (OAU) and also from the United States and France led to a cease-fire and a meeting between Hassan and Ben Bella in October 1963. The border issue remained unresolved, although it was occasionally discussed by the two countries between 1963 and 1975.[23] Tensions intensified, however, with the end of Spanish rule over the Western Sahara in 1975.[24]

Algeria's and Morocco's border dispute diverted attention from the Spanish Sahara, integrated with Spain since 1958 as "overseas provinces" of the metropolitan power. The decolonization of French and British colonies in Africa, however, increased pressure on the anachronistic Spanish position. A member of the United Nations since 1955, Spain was one of the targets of UN Resolution 1514, which called for continued decolonization. Spain's historical discourse was in transition.

Spain began a deliberate decolonization. Morocco received Spanish South Morocco (Tarfaya Province) in 1958 and Ifni in 1969. Elsewhere in Africa, Spanish Guinea and Fernando Po received independence in 1968. The Falangist government was determined, however, to hold on to the Sahara.

According to the historian Juan Pablo Fusi, Franco "said unequivocally that he would never give the territory up."[25] Indeed, Madrid began modest investments in infrastructure and practiced a paternalist colonialism.[26] The government still hoped (as Portugal did with regard to its colonies) that the Sahara would provide Spain with a wealth of resources.[27] The Sahrawis, Spain's "African brothers," had their first election in 1963 (Sahrawis could then serve in the Cortes) and a *Djemma* (assembly) of elders was established in 1967 after a 1966 referendum ostensibly demonstrated Sahrawi support of the Spanish presence.

The UN, however, remained unconvinced by Spain's actions. In October 1964, it urged Spain to conduct self-determination. By 1973, Spain declared its willingness to organize "necessary preparations" for self-determination.

Three developments accelerated these preparations. First, Spanish authorities faced political unrest in the Sahara. There was an anticolonial demonstration in June 1970, which ended in violence. On May 10, 1973, the Polisario Front was organized, followed by its first operation against a Spanish post on May 20. Second, Portugal's sister authoritarian government was destabilized by African insurgencies and overthrown by a military coup in 1974. Third, Franco's health deteriorated and with it, the Spanish government's power.

Spain declared Saharan internal autonomy in the Political Statute (*estatuo político*) of July 1974, which gave the *Djemma* a legislative capacity and inaugurated Sahrawi participation in a governing council), and announced that a self-determination referendum would be held during the first half of 1975. According to John Damis, "Spain probably still hoped up to this time that the Sahrawis would vote for independence and...rely upon Spain for economic support and military protection" while providing "a guaranteed source of phosphate for Spanish agriculture, thereby ending Spain's dependence on Morocco."[28] Thus, in 1974, the colonial administration expedited the formation of the *Partido de la Unión Nacional Saharaui* (PUNS) as a political counterpoise to Polisario.

These events worried Rabat, which had expected the eventual integration of the Spanish Sahara into a Greater Morocco. The prospect of an independent Saharan state produced political anxiety, but also created an opportunity for the unstable Alawite monarchy, which had endured two coup attempts earlier in the decade. Indeed, the crisis increased the monarchy's popularity. Annexing the Spanish Sahara became an issue of national pride.

Madrid was pressured over its vestigial colonial enclaves and its offshore islands. Spanish fishermen were even harassed. Morocco successfully delayed the projected referendum by having the Saharan question reviewed before the International Court of Justice. Rabat organized a Sahrawi *Frente de Liberación y de las Unidad* (FLU), which commenced raiding across the Moroccan border in May 1975. During that same month, Spain assured Morocco that the "legitimate" interests of neighboring nations would be taken into account. Indeed, a formula to transfer sovereignty was publicized. Nevertheless, as late as October 1975, the ailing Franco "was inclined to stand firm but he was probably at the same time unwilling to go to war."[29]

When Madrid finally concluded that decolonization was inevitable, Franco's protracted death in the fall of 1975 (he died November 20) vitiated Spanish power and produced a vacillating policy.[30] The tenuous political transition under Prince Juan Carlos (who became acting head of state on October 31), compounded by the Moroccan Green March (on November 6), ultimately forced Madrid into negotiating the Tripartite (Madrid) Accords of November 14, 1975, with Morocco and Mauritania.[31]

Spain agreed in the Tripartite Accords to transfer its Saharan administration and its authority over coastal waters to Morocco and Mauritania. Nevertheless, it reserved its right to sovereignty over the Western Sahara until the Sahrawi population expressed its self-determination, presumably through an internationally recognized referendum. Therefore, the transfer of power was actually a "de-administration" rather than a genuine "decolonization." According to Juan Pablo Fusi, "It seemed as if Spain was hurrying headlong away from that continent, as though anxious to rid herself forever of that same Africa that had nourished the career of the soldier who had ruled her for forty years."[32] Though the democratization of Spain played an important role as immediately compensating for the end of Francoism, the hasty departure or, from Polisario's perspective, the "abandonment" of the Sahara, discredited the colonial legacy and implicitly the imperial discourse. Despite the historic discontinuity created by the de-administration, there remained a disquieted Spanish interest in the Western Sahara that went beyond political and economic considerations;

the rapid withdrawal seemed to repudiate both the ideal of *Hispanidad* and the moral responsibility.

SPAIN AND THE POSTCOLONIAL PERIOD

The Tripartite Accords averted a potential military confrontation with Rabat that would have jolted the delicate democratic transition into the post-Franco era. The ambivalent de-administration also allowed Madrid some flexibility to conduct a complex and contradictory balancing policy among the contending Maghrebi parties.[33] On February 26, 1976, Spain transferred its Saharan administration to Morocco and Mauritania.[34]

Spain's political collaboration with Morocco resulted in perpetuated economic advantages. Privileges were preserved concerning fishing rights (particularly protecting the fishermen from the sensitive Canaries) and in phosphates exploration and exploitation.[35]

Furthermore, Morocco provided political accommodation. King Hassan declared on November 25, 1975, that his government would not pressure Spain over the coastal enclaves of Ceuta and Melilla until Spain recovered Gibraltar.[36] Spanish gratitude included arms shipments to the Moroccans until mid-1977, when Madrid was forced to reevaluate its bilateral engagement.

Internally, Spanish opposition political parties questioned the government's collaboration with Morocco and sympathized openly with Polisario's Sahrawi Arab Democratic Republic (SADR, proclaimed one day after Spain transferred its administration to Morocco and Mauritania on February 27, 1976). Although Spain might have evaded a military conflict with Morocco, its abrupt departure was viewed as an irresponsible act that obstructed genuine Sahrawi self-determination. Socialist Felipe González of the *Partido Socialista Obrero Español* (PSOE) visited the Tindouf refugee camps in 1976 and, along with other parties of the left, called for an official repudiation of the Tripartite Accords in March 1977. One year later, the Congress of Deputies conducted special hearings concerning the negotiation of the Tripartite Accords that underscored the political discontent. Initiatives to recognize Polisario appeared in the Cortes.

Externally, Spain faced a bitter Algeria, resentful of the Tripartite Accords and of Madrid's lack of consideration for its interests. Algiers provided important military material to Polisario and retaliated against

Madrid by promoting the Canary Islands liberation movement, *Moviemento por la Autodeterminación y la Independencia del Archipélago Canario* (MPAIAC), headed by Antonio Cubillo. Concurrently, Algiers exercised its considerable influence and convinced the OAU's Liberation Committee to adopt a resolution calling for MPAIAC support and the decolonization of the Canaries.

These Algerian actions, however, disturbed Spanish national sensibilities, including those of the left, illustrating the vestigial, yet powerful, effect of the imperial discourse. Nonetheless, Algiers realized the dangers of alienating Spain politically and economically. In particular, Algerian economic state planners projected a transmediterranean natural gas pipeline to Spain, which would expedite the export of Algerian energy to Western European markets. This important consideration prompted Algiers to defer its OAU initiative and its support of the MPAIAC.

Nevertheless, the effect of these events forced Madrid to defend its presence in the Canaries throughout Africa. Indeed, Spain's image as a nation sensitive to the interests of the Third World--an image fostered especially during the Falangist period--had been tarnished by Madrid's precipitous withdrawal from the Sahara. The political consequences of de-administration troubled Madrid and affected the changing discourse.

Compounding this uneasy situation, the fledgling SADR warned Spain that the Western Sahara's territorial waters would be patrolled and defended. Sporadic Sahrawi seaborne attacks upon the Spanish fishing fleet began in 1977. In April 1978, Polisario guerrillas seized eight fishermen. When Madrid complained to Algiers, it was advised to deal directly with the Sahrawis.

In order to be able to do that, Javier Rupérez, of the ruling *Unión del Centro Democrático* (UCD), attended Polisario's Fourth Congress in September 1978 and signed a joint communiqué recognizing the liberation movement as the only legitimate representative of the Sahrawi people. Polisario released the fishermen in October. That same month, Spain requested that the UN settle the Saharan war and expedite Sahrawi self-determination. The following spring, Prime Minister Suárez's visit to Algiers included a meeting with Polisario Secretary-General Mohamed Abdelaziz. While this did not symbolize official recognition, it underscored the UCD's new relationship with Polisario. Polisario eventually was allowed to open an office in Spain.

Closer Spanish relations with Algeria and Polisario provoked a Moroccan response. As a consequence of Rupérez's presence at

Polisario's Fourth Congress, Foreign Minister M'hamed Boucetta evoked the delicate enclave issue. Furthermore, fishing problems remained unresolved because they were linked to Morocco's demand for an agreement concerning citrus fruit exportation through Spain to European markets. This was symbolized by the unratified 1977 fishing treaty. Spanish fishing woes deepened when Moroccans seized fishing vessels and impounded catches in Spring 1980. In January 1981, Spain briefly pulled its fishing boats from the disputed waters. An interim agreement was signed in April 1981.

Madrid realized that its interests in the Maghreb could best be served by parrying Morocco with Algeria. For example, Suárez's arrival in Algeria was balanced by King Juan Carlos' visit to Morocco. The Spanish government, however, failed to reach some accommodation with Polisario.

The Sahrawi nationalists noted that, although Mauritania withdrew from the war in 1979, Spain was still engaged to the spirit if not the stipulations of the Tripartite Accord. Spain's ambiguous policy of parity left Polisario "distraught," thus provoking a resumption of attacks on the Spanish fishing fleet.[37] In 1980, thirty-eight fishermen were captured and then released at the end of the year, after Spain declared its support of "the Sahrawi people's right to self-determination, as a basis for a political solution covering the whole of the territory of Western Sahara."[38]

The PSOE's victory in the October 1982 elections raised Polisario's expectations. Before taking office as prime minister, Felipe González had opposed the Tripartite Accords. During his investiture speech, however, he declared that he intended to "strengthen and deepen...relations with...Portugal, France, and the Maghreb countries."[39] Indeed, the new premier's first foreign visit was to Morocco in order to "create a relationship of confidence."[40]

Nevertheless, chronic economic and political problems reappeared in bilateral relations. Although the fishing controversy seemed settled by a 1983 treaty (amended on January 1, 1986), Spain's entry into the European Community (EC) posed multiple threats. Morocco's economic relationship with Spain would now be conditioned by the needs of the EC and its membership. Specifically, traditional European markets for Moroccan citrus and vegetable produce were jeopardized by Iberian EC member competitors. May 1988 protocols with the EC allayed Moroccan fears, assuring Morocco that its favored position in the European economies would continue. Significantly, the long-awaited EC fishing protocol avoided recognizing Moroccan sovereignty over the Western Sahara.

Compounding this complex relationship, the enclaves issue reemerged as a consequence of a controversial 1985 aliens law affecting the Muslim population. In February 1986, former Foreign Minister Boucetta of the *Istiqlal* party repeated the familiar call for the incorporation of Ceuta and Melilla into Morocco.[41] In June, the Spanish community of Melilla targeted a prominent Muslim leader with a violent protest. Madrid, knowing that approximately 18,000 Spanish citizens lived in Morocco, appreciated Rabat's measured reaction to these troubling events.

The problems in the coastal enclaves revived the "Moorish fear" that played such an important role centuries ago in the development of an imperial discourse.[42] Indeed, just as Moroccan political parties have demonstrated remarkable unity concerning the expansion into the Western Sahara; Spain has shown similar solidarity across the political spectrum concerning the integrity of the enclaves with the metropolitan state.[43] Algeria, in support of Morocco, related the anachronistic Spanish presence to its own colonial past.[44] In a remarkable group of articles, the leading Spanish news journal, *Cambio 16*, projected a detailed war scenario between Spain and Morocco. It claimed that Melilla could be seized in four hours.[45] Despite the nationalistic clamor, neither country, at the time, could risk hostilities over the enclaves, especially while the war in the Western Sahara remained unsettled.

Polisario continued to threaten Spanish fishermen.[46] In September 1985, a Spanish fishing boat flying the Moroccan flag was attacked, resulting in the death of one fisherman. Madrid retaliated by closing Polisario's Madrid office and expelling its representative, Ahmed Boudkhari. This response has been linked to Spain's delicate sensibilities concerning terrorism from the Basque *Euzkadi to Askatasuna* (ETA) in Spain itself, although Madrid denied a comparison between the ETA and Polisario. Nonetheless, Spanish ships were targeted by Polisario in November 1986 and January 1987.

Concurrently, there was an improvement in relations between Spain and Morocco. In August 1986, Spain agreed to construct six patrol boats for Morocco.[47] Spain also agreed to construct thirty refrigerated ships for Morocco.[48] It also promoted trade with $75 million of medium- and long-term export credits given the completion of a $550 million credit line related to the 1983 fishing treaty.[49] An August 1987 television agreement permitted Spanish programs to be telecast in Morocco, thus reinforcing cultural as well as political cooperation.[50] Finally, in June 1988, a "framework agreement" covering the entire commercial relationship was signed.[51]

In spite of Spain's tilt toward Morocco during the last few years, Madrid also appreciated the strategic importance of Algeria. Before President Chadli Bendjedid's visit to Spain in the summer of 1985, Algeria's SONATRACH and Spain's ENAGAS renegotiated a liquified natural gas (LNG) contract concerning long-term purchases and prices. In an interview with the Spanish newspaper, *El País*, Bendjedid reminded Spainards that "your country has never declared itself released from this engagement [Western Saharan decolonization]." The message was clear: Spain still had a "political and moral" role to play "in regard to the decolonization of Western Sahara."[52] This was echoed on December 15, 1987, when the Spanish Congress of Deputies met in plenary session and proposed a resolution that supported the UN-OAU peace plan and called for the government to play a more active role in promoting negotiations.[53]

Even though the issues of the Western Sahara and LNG prices produced contention, Madrid and Algiers realized there was mutual need for political cooperation. On the one hand, Madrid worried about an ETA presence in Algeria. On the other hand, Algiers wanted to monitor anti-FLN dissidents living in Spain (for example, Ahmed Ben Bella). This led to antiterrorist agreements in November 1986 and September 1987.[54] Algiers has recently facilitated a dialogue between the Spanish government and the ETA, which has added a new political significance to the bilateral relationship.[55]

Concerning the Western Sahara, sanguine articles in *Jeune Afrique* contended that the Spanish press had resigned itself to the "Moroccanization of the territory."[56] Spanish tourists have frequented its beaches.[57] Nevertheless, Spain welcomed the May 1988 rapprochement between Morocco and Algeria and supported the August 1988 UN peace proposal, which Madrid hoped would lead to a self-determination referendum, finally fulfilling what would be recognized internationally as an authentic "decolonization."[58] Polisario reminded Madrid at this time that Spain's "indifference and abandonment" of the Western Sahara and its people had contributed to the war and its consequences.[59] Spain responded with a vote at the UN in October 1988 in favor of a resolution supporting direct talks between Polisario and Morocco, thereby affirming the Algerian position, which forced

King Hassan to cancel a November state visit. Relations with Polisario improved to the point that an agreement was made in January 1989 to reopen its Madrid office.[60]

King Hassan finally arrived for his state visit (the first by a Moroccan monarch since independence) in September 1989. The cordiality of the visit seemed to indicate to *El País* the end of "a period of misunderstandings and suspicions."[61] Though openly wanting to incorporate Ceuta and Melilla peacefully into his realm, King Hassan declared: "Let us develop our bilateral relations and everything will be settled little by little."[62] Agreements were announced concerning Spanish investment in public works, military cooperation (Spain is replacing France as Morocco's chief furnisher of material), annual summit meetings, continued study of a connecting bridge tunnel, and regularizing the status of Moroccan emigrant workers. Spain maintained, however, its position that the most effective procedure to expedite peace in the Western Sahara was face-to-face negotiations between the belligerents. This was reaffirmed by Foreign Minister Francisco Fernández Ordóñez before the United Nations at the end of the month.[63]

Following King Hassan's visit, Spanish-Moroccan relations again entered a troubled period. In January 1990, a Moroccan royal family aircraft mysteriously flew into Spanish airspace without identifying itself.[64] Fishing problems concerning the amount of the EC-Spanish catch and Moroccan fines were addressed by a March 1990 agreement that resulted in more legal guarantees for fishermen, coupled with remunerations to Rabat.[65]

Morocco was particularly concerned over the Spanish government's very visible reception of Polisario's leader Bachir Mustafa Sayed in May 1990. While Madrid feared that a symbolic recognition of the SADR (relating to the opening of a Polisario office) would jeopardize progress on the self-determination referendum process, the Sahrawis have received significant humanitarian assistance (300 million pesetas [$3 million] and thirty scholarships in 1989). Sayed supported Morocco's claims to Ceuta and Melilla; but he also referred to Morocco's silence concerning the enclaves in the North while "Spain washes its hands of the conflict in the South."[66] A month later *El País* reported that Moroccan intelligence services had infiltrated the Spanish Foreign Ministry with a particular interest in these Polisario-Madrid conversations. The Spanish Government was particularly displeased by this provocative action.[67]

Currently, the Gonzáles government in Spain seems to be fulfilling the PSOE's postponed promise of political support of the Sahrawi nationalists in order to edge Morocco closer toward a referendum. Concurrently, it has strengthened relations with Rabat. *El Independiente* has called this policy "two-faced" and claimed that the Socialists have a "double morality" concerning the Sahara, declaring support for self-determination while sending arms to Morocco.[68] Actually, Polisario has understood the strategic need of Spain, France, and the United States to cultivate close relations with Morocco. The president of the SADR and general-secretary of Polisario, Mohamed Abdelaziz, stated that these countries' "continued political, military, and financial backing" could be used as a diplomatic lever to persuade Morocco to end the conflict and negotiate a solution.[69] A deeper reason for Madrid's recent actions is that this incomplete decolonization has tainted the imperial legacy and has inhibited Spain's transformation to a post-Franco, postcolonial national identity.

FRANCE AND THE POSTCOLONIAL PERIOD

France's interest in Western Saharan decolonization was connected directly to its postcolonial relationships with Algeria, Morocco, and Mauritania. From 1962 to 1975, Algeria dominated Paris' relations with the Maghreb. This stemmed from President Charles de Gaulle's implementation of a privileged policy of cooperation (*coopération*) with Algeria as a "narrow door" to vast French opportunities in the Third World. Indeed, de Gaulle's substitution of cooperation for colonialism represented a remarkable transformation of discourse that preserved the identity of French greatness and independence.[70]

The French-Algerian relationship suffered as a result of hydrocarbon nationalizations in February 1971, which ended the favored relationship between the two countries. However, by the time of the death of President Georges Pompidou in 1974, a *relancement* (relaunching) had been initiated. The decision to hold the Algiers Summit between presidents Valéry Giscard d'Estaing of France and Houari Boumedienne of Algeria in April 1975 was perceived by Algeria as a symbolic gesture aimed at restoring the relationship to a privileged position.

Boumedienne greet Giscard d'Estaing warmly and declared that "the page is turned." Later during this historic state visit (the first by a French president since Algerian independence), the French president reciprocated the metaphor by announcing that it was time "to write a new page" in the history of the relationship between the two countries. This was ample proof to the Algerians that the French shared their enthusiasm for a regenerated relationship, especially as a partner in Algerian development. Their expectations would be dashed, however, by balance of trade difficulties and by problems resulting from the Western Sahara decolonization.

Despite claims of impartiality, France acted in ways that lent strength to Morocco's position. Without France's accommodation and support, Morocco could not have pursued as aggressively its Saharan ambitions. Paris encouraged the negotiation of the Madrid Accords and assisted in their implementation.[71] There were several reasons for this decision, including the following: King Hassan's strategic pro-Western orientation; the internal threats to the Alawite monarchy; the possibility of French economic opportunities; the improbability of serious Sahrawi nationalist resistance (though Polisario had conducted military operations against Spanish authorities since May 1973); the personal friendship between the two leaders; and France's wish to protect Spain's fledgling democratic movement from the perilous possibility of colonial war.[72] France's indirect involvement in Saharan decolonization would eventually lead to direct intervention.

As the war escalated, France claimed neutrality, which was at best ambiguous, especially when contradicted by economic aid and by large arms shipments sent to Morocco.[73] Giscard's public opposition to "the multiplication of micro-states" (February 1976) also implied a French endorsement of a "Greater Morocco."[74] Finally, Polisario guerrillas decided to concentrate their operations against their weaker adversary, Mauritania. Because France perceived this action as a threat to its special relationship with Mauritania, underscored by the deaths of two French technicians and the capture of others by Polisario, Giscard authorized French military operations to protect Mauritania (*Opération Lamantin*).[75]

Algiers was implicated in these events. Polisario was portrayed in some French newspapers as Algeria's "pirates" and "mercenaries." Posters appeared in Paris calling for "The Paras to the Sahara." The murder of an Algerian guardian at the Paris *Amicale des Algériens en Europe* tragically illustrated the worsening situation that was compounded by the emigrant worker expulsion issue. President Boumedienne reminded France that Africa should no longer be considered an imperialist sphere of influence.[76]

On December 2, 1977, using as a pretext the Franco-Mauritanian cooperation agreements, the French government launched air strikes against Sahrawi columns operating in Mauritania. Sorties continued later that month (December 14-15) that not only deepened French involvement, but also publicized the Saharan struggle worldwide. In a revealing statement illustrating a modified postcolonial discourse, Giscard declared: "France is a peaceful country, but it is not a weak country."[77]   In order to embarrass Giscard, Polisario handed over several captured Frenchmen on December 23 to UN Secretary-General Kurt Waldheim.

Deeply disappointed by Giscard, President Boumedienne resorted to economic reprisals, nationalizing French holdings in Algeria. Furthermore, he ordered Algerian state enterprises to stop purchases from France.   On February 9, 1978, Giscard declared, "The Evian Accords [which had given Algeria independence and which provided the framework for the postcolonial relationship] do not correspond to the actual reality of our relations."[78]   Though this could be viewed as a threat, it was actually an invitation to repair bilateral relations.

There were many reasons that pointed to a French reassessment. On the one hand, with coming legislative elections in March, Giscard's intervention had been questioned (especially from the Gaullist right). The *Patronat* had endured the undermining of its former privileged commercial position in Algeria and complained that France had dropped from being Algeria's first commercial client to its third. France could not ignore Algeria's hydrocarbon wealth nor neglect the 850,000 Algerians living and working within its borders. French intervention had symbolized a reversion to practices stemming from the past imperial discourse.   French policymakers discovered that that discourse was anachronistic and threatened their existing interests. France found it wise, therefore, to embrace once again the successful postcolonial discourse of cooperation and reconciliation.

On the other hand, Algeria could not afford an extensive political and economic crisis with France.   The emigrant worker community could only be protected effectively through an active collaboration rather than confrontation with Paris. In addition, France was still considered Algeria's most natural commercial market and partner, given geographic, cultural, and historic "predispositions."[79]   Finally, the rhetoric that repeated French complicity in Moroccan adventurism could only divert the nation's attention for so long from pressing economic issues and state-planning imperatives. On April 30, 1978, President Boumedienne declared his willingness "to discuss all the problems."[80]

The July 10, 1978, military coup that ousted Mauritania's President Mokhtar Ould Daddah also marked the end of France's direct intervention.[81]   Ironically, Giscard entertained the possibility of a Sahrawi microstate.[82] Paris may have expedited the Polisario's accord with the new Mauritanian government on August 5, 1979, which officially withdrew Mauritania from the war.[83]

The decision to terminate France's direct intervention in the conflict contributed to a political rapprochement and genuine relancement with Algeria. Before his death in December 1978, Boumedienne addressed Paris, calling for the resolution of their bilateral problems and for French assistance in ending the war.[84] On February 15, 1979, Giscard called the conflict in the Western Sahara "a decolonization program."[85] In March, Olivier Stirn, the secretary of state for foreign affairs, stated, "It is the policy of France like that of the European Community to recognize the Sahrawi people's right of self-determination.[86] During his official visit to Algeria, Jean-François Poncet stated that France was "impartial" but not "indifferent" toward finding a peaceful solution.[87]

Notwithstanding the statements for "self-determination" while arms and personal amity flowed from Paris to Rabat, France's neutrality seemed less "ambiguous" and more authentic. In December 1980, Omar Hadrami, a member of the executive committee of Polisario, contended that "France can serve as an intermediary."[88]

During the 1981 presidential campaign, the *Parti Socialiste's* "110 Proposals" included "support for the right of self-determination of...Western Sahara" and "privileged ties with nonaligned countries of the Mediterranean zone and the African continent, especially Algeria."[89] François Mitterrand's election promised a change in policy and, like González's in Spain in 1982, raised expectations among Sahrawi nationalists for a shift in French policy.

On August 5, 1981, the Quai d'Orsay received for the first time a member of Polisario. Subsequently, the liberation movement received permission to have a political office in Paris (opened March 1982). As for Algeria, Mitterrand raised the bilateral relationship to a privileged position, highlighted by the drafting of an LNG accord during a two-day visit to Algeria (November 30-December 1, 1981) that was concluded in February 1982. This accord was followed by the signing of other major agreements in 1982-83 and the drafting of "codevelopment" plans. At the same time, Mitterrand fulfilled France's arms contracts with an increasingly worried Morocco.[90]

The chronic problem of Chad, compounded by the unfulfilled troop evacuation agreement with Colonel Muammar Qaddafi, dislocated Mitterrand's Maghrebi policy. The astonishing Treaty of Oujda in August 1984 between Morocco and Libya provided Mitterrand with an opportunity to deal with Qaddafi and Chad again. This ultimately meant cultivating a stronger relationship with King Hassan, which had a negative effect upon the Algerian relationship.[91] The August 1986 abrogation of the treaty and Chadian military successes did not substantially alter Paris's relationship with either Rabat or Algiers.

Paris' recent policies toward the Western Sahara have been more passive than active. This is paradoxical given France's past military engagement and commitments in Morocco (about 265 advisers [1984] besides material).[92] Indeed, a Polisario delegation said in April 1985 that its "priority objective" was "to unblock the political state of affairs between the French government and the Polisario Front."[93] France has stated its willingness to play a more active role. This was emphasized in September 1986 by Prime Minister Jacques Chirac in Algiers. He declared that France wanted to act as a "sincere...friend of the concerned parties."[94] Nevertheless, Polisario still waited for constructive French initiatives. However, because of its multifaceted interests in Algeria and Morocco, France was careful to pursue a policy of parity.

France's interests in Morocco and Algeria are considerable. About 40,000 French citizens live in the kingdom. Morocco possesses phosphates, has a friendly leader, and occupies a strategic geopolitical location. France has also invested in the Moroccan-controlled Western Sahara and the port of El-Ayoun.[95] Algeria has hydrocarbons and great economic opportunities for French enterprises. Difficult LNG price negotiations (until the January 1989 financial cooperation accords and new gas contract) have been compounded by an acute decline in commercial activities.[96] Algeria, too, is geopolitically significant, given its "parley" abilities (for example, with Lebanon and Iran) and Third World connections. Both countries play host to French teachers and technicians (*coopérants*) who, of course, reinforce cultural and linguistic links which are particularly valued by Paris.

French policies, like Spain's, have disclosed the need to balance its complex Maghrebi interests. As French scholar Nicole Grimaud stated:

France has tried with difficulty to maintain a degree of equilibrium and neutrality; it would have liked a referendum in the Sahara, but it will go no further. It will not do anything to jeopardize the King, considering him preferable to a military regime.   Apart from a few convinced socialists, the French Administration is skeptical about the creation of a Saharan state; Mauritania's difficulties in surviving are too well know.[97]

It was no wonder that the rapprochement between Morocco and Algeria in May 1988 was greeted ecstatically.[98]   This reduced the risk of offending either Morocco or Algeria.   In addition, the UN initiatives during the summer of 1988 were also applauded, since they underscore French statements concerning a referendum.   France is now willing to play a more neutral role on the Western Saharan conflict than ever before.   For Paris, this new balance provides a less contentious position that neither denies the Sahrawis their right of self-determination--thereby reinforcing Paris' relations with Algiers--nor denies Moroccan political presumptions.   In the summer of 1990, France chaired UN Security Council meetings concerning the UN referendum process and helped mediate between Moroccan and Sahrawi positions.[99]

CONCLUSIONS

On the surface, Spain and France have pursued similar postcolonial policies of parity, effectively balancing their Maghrebi interests.   Indeed, even with friendly Socialist governments in power, Polisario learned that strategic pragmatism overruled principles.   Sympathetic rhetoric was subordinated to political and economic imperatives.

On the deeper level of discourse and practice, the two countries have approached the situation differently.   Spain has not reconciled itself with the ignominious Tripartite Accords of November 1975.[100]   Its present efforts to cooperate with all sides, including handing over the 1974 census to UN authorities, indicates its willingness to fulfill its pledge of self-determination to the Sahrawi people.   This in itself will be a significant step toward transforming the imperial discourse and reformulating relations in the postimperial period from colonialism to cooperation (like France has done), while aspiring to preserve some type of privileged influence.   It will also strengthen Spanish democracy by resolving this embarrassing and enduring problem left by the Falangist regime.   The implementation of a genuine, internationally recognized self-determination referendum is an imperative for Spain.   Nevertheless, the specter of threatening Maghrebi scenarios looms for Spain.

A settlement in the Western Sahara that excludes Polisario and Sahrawi nationalism would amplify Spain's international image as an irresponsible decolonizer. The ideal of Hispanidad would be tarnished. Indeed, several Latin American nations have recognized the SADR. A Moroccan takeover may reduce pressure on the enclaves. In another scenario, if the SADR is established, Moroccan frustrations could be vented upon the vulnerable coastal enclaves whose symbolic value to the imperial discourse has already been discussed. A nationalist movement on the Canaries could regenerate. Nevertheless, the genuine decolonization of the Spanish Sahara would be a significant step toward strengthening Madrid's generally positive image in the Third World.

The war in the Western Sahara has had a significant effect upon France's postimperial discourse. Though cooperation has replaced colonialism, the conflict endangered Frances' postcolonial Maghrebi position, which was disclosed by Giscard's radical tilt to Morocco, and military intervention against Polisario. This expressed a residual imperial discourse. Of course, France ended its direct military operations once it realized that they threatened the profoundly important (for psychological and political reasons) ties with Algeria. Paris quickly learned that poor relations with Algeria threatened France's postcolonial accomplishments and its positive image in the Third World.

Spain's complex relationship with Morocco and France's with Algeria have been the crucial determinants not only in the development of their Western Saharan policies, but also in their imperial/postimperial discourse. Inversely, both Spain and France have been most significant to the definition of Morocco's and Algeria's national identities. Morocco's own imperial discourse, a legacy of both Saadian and Alawite expansion, often expressed itself at the expense of Spain. Algeria's revolutionary discourse, founded on its own War of Liberation, continued a postcolonial socioeconomic liberating praxis against France (e.g., nationalization of French mining in 1966 and hydrocarbons in 1971), and clearly has identified itself with Polisario's struggle for Saharan sovereignty. When France intervened against Polisario, Algeria considered that intervention as one against itself.

In addition, Spain and France are also highly valued commercial clients of the Maghreb. Morocco and Algeria need to secure their regional markets and share sensitivities concerning relations with the EC. Morocco views Spain and Algeria sees France as their advocates in the EC; both North African countries would also like to be members. Spain and France have provided important trade credits to Morocco and

Algeria because they are viewed as strategic conduits to Arab and African markets.

Morocco and Algeria also share anxieties concerning their emigrant communities in Spain and especially France. The Moroccan emigrant community is the largest in Spain (20,000-40,000). Despite promises of regularizing or legalizing residence, some expulsions have concerned Rabat.[101]   There are more serious problems in France, given the flagrant anti-emigrant sentiment associated with Jean-Marie Le Pen's *National Front*. The 850,000-member Algerian community has been particularly targeted, but the Moroccan community (400,000) also has been abused. In addition, there are significant French communities in both Maghrebi countries.

The establishment of Arab Maghreb Union (UMA) in February 1989 underscored Moroccan and Algerian willingness to cooperate with each other. This does not necessarily mean that Algiers has turned its back on Polisario. Whatever the result of the self-determination referendum vote, the UMA can play a useful role toward reconciling Morocco and Algeria to the results. Maghrebi integration will certainly operate more effectively with the conclusion of a mutually recognized, authentic Western Saharan decolonization. Failure to settle the conflict would risk this new regional unity.

The latest moves toward Maghrebi cooperation may also have profound benefits for Spain and France. Negotiations on a transsaharan gas pipeline from Algeria, passing through Morocco, across to Spain, and possibly reaching France, have been proceeding smoothly.

Notwithstanding the promise of closer cooperation among these countries, there are also dangers facing these sensitive relations. Spain and France are concerned about the rise of Islamic fundamentalism in Morocco and Algeria.[102]   King Hassan's government was shaken by the publication in October 1990 of a very critical book by Gilles Perrault, entitled *Our Friend the King*, which drew attention to Morocco's human rights violations in the Western Sahara. Amnesty International and French humanitarian organizations including *France-Liberté*, presided by Danièle Mitterrand, the president's wife, have targeted Morocco. The deterioration of French-Moroccan relations prevented Mrs. Mitterand's planned visit to a Polisario refugee camp. She did meet a Polisario member's wife which caused consternation in Rabat. King Hassan also canceled his visit to France. Foreign Minister Roland Dumas tried to improve relations when he met with the king in November.[103]   The December 1990 rioting in Fez and Tangiers has compounded the king's problems.

The Gulf War has also affected these sensitive multilateral relations. The Algerian government and rival parties attacked France's direct and Spain's indirect (i.e., refueling B-52s) intervention. King Hassan's deployment of Moroccan troops in Saudi Arabia provoked domestic protests. In the Spanish enclaves Muslims proclaimed their solidarity with Iraq.[104] The Iraqi seizure of Kuwait and the resolute response to this aggression by the American-led coalition through the auspices of the United Nations have given that organization a heightened prestige and a renewed moral commitment. This should provide a corresponding decisive momentum to hold a referendum in Western Sahara to resolve finally this protracted decolonization.

Although Spain and France have strongly supported the UN's diplomatic initiatives toward settling the conflict in Western Sahara, genuine peace can only arrive from the parties directly involved. Nevertheless, Madrid and Paris cannot remain immobile concerning this diplomatic process. On the surface, an unsatisfactory Western Saharan decolonization would threaten their regional strategic interests. On a deeper level, Spain especially needs a resolution to continue the transformation of its national identity from a colonial to postcolonial state. (This process may not end until the enclaves issue is finally addressed.) For France, a settlement would reduce the risk of jeopardizing not only its relations with Morocco and Algeria, two of its most important Third World economic partners, but also its successful transition from colonialism to cooperation. Spain and France are acutely aware of the political sensibilities of their Maghrebi neighbors, however the implementation of a mutually recognized decolonization procedure would offer tangible and intangible benefits to both of these former regional imperial powers.

NOTES

1. "Level of events" refers to the thought of the French historian and philosopher Michel Foucault. Foucault's writings underscored the complexities of describing historical "discourse", in particular the discontinuity of discourse, and the way power is "codified" in relations. Spanish and French policies in transition from the colonial to

postcolonial periods reflect changes in the course of political direction and in the current of discourse, both influencing national identity.

2. For a succinct account of earlier European exploration see John Mercer, *Spanish Sahara* (London: Allen & Unwin, 1976), 77.

3. Mercer provides detailed information; see *Spanish Sahara*, 76-90. See also Tony Hodges, *Western Sahara: The Roots of a Desert War* (Westport, Conn.: Lawrence Hill, 1983), 17-24; and Maurice Barbier, *Le Conflit du Sahara occidental* (Paris: L'Harmattan, 1982), 31-37. For information on the establishment of Spanish coastal enclaves in the Maghreb, see Jamil M. Abun-Nasr, *A History of the Maghreb in the Islamic Period* (Cambridge: Cambridge University Press, 1987), 146-50. Melilla (occupied in 1457) and Ceuta (occupied in 1580) remain under Spanish control, along with the rock islets of Peñon de Alhucemas (Penon de al-Hucemas) and Peñon de Vélez (Penon de Velez) de la Gomera and the Zaffarine (Chafarinas) Islands.

4. Abun-Nasr, *A History*, 301-03. Santa Cruz was projected as a fishing post to replace a Spanish fort established along the southern Moroccan coast in 1476 by Diego Garcia de Herrera.

5. Mercer, *Spanish Sahara*, 177-78.

6. See Juan Maestre Alfonso, "Ideología y colonialismo," in *El Sahara en la crisis de Marruecos y España* (Madrid: Akal, 1975), 99-145. Raymond Carr stated concerning Spain's intensified activity in Morocco: "This sense of mission could not, of itself, have produced military intervention. That rested on the belief of most Spanish politicians that Spain would be strategically vulnerable, and would cease to count as a great power... The dilemma was clear: if Spain did not appear as a north African power, she would cease to count in the councils of Europe" (*Spain, 1808-1939* [Oxford: Clarendon Press, 1966], 518). See also F. V. Parsons, *The Origins of the Morocco Question, 1880-1900* (London: Duckworth, 1976), 27-34, for more discussion on Spain's imperial motivation and mission. Though political reasons seem most compelling, Ramon Criado contends that economics instigated Madrid's Saharan venture ("A vast conjunction of economic interest"), see *Sahara: Pasión y muerte de un sueño colonial* (Paris: Ruedo Ibérico, 1977), 11-12.

7. The chauvinistic urge was analyzed in Henri Brunschwig, *Mythes et réalités de l'impérialisme colonial français, 1871-1914* (Paris: Armand Colin, 1960) (*French Colonialism, 1871-1914: Myths and Realities*, trans. William Granville Brown [New York: Praeger, 1966]). It also relates to the idea that French culture has universal value as a *civilizing*

mission supplementing French nationalism. Like Spanish imperialism in the region, economic rationales were subordinated or supplemented to political and national interests. See also Phillip C. Naylor, "France and the Western Sahara: Colonial and Postcolonial Intentions and Intervention,"   *Proceedings of the Eleventh Meeting of the French Colonial Historical Society, Quebec 1985*, (Lanham, Maryland: University Press of America, 1987), 203-15.

8.   Frank E. Trout, *Morocco's Saharan Frontiers* (Geneva: Droz Publishers, 1969), 28. James J. Cooke details the particular role played by Eugène Etienne and the *Parti colonial* in French Saharan expansion (through organizations such as the *Comité de l'Afrique français* and the *Union Colonial français*) and consolidation in "The Maghreb Through French Eyes: 1880-1929," In Alf Andrew Heggoy, ed., *Through Foreign Eyes: Western Attitudes Toward North Africa* (Washington, D.C.: University Press of America, 1982), 52-92. See also Douglas Porch, *The Conquest of the Sahara* (New York: Knopf, 1984), 126-29. According to Carr, the Spanish statesman, Antonio Canóvas del Castillo (like Cambon) was "no rash expansionist"; nonetheless, he "pronounced that Spain's frontier was the Atlas Mountains" Carr, *Spain*, 518.

9.   Christopher Andrew, *Théophile Delcassé and the Making of the Entente Cordiale* (London: Macmillian, 1968), 153-56.

10.   The June 27, 1900, convention demarcated Spain's Saharan claim with what would be Mauritania. The October 3, 1904, secret convention circumscribed French and Spanish spheres of influence in Morocco. The November 27, 1912, convention completed demarcation as Spain received the southern portion of Morocco (Tarfaya) and a slice of the northern littoral (one-twentieth the size of the French Protectorate) (See Hodges, *Western Sahara*, 45-49).

11.   See especially Hodges, *Western Sahara*, 55-65. See also Mercer, *Spanish Sahara*, 110-16; Ross E. Dunn, *Resistance in the Desert: Moroccan Responses to French Imperialism, 1881-1912* (Madison: University of Wisconsin Press, 1977).

12.   Paris favored Algeria since it had greater administrative control over it (i.e., integrated departments). For example, when Tindouf, the Algerian southwestern city, was taken in 1934, the commanding officer was ordered "to occupy the town in the name of France and to use no Moroccan troops in carrying out that military operation" (Virginia Thompson and Richard Adloff, *The Western Saharans: Background to Conflict* [London: Croom Helm, 1980], 23). See Trout, *Morocco's Saharan Frontier*, 233-41.   Abdallah Laroui argued that "the existence

of an autonomous Algerian policy explains for the greatest part the amputation of the national territory" (*L'Algérie et le Sahara marocain,* [Casablanca: Serar, 1976], 113).   See also, Alf Andrew Heggoy, "Colonial Origins of the Algerian-Moroccan Border Conflict of October 1963," *African Studies Review* 13 (April 1970):   17-20.

13. Juan Pablo Fusi, *Franco: A Biography,* trans. Felipe Fernández-Armesto (New York: Harper & Row, 1987), 18. During the Spanish Civil War, Sahrawis fought for the Nationalists, and Loyalists were incarcerated and exiled in Río de Oro (Mercer, *Spanish Sahara,* 121).

14. According to the "'Operation Gibraltar' Memorandum," Madrid indicated to Berlin its interest in entering World War II in exchange for control over Gibraltar, French Morocco, and western Algeria (including Oran), and the "enlargement" of Spain's other African colonies. Germany dismissed this suggestion because it would alienate the more strategic Vichy France (Mercer, *Spanish Sahara,* 121-22).   See also Benny Pollack, *The Paradox of Spanish Foreign Policy: Spain's International Relations from Franco to Democracy* (New York: St. Martin's Press, 1987), 6-7.   Falangist ideology and territorial aggrandizement related to the imperial discourse. Paul Preston reflected: "The vision which linked the Civil War to the crusading spirit of the wars between Christians and Moors and the evangelical imperialism of the conquest of America was to be inflicted on Spanish society with varying intensity for more than twenty years" ("Revenge and Reconciliation," *History Today,* 39 [March 1989]: 32).

15. See Mercer, *Spanish Sahara,* 184-87.

16. Elsa Assidon, *Sahara occidental: un enjeu pour le nord-ouest africain* (Paris: Maspéro, 1978), 23.   One should survey *France outremer* and other commercially oriented publications during this period to sense the economic anticipation (and the power of the imperial discourse) that France felt toward the Sahara. (Similar arguments were also presented concerning the phosphate-rich Spanish Sahara). See also Trout for a survey of mineral exploration in the "disputed border zone" before political decolonization (*Morocco's Saharan Frontier,* 392-401).

17. See Hodges, *Western Sahara,* 73-84; and Elsa Assidon and Thomas Jallaud, "De l'Opération 'Ecouvillon' à l'intervention en Mauritanie," *Le Monde diplomatique,* February 1978, 33.

18. According to John Mercer, Loyalist veterans of the Spanish Civil War were accused of fighting alongside the Saharans (*Spanish Sahara,* 220). Until the Ifni crisis, Spain had embarrassed France by supporting Maghrebi independence movements and had established close ties with

Morocco (Thompson and Adloff, *Western Saharans*, 152-53).

19. See Mohamed el Alami, *Allal el Fassi: Partiarche du nationalisme marocain* (Casablanca: Dar el Kitab, 1975) and Attilio Gaudio, *Allal el Fassi ou l'histoire de l'Istaqlal* (Paris: Alain Moreau, 1972). "Greater Morocco" remains an enduring national objective that has been embraced by the Alawite monarchy and has produced a remarkable, though dangerous, political consensus.

20. After war broke out between Polisario forces and the FAR, Ferhat Abbas circulated a manifesto that "reminded President Boumedienne of the support that Morocco had given Algeria in its hour of need, and its authors urged him to end the fratricidal Saharan conflict and to cooperate in building a united Maghreb" (Thompson and Adloff, *Western Saharans*, 29).

21. This defense was against de Gaulle's positions to partition the country into Muslim and European enclaves and to separate the hydrocarbons-rich Sahara from the rest of the country. John Damis relates that the GPRA "categorically rejected a French proposal to organize a referendum in the Algerian Sahara" (*Conflict in Northwest Africa: The Western Sahara Dispute* [Standford, Calif.: Hoover Institution Press, 1983], 24 [citing Tahar Ben Jelloun, "Une Certitude, des questions..." *Le Monde*, March 3, 1976, 6]).

22. See Hodges, *Western Sahara*, 92-98, for a political account of the "War of the Sands."

23. The Rabat agreements of 1972 called for a recognition of present borders and the mutual exploitation of the iron deposits at Gara Djebilet. Algeria ratified them in 1973; Morocco did not until May 1988.

24. The border situation can be considered another dimension of decolonization. See Mohammed Maazouzi, *L'Algérie et les étapes successives de l'amputation du territoire marocain* (Casablanca: Dar el Kitab, 1976). For another Moroccan position see Benabdellah Abdelaziz, *Vérité sur le Sahara* (Roanne, France: Editions Horvbath, 1977). See also Robert Rézette, *The Western Sahara and the Frontiers of Morocco* (Paris: Nouvelles Editions Latines, 1975).

25. Fusi, *Franco*, 109.

26. For studies of Spanish activities during this period see Ramiro Santamaría Quesada, "Sahara," in Instituto de Estudios Africanos, *Los veinticinco años de paz en la España africana* (Madrid: Consejo Superior de Investigaciones Cientificas, 1964), 31-46; Mercer, *Spanish Sahara*, 196-217; Hodges, *Western Sahara*, 135-48; Barbier, *Conflit du Sahara*, 88-92; and Damis, *Conflict in Northwest Africa*, 12-13.

27. See René Pélissier, "Spain Changes Course in Africa," *Africa Report*, no. 8 (December 1963): 8-11.
28. Damis, *Conflict in Northwest Africa*, 51.
29. Fusi, *Franco*, 168.
30. Within government circles, there were contending groups proposing plans of decolonization. Foreign Minister Pedro Cortina Mauri favored an international referendum leading toward Sahrawi independence. The Army, a very dangerous political variable, insisted upon an honorable withdrawal. (Prince Juan Carlos's first action as acting head of state was to fly to the Spanish Sahara and reassure the army on November 2). Finally, Falangist Secretary-General José Soliz Ruiz's group supported accommodation with Morocco fearing that an independent Sahrawi state could promote the independence of the Canary Islands. In addition, the fear of a frustrated Morocco threatened the delicate situation of the Spanish enclaves of Ceuta and Melilla. Eventually this last faction's concern for a strategic decolonization convinced Carlos Arias Navarro, president of the government, who pursued the Moroccan alternative in late October. In addition, Polisario, Moroccan, and Algerian groups lobbied their interests. See Damis, *Conflict in Northwest Africa*, 64-65, Hodges, *Western Sahara*, 210-217, and Barbier, *Conflit du Sahara*, 162-64.
31. According to Benny Pollack, Spain left the Sahara for several reasons: accommodation of conservative Arab states (insuring petroleum supplies); pressure by Western Europe and the United States; and the transition to democracy. To Pollack: "A combination of all three factors produced a kind of inertia which immobilized foreign policy-designers and makers, and was not conducive to the implementation of any coherent decolonization policy for the Western Sahara " - see *The Paradox of Spanish Foreign Policy*, 98. For a succinct and critical analysis of the Madrid Accords see Francisco Villar, *El proceso de autodeterminación del Sahara* (Valencia, Spain: Fernando Torres, 1982), 345-51. Villar contended that "in November 1975 the Francoist regime, agonizing like the dictator which incarnated it, inscribed in Madrid one of the blackest pages in contemporary Spanish foreign policy" (387).
32. Fusi, *Franco*, 171.
33. See Phillip C. Naylor, "Spain and France and the Decolonization of Western Sahara: Parity and Paradox, 1975-87," *Africa Today* 34, no. 3 (Fall 1987): 7-16.
34. Col. Raphael de Valdés Iglesias, charged with supervising the transfer of power, related that the *Djemma* meeting on February 26

"does not constitute the popular consultation provided for in the Madrid agreements" (Hodges, *Western Sahara*, 237, citing United Nations General Assembly, Thirty-First Session, Official Records, Supplement 23, *Report of the Special Committee on the Situation with Regard to the Implementation of the Declaration of the Granting of Independence to Colonial Countries and People*, A/31/23/Rev. 1, 1976, 215).

35. See Richard B. Parker, *North Africa: Regional Tensions and Strategic Concerns*, 1st ed. (New York: Praeger, 1984), 137-38; Hodges, *Western Sahara*, 224; and Damis, *Conflict in Northwest Africa*, 67. *The Wall Street Journal* (July 26, 1976) reported that Morocco had to pay $90 million for 65 percent of the phosphate consortium while Spain retained a 35 percent interest.

36. Hodges, *Western Sahara*, 224, citing Hassan II, *Conference de Presse de S.M. Hassan II sur la Marcha Verte et le Sahara* (Rabat: Ministre d'Etat chargé de l'information, 1975), 16. Morocco has also supported Spanish sovereignty over the Canaries (John Damis, "The Impact of the Saharan Dispute on Moroccan Foreign and Domestic Policy," in I. William Zartman, ed., *The Political Economy of Morocco* [New York: Praeger, 1987], 196). See also Rachid Lazrak, *Le Contentieux territorial entre le Maroc et l'Espagne* (Casablanca: Dar el Kitab, 1974).

37. Hodges, *Western Sahara*, 353. Besides being "distraught," Polisario wanted to take advantage of the fishing difficulties between Madrid and Rabat.

38. Ibid., citing *Le Monde*, December 19, 1980.

39. Eusebio Mujal-Léon, "Rei(g)ning in Spain," *Foreign Policy*, no. 51, (Summer 1983): 106.

40. Hodges, *Western Sahara*, 354.

41. *Agence France Presse, Sahara* series (*AFP*), February 21, 1986.

42. According to Thomas McKirk: "Generals want to keep them [the enclaves] for reasons more sentimental than strategic" (Trouble Stirs in Spain's North African Enclave" *Christian Science Monitor*, December 16, 1986. Mujal-Léon related that "ultranationalists" associate the enclaves as "part of [the Spanish] heritage of unity, dignity and national honor" ("Rei(g)ning in Spain," 109). Though no "ultranationalist," Felipe González supports the enclaves' integration with metropolitan Spain.

43. See Juan Goytisolo, *El problema del Sáhara* (Barcelona: Editorial Anagrama, 1979), 107-16.

44. S. Aguenious, "Melilla: Entre l'abandon et al surenchère," *Révolution africaine*, no. 1171 (August 8-14, 1986): 23. The article compared the Spanish right-wingers to the OAS. Juan Goytisolo perceived a "pied-noir mentality" in the enclaves (*El problema*, 109-10).
45. *Cambio 16* (international edition), no. 742 (1986): 20-27.
46. In July 1986 a Spanish trawler was attacked (*Grand Maghreb*, [1986]: 362). On September 11, the *AFP* reported an alleged Polisario seaborne assault upon a Spanish boat. Ten days later Polisario denied the attack "imputing the responsibility for this action on Morocco and Spain." According to the Sahrawi communiqué: "The objective of this crime is to manipulate Spanish public opinion." It added: "This tragic act devolves on Morocco and the Spanish government, which permits its citizens to venture into a war zone" (*AFP*, September 21, 1986).
47. Economist Intelligence Unit, *Morocco: A Country Study*, no. 3 (1986): 15. Another indication of Spanish and Moroccan military cooperation was the June 1986 "Atlas 86" joint air force exercises. Morocco has disclosed its interest in purchasing two corbetas-class warships from Spain (*El País*, March 13, 1989).
48. *Africa Research Bulletin* (Economic Series) 24, no. 7 (1987): 8776.
49. Economist Intelligence Unit, *Country Report: Morocco*, no. 4 (1987): 30.
50. See José Manuel Fajardo, "Marruecos, ovidos de España," *Cambio 16*, no. 832 (1987): 156-58.
51. See Economist Intelligence Unit, *Morocco: A Country Study*, 10-11.
52. "Nous avons beaucoup de choses à nous dire," *Révolution africaine*, no. 1114 (1985): 16.
53. The Spanish Association of Human Rights bestowed its 1987 prize to the Sahwari population of the occupied zone (*SPSC [Sahara People Support Committee] Newsletter* 8, no. 3 [December 1987-January 1988]).
54. *Africa Research Bulletin* (Political Series) 24, no. 8 (1987): 8609-10.
55. *El País*, February 1, 5, 11, 12, 1988; January 27, February 13, 17, 1989; and *Christian Science Monitor*, January 31, 1989. Algeria's role as a recognized "mediator and moderator" has become more involved in this intra-Spanish negotiation (*El País*, January 27, 1989).
56. Abdelaziz Dahmani, "Sahara: Pas de solution à l'horizon." *Jeune Afrique*, nos. 1336-1337 (1986): 72. See also Thomas Moffett III, "Morocco Winning Hearts and Minds," *Christian Science Monitor*, April 12, 1989.

57. Abdelaziz Dahmani, "Sahara: un prochain paradis touristique?" *Jeune Afrique*, no. 1331 (1986): 40-41.

58. *El País*, August 29, 1988. According to Maurice Barbier, Polisario has always received encouragement in Spain because of "a certain malaise" that seemed "like a betrayal in regard to the Sahrawi people" (Barbier, *Le Conflit du Sahara*, 244). The Spanish Government's position reflects the general post-Franco "continuation and change." The Spanish democracy has had an equivocal attitude toward the Falangist-negotiated Tripartite Accords (see Villar, *El proceso*, 387). That equivocation also expresses the dilemma of a discourse in transition. Spain also projects itself as competing with France as a "privileged interlocutor" between the Maghreb and Europe (Villar, *El proceso*, 387).

59. *El País*, August 30, 1988.

60. *El País*, January 26, 1989.

61. *El País*, September 25, 1989.

62. *AFP*, September 25, 1989.

63. *El-Moudjahid*, September 29-30, 1989.

64. *El País*, January 5, 1990.

65. *El País*, March 21 and 22, 1990.

66. *El País*, (semanal), May 21, 1990.

67. *El País*, (semanal), June 25, 1990.

68. *El-Moudjahid*, September 29-30, 1989.

69. "Update," *Africa Report*, 31 (May - June 1986): 57.

70. According to Edward A. Kolodziej: "The objectives served by colonialism would still be honored [by the policy of cooperation] -- grandeur, security, economic gain, cultural radiation, a sense of universal mission, and moral vindication." *French International Policy Under De Gaulle and Pompidou: The Politics of Grandeur* (Ithaca, New York: Cornell University Press, 1974), 448. Maurice Couve de Murville considered the policy of cooperation as "the means to purse the civilizing work and development conducted by the colonial power" (*Une politique étrangère, 1958-1969* [Paris: Librairie Plon, 1971], 434).

71. The "Marrakech Plan" was a series of military agreements for French arms transfers to Morocco. (Tony Hodges, *Historical Dictionary of Western Sahara* (Metchuen, New Jersey: Scarecrow Press, 1982), 222-23, citing *Le Nouvel Observateur*, no. 591 [1976]).

72. Nicole Grimaud also states that France may have wanted to make amends for favoring Algeria in border disputes during the colonial period (*La Politique extérieure de l'Algérie* [Paris: Karthala, 1984], 98). This, too, revealed the enduring effect of the imperial discourse, especially

during Giscard's presidency.

73. See Barbier, *Conflit du Sahara*, 308-15. See also Assidon, *Sahara*, for a sector listing of economic assistance (pp. 143-48).

74. Grimaud, *Politique*, 98, citing *Le Nouvel Observateur*, no. 586 (1976).

75. See Hodges, *Western Sahara*, 114-19, 247-256 and Barbier, *Le Conflit du Sahara*, 248-50. Assidon relates this invention with other French actions in *Sahara*, 117-27. An attack on May 1, 1977, at the Zouerate iron ore center killed two French technicians while six others were captured. Two more Frenchmen became hostages on October 25 along the Zouerate-Nouadhibou railway.

76. See Paul Balta and Claudine Rulleau, eds., *La Stratégie de Boumediène* (Paris: Editions Sindbad, 1978), 249-53 (speech of November 14, 1977). The threat of French military intervention against Polisario was also viewed as endangering Algeria politically and ideologically (Youcef Bournine, "L'Objectif de la France colonial," *El-Moudjahid*, November 6, 1977). Algeria held France responsible for the murder at the Amicale (*El-Moudjahid*, November 10, 1977).

77. Jérome Dumoulin, "Sahara: Le Dispotif français," *L'Express*, no. 1381 (December 26, 1977 - January 1, 1978): 36.

78. *Le Monde*, February 11, 1978.

79. During Giscard's April 1975 visit to Algeria, Boumedienne asserted: "Algeria and France are predisposed by their history and their spirituality" (Houari Boumediène, *Discours du Président Boumediène (2 January 1975-3 December 1975)* (Algiers: Ministère de l'Information et de la Culture, 1976), 87. President François Mitterrand characterized French-Algerian relations in 1989 as "life in common" (*Le Figaro*, March 11-12, 1989).

80. *Le Monde*, May 7-8, 1978.

81. According to Anne Lippert: "It seems likely that the French were aware of the move made by the Mauritanian military forces and did nothing to hinder it" ("The Struggle in the Western Sahara and Foreign Intervention," paper distributed by the Saharan People's Support Committee, n.d., citing a conversation with Amis de la RASD).

82. The "SADE Plan" called for a federated Sahrawi state associated with Mauritania but with substantial loss of territory to Algeria (see Damis, *Conflict in Northwest Africa*, 138-39).

83. David Lynn Price, *Western Sahara* (Beverly Hills, Calif.: Sage Publications, 1979), 69-70.

84. *Annuaire de l'Afrique du Nord, 1978* (Paris: Editions du Centre National des Recherches Scientifiques, 1980), 348.

85. Tony Hodges, "Valéry Giscard d'Estaing," *Historical Dictionary*, 152.

86. Association France-Algérie (AF-A), *Algérie informations*, no. 54 (1979): 7.

87. AF-A, *Algérie informations*, no. 57 (1979): 13.

88. Amis de la RASD, *Sahara Info*, nos. 50-51 (1980-81): 6. Boumedienne believed as early as April 1976 that France could have mediated the conflict (Ania Francos and Jean-Pierre Séréni, *Un Algérien nommé Boumediène* [Paris: Stock, 1976], 343).

89. François Mitterrand, *Politique 2, 1977-81* (Paris: Fayard, 1981), 314, 323.

90. See Tony Hodges, "François Mitterrand, Master Strategist in the Maghreb," *Africa Report*, no. 28 (May-June 1983): 17-21. According to Nicole Grimaud, France's favoring of Algeria influenced, in part, Morocco's decision during the 1981 OAU summit to support a self-determination referendum for the Western Sahara ("Algeria and Socialist France," *Middle East Journal* 40 (Spring 1986): 258.

91. There were problems concerning LNG pricing and French financial aid as well as the aspects of the policy of cooperation. See Grimaud, "Algeria and Socialist France," 260-61.

92. Werner Ruf, "The Role of World Powers;   Colonialist Transformations and King Hassan's Rule," in Richard Lawless and Laila Monahan, eds., *War and Refugees: The Western Sahara Conflict* (London and New York: Pinter Publishers, 1987), 81. Ruf provides useful statistics on French and American military financial assistance. While arms dealing is very important to France, Dassault-Breguet, fearing Moroccan purchases of American F-16s, criticized the government for not supporting the sale of 20-25 Mirage 2000s to Rabat (*Le Monde*, July 23, 1986). France has also made a determined effort to market arms to Algeria.

93. Amis de la RASD, *Sahara Info*, no. 73 (1985): iii. French personnel have not been specifically targeted, however Polisario forces shot down two private French aircraft in December 1985 and October 1986, killing the pilot of the first plane.

94. *AFP*, September 13, 1986.

95. David Seddon, "Morocco at War," in Lawless and Monahan, eds., *War and Refugees*, 123.

96. The elasticity in hydrocarbon markets and particularly the drop in oil prices (linked to Algerian LNG pricing systems) has produced very low prices ($1.97/million [MM] Btu) paid by Gas de France (GDF) especially when compared to the 1982 accord ($5.20/MMBtu with GDF paying $4.65/MMBTu) (Economist Intelligence Unit, *Algeria: Country Report*, no. 4 [1987]: 15; John Entelis, *Algeria: The Revolution Institutionalized* [Boulder, Colo.: Westview Press, 1986], 122). In 1984 France imported from Algeria 24.9 billion French francs (FF) and exported 23.6 billion FF, but these numbers tumbled precipitously by the end of the decade. The January 1990 financial accord earmarked 7 billion FF in credits. The new gas price was projected as just under $2.30/MMBtu (*AFP*, January 26, 1989). (Furthermore, French and Spanish oil companies have renewed interest in Saharan exploration given new, more liberal Algerian investment regulations.) France exported 12.8 billion FF to Algeria and imported 9.45 billion FF in 1989, which was actually a considerable improvement. While Algeria remains France's most important Third World market, Morocco's commercial volume is also significant (10.3 billion FF in French exports to Morocco and 8.6 billion FF in imports) (Economist Intelligence Unit, *Algeria: Country Report*, no. 2 [1990]: 22 and *Morocco: Country Report*, no. 2 [1990]: 20).

97. Grimaud, "Algeria and Socialist France," 262.

98. AF-A, *Algérie informations*, no. 151 (1988): 50.

99. In April 1989, Polisario's representative in France, Sayed Baba, renewed the call for France to serve as a moderator/mediator ("a messenger of peace") between the belligerents and to use its influence in the UN Security Council (*El-Moudjahid*, April 11, 1989).

100. Spanish colonial and postcolonial neglect of the Western Sahara correlates particularly with its historic policy toward its African colonies. Nevertheless, Spanish aid programs in the Third World have directed significant sums to former Spanish colonies (e.g. Equatorial Guinea) (*El País*, January 3, 1990).

101. Moroccan immigrants greeted Hassan during his September state visit. In 1989, 1,538 Moroccans were forced to leave Spain (*El País* [semanal], June 11, 1990). About 4 percent of the illegal immigrants have been regularized (*El País* [semanal], July 9, 1990).

102. There were fundamentalist protests in Morocco in May 1990. Islamic revivalism has been cited as a cause of the October 1988 "events" (riots) in Algeria. Furthermore, the Islamic Salvation Front (FIS) won local elections in Algeria in June 1990.

103. "Update," *Africa Report* 36 (January-February 1991): 8, 11.
104. See Manuel Cerdan and Antonio Rubio, "La Tensión bélica tiene eco Ceuta y Melilla," *Cambio 16*, no. 1003 (1991): 20-25.

3

The United States in the Saharan War: A Case of Low-Intensity Intervention
Stephen Zunes

INTRODUCTION

The war in the Western Sahara has not occupied the attention of United States policymakers as much as conflicts elsewhere in the world. Yet for most of the past fifteen years, the United States has been perhaps the most important extracontinental actor of the conflict, providing significant political, economic, and military support for Morocco's war effort. Meanwhile, the United States has demonstrated little support for a negotiated settlement, only recently giving an unqualified endorsement of United Nations peace efforts.

The United States and Morocco have a longstanding special relationship. They have had a treaty of friendship since 1787, the longest unbroken peace agreement the United States has maintained with any country in the world. Morocco has a population of over twenty-three million, making it the second largest Arab country. Morocco is also rich in mineral resources that may become more important to the United States in coming years.[1] It is strategically located in the northwest corner of Africa, bordering both the Atlantic and Mediterranean coasts, including the Strait of Gibraltar. Since 1950, Morocco has received more U.S. aid than any other Arab country, except for Egypt,[2] and more than any African country, except for Ethiopia under Emperor Haile Selassie.[3] Indeed, over the past decade, Morocco has received more than one-fifth of all U.S. aid to the continent, totaling more than $1 billion in military assistance alone.[4]

The modern-day special relationship between these two countries developed in earnest only with the signing of the Madrid Accords in

November 1975, which ceded Spanish administrative control of the Western Sahara to Morocco.[5] Indeed, the United States played a major role in pressuring a reluctant Spain to sign the accords, citing the possibility that the failure to meet Moroccan territorial demands might result in the overthrow of Morocco's King Hassan II, a strong American ally.[6] The rigidly bipolar perspective of the U.S. State Department under Secretary Henry Kissinger also played a role in the decision. Kissinger, a firm believer in the need to maintain a balance of power between allies of the Soviet Union and allies of the United States, said in Madrid that "the United States will not allow another Angola on the East flank of the Atlantic Ocean."[7] Still another concern, coming soon after Portugal's sharp turn to the left following the overthrow of the Marcello Caetano regime the year before, was that the Spanish might be able to concentrate on possible domestic turmoil following Franco's death rather than on a conflict in North Africa.[8] General Vernon Walters, then a special envoy, played a particularly important role in the 1975 negotiations.[9] A friend of Hassan since the general's days as an intelligence agent in Vichy-controlled North Africa, Walters was dispatched by Kissinger to convince the Spanish government, then preoccupied with a possible succession crisis during Franco's terminal illness, of the need to acquiesce to Moroccan territorial demands. Walters apparently tied Spain's cooperation on the Western Sahara with the renewal of the lease for U.S. air and naval bases on generous terms and with Spain's request for $1.5 billion in new U.S. weapons.[10] Within two months of the signing of the Madrid Accords, a five-year U.S.-Spanish treaty was signed that included agreements favorable to Spain. Walters, who has spoken quite candidly about other secret missions with which he was involved, such as arranging Kissinger's secret trips to China in 1971 and setting up the Paris peace talks between the United States and North Vietnam in 1968, has kept silent on his role here, saying, "It would look like the King of Morocco and the King of Spain are pawns of the United States and that wouldn't be in anybody's interest."[11]

As Moroccan troops moved into the Western Sahara in November 1975, the United States sent the aircraft carrier *Little Rock* to the North African coast and promised that "twenty F-4 jets are ready on the carrier" to assist the Moroccan forces in the event that the Moroccan invasion was challenged by Algerian or other armed forces.[12] In addition, the United States announced its intention to deliver twenty-four F-5E fighter planes[13] and $36 million worth of armored vehicles, while special steps were taken to rush these and other equipment to Morocco and Mauritania.[14]

The United States also sought to block diplomatic efforts to curb the Moroccan conquest. Allan Nanes, a specialist in U.S. foreign policy for the Congressional Research Service of the Library of Congress, described this as a shift to a U.S. policy that "would not automatically reject a territorial transfer brought by force."[15] At the United Nations, U.S. Ambassador Daniel Patrick Moynihan fought successfully to block effective UN action. In describing the episode, Moynihan observed that "the United States wished things to turn out as they did, and worked to bring this about. The Department of State desired that the United Nations prove utterly ineffective in whatever measures it undertook. This task was given to me, and I carried it forward with no inconsiderable success."[16]

The Western Sahara has been in a state of war ever since, with the Moroccans asserting their sovereignty through military force, and the Sahrawis likewise resisting the occupation army. A battle has been raging on the diplomatic front as well, but neither has yet brought the situation any closer to a solution than it was in 1975. This chapter examines the evolution of U.S. policy during that period and seeks to understand the ramifications and possible motivations for U.S. policy in the Western Sahara conflict.

EVOLUTION OF CARTER ADMINISTRATION POLICY

Some modern diplomatic historians have attempted to contrast Jimmy Carter's idealism in the international arena with both Kissinger's *Realpolitik* of the Richard Nixon and Gerald Ford State Department and the right-wing ideologues of the Ronald Reagan administration. Yet despite some differences in emphasis, there appears to be a high degree of continuity in the U.S. policy since the signing of the Madrid Accords.

In the period between the Moroccan takeover of the Western Sahara and the latter half of the Carter administration, U.S. military aid to Morocco increased dramatically, although it remained at a moderate level. The total of U.S. military aid rose from $4.1 million in Fiscal Year (FY) 1974 to $99.8 million in FY 1978.[17] Part of the reluctance of the Carter administration to become more directly and openly involved during that period stemmed from its formal nonrecognition of the Moroccan claims to the Western Sahara, a 1960 agreement prohibiting use of U.S. arms by Morocco outside its internationally recognized borders, and the U.S. Arms Export Control Act, which limits the use of American weapons by recipients of military aid to defensive purposes.   Early in Carter's presidency the administration had to acknowledge that the United States was tolerating the use of its weapons in the Western Sahara.[18] The State Department claimed that the use of U.S.-supplied F-5 aircraft in the Western Sahara by the Moroccan air force was not a "substantial violation" of U.S. law.[19] Despite concerns expressed by some Congressional liberals, Congress bowed to administration pressure and refused to block the sales.

Meanwhile, former U.S. officials were engaged in clandestine arms shipments to Morocco. Henry Kissinger and Vernon Walters found new military connections for Morocco in Jordan, Iran, Taiwan, South Korea, and South Africa. In 1978, they supervised secret transfers of guns, ammunition, and planes from those countries. Government documents and interviews with some of the key players indicate that Walters received at least $300,000 for his work with Morocco from a company that specializes in selling sophisticated military technology to foreign governments in 1980, barely one year after he left the CIA.[20]

In May 1979, the State Department approved a proposal from Northrop Page Communications to construct a $200 million electronic detection system to help the Moroccans locate elusive Polisario fighters in the desert.[21] Direct American counterinsurgency support had begun. During the remainder of the Carter administration, large shipments of weapons ordered specifically to assist Moroccan forces in the Western Sahara were sent by the United States.

Still, President Carter stated that the sale was "defensive," reinterpreting the 1960 agreement to include defense of Moroccan-held territory seized by military force. The arms sale was also approved on the grounds that the Polisario had launched attacks into Morocco itself. Additional concern was raised by Algerian and Libyan arms supplies to the Sahrawis.

The change in Carter administration policy came within the context of the rightward drift in foreign policy that occurred in the latter half of its term in office. With Polisario winning a string of military victories and the stability of King Hassan's throne in question, the United States did not wish to lose another ally so soon after the Iranian revolution, a reasoning that continued during the Reagan administration. Critics, however, observed that the Shah of Iran fell despite and, in part because of, the Shah's reliance on U.S. arms and his refusal to recognize the opposition.[22]

The scale of President Carter's military buildup was questioned by Secretary of State Cyrus Vance, who favored increasing the shipment of defensive weapons only, and the Arms Control and Disarmament Agency. However, none of President Carter's inner circle even considered a cutoff of arms.[23] The United States was increasingly explicit in its opposition to Polisario winning its war against Moroccan occupation forces.[24]

Support in Washington for Morocco was not automatic. Indeed, given the widespread concerns over the implications of such a policy toward international law and impact on U.S. relations with Africa, there were occasional questions raised on Capitol Hill by Congressional liberals. However, Morocco was prepared for such potential opposition. Late in 1978, the Moroccan government hired the public relations firm of DGA International to promote its cause in the United States at a cost reportedly amounting to almost $900,000 for six months of lobbying, and similarly hired the firm of Hill and Knowlton for approximately $100,000 per year.[25]

Much of Morocco's public relations successes could also be attributed to Moroccan Ambassador Ali Benjelloun, who, during this period, replaced the Shah's Ambassador Ardeshir Zahedi as the most gregarious diplomatic host in Washington, developing the skills of charming decision-makers at opulent gatherings into an art form. He feted Florida Senator Richard Stone just a few weeks before Stone proposed that Congress boost military sales credit to Morocco by amending the International Security Assistance Act. Ambassador Benjelloun gave black-tie dinners for House Foreign Affairs Committee Chairman Clement Zablocki and State Department director of North African affairs, James Bishop. Within a few months of this diplomatic offensive, the change in Carter administration policy was official. The lavish parties, dinners, and luncheons with exotic Middle Eastern cuisine, often accompanied by belly dancers, took place during this critical juncture as often as three times a week, while opposition to the shift in administration policy was muted.[26]

REAGAN ADMINISTRATION POLICY

Despite the increased support from the Carter administration and Congress, lingering American concerns about international law and human rights issues caused the Moroccan government some worries about what they saw as an ambivalent attitude from Washington. The Reagan election victory in 1980 was met with great enthusiasm by Moroccan officials. According to Lissan Eddine Daoud, assistant director of the Maghreb Arab Press, Morocco's official news agency, "We believe in God in this country and God balances things, so we got Mr. Reagan."[27]

In one of his first major ambassadorial appointments, President Reagan appointed Joseph Reed, a friend of King Hassan's, to become ambassador to Morocco. The only noncareer ambassador in the Middle East, Reed had worked closely with David Rockefeller (a close friend of the king) as his executive assistant and vice-president of Chase Manhattan Bank from 1969 to 1981. Reed was particularly eager for greater U.S. support for King Hassan's military struggle in the Western Sahara,[28] stating that

Morocco is at the strategic straits of the Mediterranean. It is clear how Morocco is important to the survivability of Europe. My mandate is to illustrate to our friends around the globe that the Reagan Administration wanted to single out Morocco as the primary example of how America supported a proven ally and friend.[29]

When presenting his credentials to King Hassan on November 6, 1981, he stated that

the United States is the true friend of Morocco. The leadership of the Reagan Administration has stated that your country's concerns are my country's concerns. The United States will do its best to be helpful in every area of need that may arise. Count on us. We are with you.[30]

According to Morris Draper, Deputy Assistant Secretary of State for Near Eastern and South Asian Affairs, in Congressional testimony in March 1981, "it would not be in the spirit of this administration's policy if support for America's traditional and historic friends--to meet reasonable and legitimate needs--were to be withheld or made conditional other than under extraordinary circumstances."[31]

Thus, the Reagan administration made clear to Congress that it regarded Morocco's war in the Sahara as "reasonable and legitimate."

A parade of American officials visited Morocco when the Reagan administration came to office. Lannon Walker, the Acting Assistant Secretary of State for African Affairs, met with CIA agents in Rabat, Morocco, in March 1981.[32] Frank Carlucci, former Deputy Director of the CIA and later Secretary of Defense, paid a three-day visit in mid-June 1981,[33] and Bobby Inman, Deputy Director of the CIA, visited in late November 1981. Lt. General James Williams, Director of Defense Intelligence Agency, went to Morocco in September of that year.[34]

In early November 1981, Francis West led a delegation of twenty-three high-level Pentagon and State Department officials to Morocco.[35] The following month, Secretary of Defense Casper Weinberger went to Rabat for direct negotiations with King Hassan.[36] Admiral Thomas Hayward, Pentagon Chief of Naval Operations, visited on February 23, 1982.[37] Secretary of State Alexander Haig met with King Hassan on February 12, 1982,[38] and Senate Foreign Relations Committee Chairman Charles Percy visited on December 22, 1981, and promised greater U.S. economic assistance.[39] Vice President George Bush visited Morocco in September 1983 and Jeanne Kirkpatrick, U.S. Ambassador to the United Nations, visited Moroccan-occupied Sahara that same month.[40] Subsequently, there were visits by Weinberger, his successor Carlucci, Secretary of State George Schultz, and Undersecretary Richard Murphy.[41]

This personal attention given by U.S. representatives was matched by a dramatic increase in military support. During the first week of the Reagan administration, the United States announced that it was going through with a sale of 108 tanks to Morocco. The decision to deliver weapons, initially announced by the Carter administration in 1980, was based on its judgment that Morocco had demonstrated a "willingness to help achieve a cease-fire, to negotiate the relevant Western Sahara issues, and to cooperate with the international efforts to mediate the dispute."[42] This decision came only days after the Algerian government--which was Polisario's primary supporter--had played a key role in the release of American hostages in Iran. Many diplomats considered the timing of the arms sale highly insensitive.

Algeria had made overtures for better relations with the United States, and ties had improved somewhat, but the Reagan administration defended the tank sales on the grounds that Morocco need to protect itself from the threat of Algeria. However, administration officials were unable to produce any evidence suggesting aggressive intentions by the Algerians.

Military aid to Morocco during the first two years of the Reagan administration increased dramatically. By 1982, there were approximately 130 U.S. military advisors supporting the Moroccan armed forces,[43] including members of the Special Forces (Green Berets),[44] as well as U.S. military attachés seen wearing Moroccan uniforms in the Western Sahara battle zone.[45] Over $1 million was being spent annually for training Moroccan military officers,[46] and training was provided for counterinsurgency commandos and pilots.[47] C-130 aircraft with side-looking airborne radars were supplied, along with other reconnaissance and intelligence assistance, possibly via satellites.[48] Moroccan officials acknowledge that the United States was providing Morocco with "technical assistance regarding Polisario movements and bases in the Western Sahara."[49] Francis West, U.S. Assistant Secretary of Defense for International and Security Affairs, suggested to the head of the Moroccan Air Force that the Moroccan military shift to more mobile and aggressive tactics,[50] adding that the United States would provide the necessary training.[51] Such efforts, in addition to the U.S.-designed wall cordoning off Moroccan-occupied territory, substantially contributed to Morocco being able to counter the military advantages which Polisario had enjoyed by 1983.

Among the weapons that the Reagan administration sent to Morocco were controversial antipersonnel ordinance. During November and December 1981, the United States delivered one hundred cluster bombs (CBU-58s). The United States also agreed to send additional CBU-58 and CBU-71 cluster bombs. Unlike the shipment of such weapons to Israel, which carried stipulations as to their use, there were no such special restrictions on Morocco.[52]

The Reagan administration proposed to give Morocco $100 million in loans for U.S. arms purchases for FY 1983, half of which would be given at subsidized rates of interest.[53] However, on May 11, 1982, the House Foreign Affairs Committee voted to cut that figure in half and eliminated the interest rate subsidy. Furthermore, it prohibited U.S. military advisors from visiting or "performing official functions in the Western Sahara" as well as "any training which has as its principal purpose improving the ability of the Moroccan armed forces to carry out offensive counterinsurgency military activities in the Western Sahara."[54] The bill never reached the floor, however, since foreign aid went through as part of a continuing resolution. At the last minute Senator Robert Kasten slipped in the administration's $100 million, which passed along with the continuing resolution, to the irritation of many who expressed concern that the additional money would have to be taken out of aid to other countries.[55] Aid continued at moderately high levels for the next several years, with military sales averaging between $50-$60 million and direct military aid at a slightly higher figure.[56]

In FY 1989, U.S. military aid to Morocco stood at $43 million, despite fiscal constraints that led to cutbacks in foreign aid to most Third World countries.[57] For FY 1991, President George Bush requested $40 million in military grant aid for Morocco.[58] The major impetus appeared to be coming from Congress, not the Reagan or Bush administrations, with particular advocacy coming from Hawaii's Democratic Senator Daniel Inouye. Much of the Moroccan success can be attributed to effective lobbying. The Moroccan government is now represented in Washington by Neal and Company, a highly successful lobbying firm that includes Egypt, Pakistan, and El Salvador among its clients.[59]

For the first several years of the war, Polisario matched increases in Moroccan military hardware with better equipment of their own provided by Algeria and, for a time, by Libya. Polisario apparently used SAM-6 antiaircraft missiles when they downed five Moroccan planes at the battle of Guelta Zemmour on October 13, 1981.[60] The use of such sophisticated weapons, combined with continued Polisario military successes, led to a major shift in U.S. aid program in order to restructure the Moroccan war effort to make the Moroccans into a more effective fighting unit.

Part of the weakness in the numerically superior and better armed Moroccan forces could be explained by the Moroccan army's highly centralized structure of command, communication, and control.[61] For example, a field commander had to go through Rabat to get air power to respond to a Polisario attack; by the time the Royal Moroccan Air Force (RMAF) would arrive, the highly mobile guerrillas would have disappeared.[62]

A revealing study of the significance of the U.S. role in the Sahara war was presented in a book by Lt. Colonel David J. Dean of the U.S. Air Force's Airpower Research Institute titled *The Air Force Role in Low-Intensity Conflict*.

By the end of 1980, the use of U.S.-supplied C-130s for command, control, and surveillance resulted in "a series of strikes that had a serious impact on the Polisario. These attacks not only led to a high attrition of the rebel forces but also denied them the ability to operate freely in the desert."[63]

The training and arming of the RMAF has proved to be decisive.

According to Lt. Col. Dean, the RMAF

> plays a key role in every phase of this desert war. The Royal
> Moroccan Air Force has set the pace for the conflict. Its actions
> have at times denied the Polisario fighters and the freedom of
> movement so critical to their success and have led the Polisario
> to obtain high-technology weapons to drive the Moroccan air
> force from the battlefield.[64]

Unfortunately for the Moroccans, however, the use of sophisticated
antiaircraft weaponry by Polisario led the Moroccan Air Force to
become ineffective for a time, with the important exception of air
resupply provided by U.S.-made C-130 transport planes.[65] By the end
of 1981, thirty U.S. instructors began training Moroccan pilots in
antimissile tactics, and within a few months an additional team of
twenty-five had been sent to train Moroccan troops in counterinsurgency
tactics.[66] According to Dean and other strategic analysts, such support
played a major role in countering the military advantage previously
enjoyed by Polisario.

The Reagan administration claimed that increased military support of
the heavily armed 150,000-strong Moroccan army against nomadic
Polisario guerrillas was geared to "redress the balance" that the
administration asserted favored the Polisario. During this same period,
Robert Flaten, director of the North African desk at the State
Department, claimed that the UN recognized Morocco as the
administrative authority in the Western Sahara.

While the Reagan administration was dramatically increasing its
diplomatic activity with Morocco, it cut off the limited contact with
Polisario established during the Carter administration.[67] A House
Committee on Foreign Affairs staff study commission to the region in
1982 criticized the administration for "prohibiting even discreet and low-
level diplomatic contact with the Polisario"[68] as well as the
administration's "over-reliance on the military component in United
States-Moroccan relations."[69]

Economic aid in Morocco was also on the rise, even as aid to poorer
countries was being cut back. Such aid was directly linked to supporting
the war effort, since nearly half of the annual budget is related to the
war and the resulting foreign debt.[70] There is little likelihood that
Morocco could sustain the economic costs of the war were it not for
generous U.S. assistance.

THE U.S. GOVERNMENT AND THE PEACE PROCESS

The official position of the U.S. government on the Western Sahara has been that it is "neutral as regards the final status of the Western Sahara territory."[71] While not formally recognizing the Western Sahara as part of Morocco, the United States does recognize Moroccan administration of the territory.[72] While the United States has formally declared that "a military solution to this conflict is neither possible nor desirable" and that "no side can win a clear-cut victory in military terms,"[73] the arming and training of the Moroccan armed forces for counterinsurgency warfare appears to indicate U.S. support for some sort of military solution. Since the increase in sophistication of arms procured by the Moroccans led on several occasions to a corresponding escalation by Polisario, and since Polisario has not appeared anywhere close to defeat, the result was to prolong the conflict, increasing casualties on both sides and putting a negotiated settlement further out of reach.

While the Carter administration contended that arms aid was tied to Moroccan efforts to end the fighting, the Reagan administration made it clear that such concerns were divorced from the consideration of aid requests. Morris Draper, Deputy Assistant Secretary of State for Near Eastern Affairs, testifying before a hearing of the House Subcommittee on Africa on March 25, 1981, stated, "We will not...make decisions on military equipment sales explicitly conditional on unilateral Moroccan attempts to show progress toward a peaceful negotiated settlement."[74]

Both the Carter and Reagan administration claimed that such military aid increased the chances of a peace settlement. Yet despite such pronouncements and congressionally mandated language in the 1980 foreign aid legislation that U.S. aid "should be related to Morocco's willingness to help achieve a cease-fire, to negotiate the relevant Western Sahara issues, and to cooperate with international efforts to mediate the dispute,"[75] the aid appears to have had the opposite effect. Soon after the announcement of the large-scale increase in aid in October 1979, Hassan vowed in a nationally televised address that Morocco would never discuss a withdrawal from the Western Sahara and would fight "forever and forever" to maintain its control.[76] Later that month, Hassan was scheduled to go to Monrovia, Liberia, for the Organization of African Unity (OAU) meeting hosted by the leaders of Nigeria, Tanzania, Sudan, and Guinea to discuss the Western Sahara situation. Buoyed by the announcement, less than three days before the scheduled meeting, of the increased aid by President Carter, King Hassan abruptly decided not to attend.[77]

The Carter administration stated in early 1980 that the supply of counterinsurgency weapons to the Moroccan government would "give Morocco a sense of support that can contribute toward negotiation of a solution which reflects the wishes of the inhabitants."[78] However, King Hassan remained as adamant as ever in his refusal to negotiate with the Polisario Front.

A new peace offensive was launched at the June 1983 meeting of the OAU in Addis Ababba, Ethiopia. The OAU reaffirmed the right of Sahrawi self-determination, and called for direct negotiations for a cease-fire and the emplacement of a UN-OAU peacekeeping force during the referendum. Polisario and Morocco scheduled a meeting in September, hosted by OAU committee of six nations: Sudan, Guinea, Senegal, Tanzania, Mali, and Sierra Leone.

The OAU, as one of the world's most important forums on nonalignment, did not fit into the Reagan administration's bipolar view of the world, where Africa was neatly divided between East and West. Therefore, the United States persisted in efforts that would both strengthen Morocco and cripple the OAU. Just prior to the scheduled meeting, U.S. Vice President George Bush met with King Hassan in Morocco, and Morocco subsequently decided not to attend. Less than a month later, Morocco launched a military offensive in the Western Sahara.[79]

The Reagan administration discounted an initiative made late in the Carter administration to partition the country, with the northern half going to Morocco and the southern half becoming the SADR. The Polisario had already rejected this proposal, because virtually all the country's mineral wealth lies in the northern half, thus making the proposed Polisario ministate economically unviable. And considering Morocco's rush to annex the former Mauritanian sector in 1978, it was unlikely that King Hassan would have accepted such a proposal either.

The 1982 House Committee on Foreign Affairs staff study mission observed that

> the qualitative change in military assistance the United States is providing may well have a negative impact on the achievement of a political solution in the Western Sahara....The concrete assistance and symbolic message these kinds of military cooperation send appear counterproductive to the U.S.

commitment to a political solution.[80]

The report further criticized the Reagan administration's failure to communicate concerns over King Hassan's opposition to efforts by regional and international bodies for a negotiated settlement or even to acknowledge that such opposition existed.[81]

Meanwhile, the United States continued its efforts to block effective action by the United Nations. It lobbied to prevent the Western Sahara situation from being placed on the agenda of the Decolonization Committee.[82]

Such concerns about these regional issues may have reflected a desire of the United States to exploit divisions among African states over the Western Sahara issue to its own advantage. In February 1982, the OAU admitted the SADR as its fifty-first member.

The United States lobbied a number of pro-Western African leaders, using aid as leverage, to refuse admission of the SADR and encourage the failure of the OAU.[83] The United States circulated a secret document stating that "the admission of the SADR to the OAU would be a grave mistake" and urging that African states boycott the summit that was to be held in Libya that August.[84] The United States desired to thwart diplomatic gains of Polisario, and embarrass Muammar Qaddafi in the process.

When the OAU attempted to hold its 1982 summit, Morocco and its allies boycotted the meeting and made a quorum impossible, thus creating perhaps the greatest crisis in the OAU history and threatening to split the organization apart. Though the OAU had successfully weathered other crises, such as the controversy over the recognition of the Popular Movement for the Liberation of Angola (MPLA) government of Angola during 1975 and 1976, there were elements in the Western Sahara controversy that were unprecedented: it was the first time the OAU had failed to convene, and it involved the de facto accusation that a fellow African state was engaged in colonialism.

Warnings by U.S. Representative Stephen Solarz in 1979 that arming Morocco would "encourage intransigence rather than flexibility" and that it would "prolong the war rather than shorten it" appear to have been correct.[85] The chances of a successful negotiated peace settlement would likely have been greater were it not for U.S. diplomatic, economic, and military support of the Moroccan war effort.

THE RISKS IN U.S. POLICY

One major risk cited by critics of U.S. support for Morocco in the Western Sahara was in its consequences on international order. Traditionally, nation-states--particularly great powers such as the United States--have upheld international law not for fear of sanctions as much as for the perception that maintaining international order prevents global instability that could threaten that nation's vital interests worldwide. With some notable exceptions, primarily within their tightly controlled spheres of influence, the United States and other major powers have been willing to sacrifice short-term policy interests rather than risk losing the long-term advantages of maintaining international stability that could be jeopardized if these major powers engaged in or tolerated a precedent-setting act of aggression.

Such traditional concerns have apparently been ignored by U.S. policy planners, leading some critics to fear that the United States has allowed for the establishment of a potentially dangerous precedent. According to Congressional testimony on Morocco's war in the Western Sahara by Thomas Frank of the New York University Law School,

> this is the first instance--with the possible exception of West Irian [Western New Guinea], where there was at least an attempt to make a show of consultation--in which a former colony has been dismantled by another former colony before being allowed to become independent, thereby being denied its right to self-determination; and, as such, it constitutes a particularly destabilizing precedent for Africa and indeed the whole world.[86]

Of similar concern is that Morocco's actions break with the policy of strict adherence by African states to the old colonial boundaries, no matter how arbitrary, unless there is full agreement by all parties involved. (It is noteworthy that Morocco's southern boundary is not arbitrary; no Moroccan ruler until the present has controlled territory south of the Draa River and there are clear distinctions in language, dress, and customs between Moroccans and Sahrawis.)[87] By supporting Morocco's takeover of the Western Sahara, critics fear the United States could be giving its stamp of approval of actions that, if taken by other African states, could plunge the continent into chaos.

Another risk comes from the consequences of the United States' relative diplomatic isolation in its support of Morocco. The world response to Moroccan policy has been overwhelmingly condemnatory. Votes in the United Nations General Assembly have been overwhelmingly in favor of Sahrawi self-determination and direct negotiations between Polisario and Morocco.

Meanwhile, seventy-five nations have formally recognized the SADR, including twenty-seven African countries and fourteen Latin American countries. Recognition is not limited to radical states, but includes such conservative African governments as Togo and Rwanda, as well as influential moderate Latin American states like Mexico and Venezuela. Polisario has been endorsed by several international forums including the Non-Aligned Movement and the Arab Steadfastness Front.[88] Polisario has also gained a sympathetic response in Europe, particularly in Spain, which has repudiated the Madrid Accords. European Community (EC) officials have met publicly with Polisario leaders, and dialogue with the governments of France and Spain is continuing quietly.[89]

The Reagan administration's tough pro-Moroccan stance and involvement in the internal conflicts of the OAU could have had serious consequences for U.S. relations with the rest of the continent, relations already strained as a result of U.S. ties with South Africa. The OAU has been particularly concerned with the U.S. refusal to see this African conflict in an African context, fearing that the United States viewed the conflict from a kind of Cold War myopia that has already had a deleterious effect on regional conflicts in Central America and the Middle East.[90] There has also been concern that U.S. support for Morocco might encourage similar military adventurism by other African states. Indeed, observers argue that Qaddafi was emboldened by the Moroccan takeover of the Western Sahara to launch attacks against disputed territories in northern Chad. The Treaty of Oujda between Libya and Morocco was based in part on their desire to negate each other's opposition to their claims against territories to their south. The Iraqi invasion of Kuwait in August 1990 strengthened this concern.

Another concern by critics of U.S. policy, particularly in Congress, has been its ramifications for relations with Algeria. Algeria has been increasing its ties to France and attempting to lessen its dependency on the Soviet Union. It has made clear that U.S. support for Morocco is the only real obstacle to closer relations. Some observers, citing figures from the International Institute for Strategic Studies, fear that increased

U.S. aid to Morocco will shift the military balance enough in Morocco's favor that it will be tempted to launch a major war, which until the recent military buildup was impossible due to Algeria's military superiority.[91] The construction of the sixth earthen wall in the Western Sahara, which brought Moroccan forces close to Algeria's relatively vulnerable southwestern border, raised additional concerns.[92] In the past, King Hassan has threatened to attack Sahrawi refugee camps in southwestern Algeria as more sophisticated U.S. military hardware came into his possession, declaring that he "will not hesitate to violate the Algerian border."[93] There were several small-scale border clashes in the late 1970s.[94] This led even members of the U.S. foreign policy establishment, who had generally not raised moral or legal concerns about arming Morocco, to question U.S. policy in the region.[95] They pointed out that Algeria supplies 7 percent of the oil and much of the liquified natural gas imported into the United States annually, making Algeria a far more important country to the United States than Morocco in economic terms.[96]

Successive U.S. administrations have hoped that Algeria would abandon the Polisario, especially recently, with the future rule by the Algerian National Liberation Front (FLN) in doubt and severe economic problems leading that country to increase its ties with Morocco and decrease its financial assistance to Polisario. However, popular support in Algeria for the Sahrawi cause extends to the Islamic opposition as well, and economic cooperation with a neighboring country does not preclude strong political disagreements. In addition, many Algerians believe that it would be a dangerous precedent to Morocco's neighbors should Moroccan aggrandizement prove successful in the Western Sahara. (Morocco, in addition to its claims on the Western Sahara, has also claimed at times all or part of Mauritania, Algeria, Mali, and Senegal). Nor would Algeria likely jeopardize its standing as a leader of the Non-Aligned Movement by allowing a victory for what many see as colonialism.

Critics also expressed concern over the possibility of the United States being dragged into a military quagmire. While the Moroccans have significantly increased the amount of territory under their control during the past five years, they are as far as ever from a total victory. Moroccan forces are stretched thin along the 2,400-kilometer wall,[97] with Polisario attacking at will and with little opportunity for offensive actions by the Moroccans. Unless ended by a negotiated settlement, such a war of attrition could last for an indefinite period with little guarantee of an outcome favorable to the Moroccans and--given Morocco's chronic economic and social problems--would likely require increased U.S. military support.

Still another risk to U.S. interests is that the ongoing Western Sahara conflict may lead to the fall of the pro-American Alawite dynasty in Morocco.   Although the United States believes that Moroccan withdrawal from the war would provoke a popular reaction that would lead to Hassan's overthrow, many observers believe that the economic crises resulting from the war are actually a greater threat to the king's survival. Polisario is not interested in Hassan's downfall, believing him to be a relatively moderate and stabilizing force as compared with even more hard-lined potential successors.[98]

There is a chance that Hassan, like the Caetano regime in Portugal and France's Fourth Republic, is doomed because of his pursuit of what many in Morocco, albeit still a minority, see as an unjust, unnecessary, and unwinnable war. As far back as 1979, several U.S. government agencies reported that King Hassan was losing control; the CIA even questioned his ability to last out the year.[99] Yet despite high inflation, labor unrest, and a lowered standard of living as a result of the war, Hassan has somehow managed to stay afloat, at least for now, due to generous U.S. economic assistance and Hassan's highly developed political skill. However, there are serious risks involved in U.S. support for the Moroccan war effort; its damaging effects on the Moroccan economy could lead to the establishment of a regime far less friendly to the interests of the United States.

According to Tony Hodges, one of the world's leading authorities on the conflict,

> one of the ironies of U.S. policy of the Sahara is that, by enabling King Hassan to sustain his war, it is indirectly helping to worsen his country's economic difficulties, to exacerbate the social tensions in his kingdom, and to undermine his regime's political stability--the very opposite of Washington's objectives. By contrast, Polisario, whose forces appear to have suffered relatively few losses, and Algeria, which is economically much stronger than Morocco, can afford to sit out this long war.[100]

THE IMPACT ON MOROCCAN POLITICAL ECONOMY

This raises the important issue of how the development of the special relationship between the United States and Morocco is affecting Morocco itself, particularly with regard to the increasing costs of the war and the domestic political structure.

King Hassan is one of the world's few remaining absolute monarchs. He possesses impressive intellectual and political skill (as well as a French law degree), but rules his country much as the three-hundred-year-old Alawite dynasty has always done. The king has a reputation of often being moody and reportedly suffers from emotional problems. Not inappropriately, Hassan wrote his political science dissertation on Machiavelli.[101] Hassan's lifestyle is lavish; his advisors are uncritical; corruption is widespread; and the constitution forbids criticism of the king.[102]

The sixty-year-old monarch has a history of cultivating opposition views on important matters followed by tough crackdowns, especially against labor unions. In 1981, there were massive repression and jailing of students sympathetic to the Sahrawi cause. Though supporters of Moroccan annexation took control of Morocco's national student union from pro-Sahrawi students, they have supported the right to dissent, and have led student strikes and demonstrations against the repression.[103]

Amnesty International has been consistently critical of the Moroccan human rights situation, both in the occupied territories and within Morocco itself. One recent report documented the detention of hundreds of political prisoners, as well as reports of torture and ill-treatment of prisoners and deaths in detention.[104] One U.S. diplomat referred to the Amnesty International studies as "100 percent accurate".[105] The State Department's annual human rights report was also unusually frank in its assessment of Morocco's human rights violations.[106]

In the past, the war effort had considerable popular support in Morocco. Today, however, there appears to be little enthusiasm outside of the country's political leadership. While most Moroccans support the war effort publicly, given that it is illegal to do otherwise, the exact scale of support is hard to gauge. In April 1979, Morocco's entire political elite, ranging from conservative monarchists to the Communist party, formed the National Defense Council in support of the takeover of the Western Sahara.[107] The opposition Socialist party is actually more hardline than the king on the issue.[108]

The military, always a key element in Moroccan politics, is itself divided on what to do next. There have been rumors of purges and even a possible coup attempt. General Ahmed Dlimi, commander of the Moroccan armed forces, was killed January 15, 1983, in a suspicious car accident. Dlimi had been meeting with Algerian and French officials just before his death, and possibly with representatives of the Polisario as well, and forces within both the military and the royal palace were troubled by his desire for a negotiated settlement to the war and his concern about growing Moroccan ties with the United States and the use of Morocco for U.S. foreign policy goals.

The war costs Morocco over $1.5 million a day.[109] The often stated goals of a more equitable distribution of wealth, improved housing and health care, and universal education have been indefinitely delayed by the conflict. A severe austerity program launched in 1979 cut back everything except the military and internal security, and the situation has improved little since then.

The war has exacerbated Morocco's economic crisis. The country is dependent on foreign imports for 80 percent of its oil; it is faced with tariff restrictions by the EC; it has a high demographic growth rate; and it has suffered from a crash on the world market for phosphates and other raw material exports. In addition, the admission of Greece, Spain, and Portugal to the EC has limited exports of Moroccan citrus, wine, tomatoes, and olive oil.[110]

Furthermore, Morocco suffered from a devastating drought in the late 1970s and again in the mid-1980s, and experienced other natural disasters, including a recent attack of locusts. As many as a thousand people a day leave the countryside for the cities, creating vast sheet metal shanty towns called *bidonvilles*. The result is a potentially unstable employed and disaffected urban population.[111]

In March 1981, the International Monetary Fund (IMF) granted a standby credit of $988 million, at the time constituting the second largest bailout in IMF history.[112] As is the case with such loans, the IMF imposed austerity conditions that forced the government to raise prices on basic foodstuffs by as much as 72 percent.[113] There were massive protests led by the socialist-dominated trade unions, which included a general strike that resulted in the arrests of 6,000 to 8,000 people, among them top trade unionists and leftist political leaders.[114] Their newspapers were banned. Protests in Casablanca led to the deaths of as many as 900 people at the hands of government forces.[115] The king rescinded the measure two weeks later, but significant, if less dramatic, increases went into effect in December 1982, creating further unrest.

Subsequent reform efforts supported by the IMF have led to an economic rebound; but as with similar countries experiencing an economic recovery based on liberalized trade and financial policies, the benefits are yet to reach the majority of the population. With a foreign debt of over $20 billion, continued high unemployment, and an export-oriented economy vulnerable to external pressures, it is unlikely that a full recovery is possible as long as Morocco has to maintain its occupation of the Western Sahara. In addition to the costs of maintaining a large armed presence along the wall, there are the costs of internal security, and the enormous expenses from ambitious development projects in the occupied territories directed at encouraging immigration from Morocco and gaining the support of the remaining Sahrawi population.

At least 40 percent of the consolidated national budget goes to military-related expenditures.[116] The country's limited technical and management skills are concentrated on the war effort instead of on rebuilding the economy. Workers are striking in increasing numbers against having their wages sacrificed for the "national cause," and the heavily taxed middle class are privately expressing antiwar sentiments.[117] Economic discontent led to a national general strike and violent riots in Fez and Tangier in December 1990.[118]

PREVAILING THEORIES OF POLICY

The standard justification in support of U.S. military assistance of its allies against armed resistance movements is the concern over Soviet penetration into the area in question. Whatever the merits or demerits of such concerns in other areas of U.S. policy interests, this does not seem to apply to the situation in the Western Sahara.

Far from being Soviet-aligned Marxists, members of Polisario see themselves as deeply religious nationalists, not unlike the resistance movement in Afghanistan. There is an understandable confusion among them as to why the United States refers to the Afghans as freedom fighters and the Sahrawis, who also see themselves as victims of foreign aggression, as terrorists.

Within this Islamic context, Polisario does espouse a kind of vague indigenous socialism. It has freed black slaves owned by some traditional Sahrawi nomads,[119] and has announced its intention to nationalize the mines.[120] Polisario has pointedly declined to identify itself as Marxist, however, saying that the ideological direction of the nation is up to the Sahrawis themselves, not to a vanguard party.[121] Many observers identify Polisario with the early Front for the Liberation of Mozambique (FRELIMO) in Mozambique or with the nationalism of Amilcar Cabral and the African Party for the Independence of Guinea-Bissau and Cape Verde (PAIGC) in Guinea-Bissau. Polisario's decentralized system of governance and its participatory-democratic structure is in sharp contrast to the Marxist-Leninist model favored by many other Third World nationalist movements.[122]

According to Hodges, "Polisario has never espoused Marxist principles, even verbally, and, as a proudly nationalist movement, it would be most unlikely to end up beholden to any foreign power after successfully concluding its long and difficult struggle for independence."[123]

There have been no confirmed reports of Polisario receiving military aid from the Soviet Union, a fact acknowledged by the U.S. government.[124] Indeed, they are the only liberation movement in Africa that has never received military aid directly from the Soviets, Chinese, or Cubans. The only known recipient of direct arms shipments from the East bloc in the conflict is Morocco, which has received arms from Rumania.[125] Neither the Soviet Union nor any former East bloc country has recognized the SADR. In fact, the Soviet Union is Morocco's largest trading partner, importing large amounts of phosphates since the United States halted exports following the Soviet invasion of Afghanistan.[126] A 1978 multibillion dollar agreement between the Soviet Union and Morocco, the largest ever between the USSR and a Third World country, includes agreements for Soviet exports of oil, chemicals, lumber, and cargo ships.[127] Though the Soviet Union has closer diplomatic ties with Algeria, its trading relationship with Algeria is minuscule by comparison.

Soviet trawlers regularly take advantage of the rich waters off Morocco's Atlantic coast as well as off the coast of the Western Sahara, and Polisario forces have even fired upon Soviet fishing vessels for engaging in such activities, which they consider an illegal infringement of Sahrawi territorial waters.[128] The Soviet-aligned Moroccan Communist party, PPS, has consistently supported the takeover of the Western Sahara.[129] Nor has there been any substantiation of Moroccan charges of the presence of Cuban and East German personnel with

Polisario. Polisario's diplomatic contacts are far closer to the Western European socialist parties than they are with any communist parties.

The concern over Libyan influence in North Africa, a justification for U.S. military aid to a number of countries in the region, certainly does not apply to the Western Sahara situation either. Libya, in its 1984 treaty with Morocco, tacitly agreed not to challenge Morocco's claim on the Western Sahara and to continue a previously self-imposed embargo on arms to Polisario.[130] The Treaty of Oujda was revoked by King Hassan in August 1986, but there has been no evidence of renewed Libyan military support of Polisario. Well before the rapprochement between Morocco and Libya, Libyan leader Muammar Qaddafi was reluctant to get involved in the conflict on any level, refusing to even recognize the SADR until April 1980, presumably because his strong ideological position in support of pan-Arab unity would be contradicted by support of the creation of yet another Arab state. Even when Libya formally recognized the SADR, Qaddafi expressed his desire for a union between Mauritania and the Western Sahara.[131] And at the peak of Libyan support for Polisario, during the 1980-83 period, Qaddafi's role in the conflict was far less than that of Algeria. Libyan involvement during that period was greatly exaggerated by Hassan, presumably as a means of gaining greater sympathy for his cause from the United States.[132]

Nor could the United States reasonably support Moroccan claims that the Polisario Front is essentially an Algerian creation composed largely of Algerian mercenaries. Until 1975, the Algerians supported another independence group, and threw their support to Polisario only reluctantly.[133] In addition, there is some evidence suggesting initial Algerian acquiescence to the Moroccan takeover.[134] There is similarly little reason to support the Moroccan claim that the war is one over Algerian expansionism in order to gain access to the Atlantic Ocean through the takeover of the Western Sahara. Algeria is hardly a land-locked country: it has over seven hundred miles of coastline on the Mediterranean Sea, including several prominent ports, and at least 98 percent of the population resides closer to the Mediterranean than the Atlantic. Virtually all roads and rail lines for international commerce are directed toward the Mediterranean and none toward any of the Western Saharan ports. Only the iron ore deposits near Tindouf could logically be routed westward, and there is no reason that Algeria would not be able to work out an agreement with Morocco should they desire, or, alternatively, to route iron ore through Mauritania and hook up with the rail lines at Zouerate Fe. In addition, Algeria has its own processing facilities and steel plants, thus there is little reason to export raw iron ore in the first place.[135]

There is similarly no reason to suspect that Polisario would be a destabilizing influence in the region. The General National Program of Polisario, adopted at their Fourth Congress in 1978 states that, "Our fight is a liberation war, for national independence, and is not intended to overthrow foreign regimes."[136] Polisario has similarly pledged not to fight for the Sahrawi-populated Tarfaya region in southern Morocco, which is contiguous with the Western Sahara.

One possible explanation for U.S. policy is that there would be distinct economic advantages for having the Western Sahara under the control of a strong U.S. ally. As an underpopulated desert country, its economic promise to the United States certainly could not be explained by the traditional Marxist analysis of a needed market for surplus production or a source of cheap labor. However, the Western Sahara does possess extraordinary mineral wealth, which in addition to casting doubt on claims that an independent Sahrawi state would not be "viable," demonstrates why countries such as the United States might perceive themselves as having great interests at stake. The Western Sahara boasts the world's fourth largest deposits of phosphates, an important source of fertilizer, with an estimated value of $6 billion.[137] Important fishing grounds lay off its shores. The Western Sahara also has proven, but largely underdeveloped, deposits of uranium, titanium, zinc, copper, coal, natural gas, and oil. The U.S. nuclear industry has special interests in the possible exploitation of uranium codeposited with the phosphates. Not only is there a chance of discovering a major field, but phosphoric acid is helpful for uranium mining and milling. Westinghouse has already offered to sell its uranium extraction technology to Morocco.[138] The Moroccan government has already assumed mineral rights in the territory, having granted British Petroleum and Phillips Petroleum prospecting rights covering more than 20,000 square miles off the coast between Al Ayoun and Cape Bojador.[139]

However, the economic costs for the United States in bankrolling the Moroccan war can hardly be justified for the sake of mineral wealth that is largely speculative. There is a glut on the world market for phosphates, and the United States is the world's largest producer, so it clearly does not need access to those markets, particularly since friendly Morocco is the world's third largest producer.[140] Even should the Sahrawis establish full control of their territory, there is no reason why they would not allow trade with the United States and other countries. Thus, there seems to be little evidence to support a purely economic explanation of the United States' role in the conflict.

U.S. POLICY AS A MANIFESTATION
OF REGIONAL CONCERNS

Given the lack of credibility to the explanations behind current U.S. policy cited above, it becomes necessary to search for alternative theories.   Unfortunately, as a contemporary conflict, very little documentation is publicly available that would provide a definitive explanation for what actually motivates U.S. policy in the region.

The most likely explanation involves a version of what Michael Klare has referred to as "surrogate strategy,"[141] also known as the "Nixon Doctrine" or the "Guam Doctrine." Growing out of the Vietnamization program, which resulted from the widespread concern in the United States over American casualties in Indochina, surrogate strategy became a cornerstone of U.S. foreign policy toward the Third World in the early 1970s.   When domestic opposition made direct U.S. intervention in Third World conflicts politically prohibitive, U.S. policy planners sought alternative methods of U.S. power projection against revolutionary movements and hostile governments. The result was a policy where the United States would arm reliable Third World allies to play the role of regional police in trouble spots to contain the threat of leftist insurgencies and maintain conservative pro-U.S. governments. The most highly developed model of this policy was manifested in U.S. support for the Shah of Iran, where the United States sold $20 billion of military equipment and supplied as many as 20,000 advisors to build up a force capable of policing the strategically important Persian Gulf. Such force was utilized when leftist rebels in Oman's Dhofar province threatened the throne of Sultan Qabus ibn Said in the early 1970s. Iranian forces, under U.S. guidance, played a decisive role in completely defeating the insurgency by 1975.[142]

The Islamic Revolution in Iran demonstrated the disastrous consequences of placing such enormous strategic importance on a single leader. The resulting reevaluation by U.S. policy planners of effective means of controlling Third World rebellions that would lead to neither a drawn out counterinsurgency war by U.S. soldiers nor a dependency on unstable dictators to take on such a role led to the development of the

Rapid Deployment Force, or RDF. The creation of the RDF in 1979 placed the United States in charge of counterinsurgency operations, but theoretically ensured that it would have enough concentrated force at its disposal that an insurgency could be crushed or a government overthrown within the time limitations of the War Powers Act of 1973 (which mandated that a president cannot send U.S. troops abroad for more than sixty days) and before sufficient domestic opposition to the war could materialize. In return for U.S. military support, Morocco has offered Moroccan facilities for the RDF, now known as U.S. Central Command, as well as overflight rights, in a six-year agreement signed in 1982.[143] The agreement is to continue in effect unless either party decides to terminate it, with two-years notice.[144]

This by no means implies that the United States has totally abandoned the surrogate strategy. Indeed, the relationship with Morocco is perhaps the best example of the use of allied Third World countries to support U.S. policy interests in their part of the world. The Moroccans have willingly played a role as a surrogate for U.S. interests in Africa, even offering their armed forces in situations where the domestic repercussions precluded the direct deployment of U.S. forces. Twice in the late 1970s, Moroccan forces helped suppress uprisings against pro-U.S. Zairian President Mobutu Sese Seko. In 1977, the United States and France coordinated the deployment of fifteen hundred Moroccan troops to Zaire's Shaba province, the center of the rebellion. In 1978, yet another fifteen hundred Moroccan troops were airlifted by the U.S. Air Force as the mainstay of an "African Defense Force" (also consisting of token contingents from Togo, Gabon, Senegal, and the Ivory Coast) to suppress a second uprising.[145]

There are indications that the United States armed the National Union for the Total Independence of Angola (UNITA), the South African-backed rebel movement in southern Angola, through Morocco as a means to circumvent the Clark Amendment, which prohibited direct American support of Angolan opposition groups.[146] (The amendment has since been repealed and the United States armed UNITA directly.) In addition to acting in the role of conduit, captured UNITA guerrillas have admitted to being trained in Morocco.[147] Jonas Savimbi, the UNITA leader, spent considerable time in Morocco as part of his diplomatic efforts.[148]

A joint U.S.-Moroccan military training center has been utilized for training UNITA, the Mozambican National Resistance (MNR), the South African-backed group fighting the Mozambiquan government,

Mauritanian insurgents, as well as such figures as Bob Denard, the mercenary who led the 1978 coup against the government of the Comoro Islands.[149]

Morocco is also the base for U.S.-backed Libyan exiles opposed to Qaddafi government.[150] Moroccan troops played a role in the overthrow of the Chadian government in 1982.[151] The ninety-two-man invasion force that attempted to overthrow the socialist government of Benin in 1979 was trained in Morocco.[152] Also in 1979, King Hassan dispatched one hundred troops to Equatorial Guinea in support of Colonel Teodoro Nguema Mbasago after his successful coup d'état,[153] which has since grown to a permanent force of four hundred.[154] Morocco is the known center for CIA activities in North Africa and a number of prominent CIA officials pass through Morocco regularly.[155] Hassan has also dispatched security personnel to support conservative Arab monarchies in the Persian Gulf region.[156] And in August 1990, Hassan dispatched troops to Saudi Arabia following the invasion of Kuwait by Iraq.

Morocco has played a supportive role for U.S. diplomatic initiatives as well. Morocco was the site of meetings between Egyptian representatives and Israeli and other Jewish leaders to lay the ground work for Anwar Sadat's trip to Jerusalem in 1977.[157] Though supportive of Sadat's initiatives, the Moroccans, under pressures from their Saudi benefactors, publicly opposed the Camp David Accords and broke relations with Egypt. Still, despite their formal opposition, and their sending three combat brigades to fight Israel in the Golan Heights during the 1973 war,[158] Morocco is considered to be one of Israel's closest contacts in the Arab world, with clandestine meetings reported periodically with high Israeli officials, culminating with the July 1986 meeting between Hassan and Israeli Prime Minister Shimon Peres in Rabat. In November 1982, Hassan offered Lebanese President Amin Gemayel thirty-nine hundred Moroccan troops for use in the multinational peacekeeping force in Lebanon, a move reportedly blocked by Israel.[159] In the spring of 1982, King Hassan met with President Reagan as the representative of the Arab League following the Fez summit at which Arab leaders signalled a new willingness to recognize Israel in return for the establishment of a Palestinian state. Hassan was chosen not only for his role as ruler of the host country, but also because of his acknowledged position as the Arab leader closest to President Reagan. Despite the fact that this peace initiative by the Arab governments toward Israel was rejected, in part because of the Reagan administration's only lukewarm support, U.S.-Moroccan relations were not adversely affected.[160]

After the experience in Iran, the U.S. government is more reluctant to rely too heavily on a surrogate power to police the region and, in addition to Moroccan support for possible deployment by U.S. Central Command forces, has attempted to combine Morocco's role as a surrogate with a more direct U.S. military presence. In February 1982, Secretary of State Alexander Haig announced the formation of a joint military commission, and stated the administration's desire for substantially increased military support for Morocco. U.S. and Moroccan personnel have conducted joint amphibious maneuvers and other military exercises.[161] The United States closed the last of its four air bases in Morocco in 1963 and closed its last communications station in 1978. However, declassified official memoranda indicate that the United States has held on to emergency transit, staging, and refueling rights at the four former U.S. bases.[162] Similarly, two telecommunications centers, although operating under the pretext of civilian functions, apparently also help link U.S. fleets in the Atlantic and the Mediterranean.[163] There are indications that the United States may seek permission to reopen at least one of the bases, provision for which may have been included--along with other special arrangements--in the still-secret six-year agreement signed in May 1982.[164] Morocco's location would be important to the U.S. Central Command both for refueling rights and for the use of airspace, although King Hassan has reportedly stated his unwillingness for the United States to use Morocco in any military operation against any "Arab country friendly to Morocco." Under the 1982 U.S.-Moroccan agreement the Moroccan government has made the military part of Casablanca's international airport and the Sidi Slimane military air base available to U.S. forces.[165]

The U.S. Navy regularly uses Moroccan ports. According to Thor Kuniholm of the Moroccan desk at the U.S. State Department, "One thing we're getting is naval ships' visits there, and the Navy is very interested in that. That's a high priority for the Navy, because it is becoming increasingly difficult to find ports in the Middle East where American ships are welcome."[166] In addition, the harbor at Tangier is sufficiently large for U.S. nuclear-powered aircraft carriers.

At a time when U.S. bases in Greece and Spain are still under a degree of scrutiny by those countries' governments, Moroccan bases are of particular interest. A large U.S. military presence would be far more plausible here than in most Middle Eastern countries, since Morocco's geography, history, and culture have created a climate unlikely to breed a xenophobic reaction, as occurred in Iran.

Such growth in the U.S. military presence in Morocco should also be seen in the context of larger U.S. global strategy, such as the effort to extend U.S. naval operations below the southern limit of NATO. This effort includes the expansion of facilities in the Azores, the proposed new NATO base in Portugal's Madeira Islands, and closer links to the French bases in Senegal and Gabon, British facilities on Ascension Island, and South African bases at Walvis Bay in Namibia and Simonstown at South Africa's Cape of Good Hope. In addition, such moves would serve to counter the influence of nonaligned powers such as Algeria, which is developing close relationships with Mauritania and other countries in the region.

In addition, as a result of antinuclear sentiment in Europe and an increased dependence on air-launched cruise missiles because of the removal of ground-launched cruise missiles from Europe under the INF Treaty, Morocco becomes a logical base for American nuclear weapons.

There thus appears to be a mutually beneficial relationship--from the perspective of the two countries' governments--emerging from this unprecedented cooperation between the United States and Morocco. Though Morocco appears to be more of a backup to U.S. global strategy than a crucial cornerstone, it fit well with the Reagan administration's concept of a "strategic consensus" between the United States and its allies against Soviet influence and radical Third World governments.[167] From Morocco's point of view, it now has superpower support for its territorial ambitions. The House Committee on Foreign Affairs staff study mission noted that some Moroccan officials see "U.S. military assistance and the new access and transit agreement as indications for U.S. commitment to provide Morocco with a security umbrella."[168]

CONCLUSION

Clearly, a special relationship does exist between the United States and Morocco, where clear strategic interests have led them to build one of the closest relationships the United States has with any Middle Eastern or African country. Unfortunately, this relationship bears a disturbing resemblance to the special relationship between the United States and Iran, which had disastrous results for both countries.

The U.S.-Moroccan relationship was built largely on expediency. Morocco was willing to surrender its potential role as a leader in the nonaligned world in return for American support, even if this meant serving as a surrogate for U.S. interests and threatening Arab and African unity. The United States was often willing to openly contradict its stated foreign policy aims by supporting what is generally recognized as an act of aggression by one state against another, in return for establishing this kind of relationship with an important actor in an increasingly hostile Third World.

While U.S. military aid and cooperation with Morocco continues unabated, there were signs late in the Reagan administration, which have continued under President Bush, that the United States might finally be willing to support a negotiated settlement. U.S. officials have increasingly emphasized the necessity of a negotiated settlement and acknowledged the futility of a military solution. Efforts by the OAU and UN have received explicit State Department endorsements.[169]

The U.S. response to Polisario's accidental downing of a U.S. plane leased by the Agency for International Development in December 1988 was muted. Polisario, upon confirmation that their forces were responsible, issued an immediate apology and U.S. officials acknowledged that it was indeed a case of mistaken identity. It would have been easy for U.S. officials to have capitalized on the incident to create anti-Polisario sentiment, but this carefully measured response appeared to be a deliberate effort by State Department officials to ease tensions in light of increased diplomatic activity concerning the conflict.

A major reason for this apparent shift in U.S. policy may be that despite tacit support of Moroccan claims that the Polisario had been eliminated as a military threat, U.S. officials may finally be acknowledging that the war is indeed at a stalemate. Reports of an imminent withdrawal of Algerian support of the Polisario (which have circulated periodically since that country's rapprochement with Morocco) have all proven groundless.[170] The growing fiscal crisis is Morocco and a global trend toward the resolution of regional conflicts may have given impetus to those in the U.S. government willing to press Morocco to compromise.

In times of fiscal restraint in the United States, foreign aid has traditionally been a tempting target for reductions. Given that the largest recipients of U.S. aid (Israel, Egypt, and Turkey) have their budgets essentially guaranteed at current levels, and with several allied governments in the Third World seriously challenged by popular uprisings, it is governments like Morocco that may soon be noticing substantial cutbacks in U.S. aid. Morocco's other two major sources of aid are also less than reliable: France's Socialist government has often been ambivalent about Morocco's Western Sahara policy; the world oil glut and the costs of the Gulf War has limited the level of Saudi contributions. Should current negotiations progress and Moroccan intransigence become increasingly apparent, Morocco may feel the pinch even sooner.

For now, however, most attention is on the United Nations and recent progress toward holding a referendum to determine the fate of the territory. The United States, in both the General Assembly and the Security Council, has voted with the majority in support of the secretary-general's peace efforts.

This newfound U.S. interest in the peace process may be attributed to several factors. First, this may simply be a reflection of the generally cautious and pragmatic approach that the Bush administration has demonstrated in several foreign policy areas. Second, the Cold War has effectively ended, negating some of the ideological rationale that often led the United States to support certain questionable policies of Third World allies; this also lessens the need for Morocco to play a surrogate counterweight for perceived Soviet designs in Africa. Finally, the successes of the "resurgent UN," and a willingness by the United States to support such efforts, has allowed the United States to support the call for a UN-sponsored referendum. The consensus at the UN for a peaceful resolution of the conflict is so strong that it would have been politically difficult for the United States to equivocate. In addition, acceptance of a plebiscite has been made easier, due in large part to a belief among U.S. diplomatic personnel that Morocco would win.[171]

Still, while the United States is not interfering with the peace process, there has been little more than rhetoric to support it. Similarly, there appears to be no willingness to pressure Hassan should he balk at the UN efforts. One test of the sincerity of U.S. intentions is whether the United States--the primary financial supporter of the UN--is willing to fund the presence of adequate United Nations personnel to ensure that a referendum held under foreign military occupation is conducted fairly.

Should the Sahrawis win independence through a referendum or some sort of compromise, it could be said to be despite rather than because of the United States. Should Morocco, through a referendum or other means, hold on to the territory, the credit could go in part to the more than fifteen years of U.S. support. In any case, the U.S. role in the Western Sahara conflict has generally not been consistent with the goal of a just and lasting peace and, whatever the final outcome, historians are unlikely to look favorably upon the U.S. policy in this troubled region.

NOTES

1. U.S. Congress, House Committee on Foreign Affairs, Subcommittees on Africa and on International Security and Scientific Affairs, *Hearings on Arms Sales in North Africa and the Conflict in the Western Sahara: An Assessment of U.S. Policy*, 97th Cong., 1st sess., March 25, 1981, 42. The State Department emphasized Morocco's importance repeatedly, especially when Congress was considering foreign aid requests. According to State Department figures in this report, manganese and cobalt, for which the United States is 100 percent dependent on imports, are mined in Morocco. Nearly half of the world's known phosphate reserves--an important source for fertilizer that may be in short supply in coming decades--comes from Morocco. With the assistance of U.S. firms, Morocco is beginning to develop its vast oil shale deposits, estimated at 15 percent of the world's total reserves. There are also deposits of antimony, zinc, lead, coal, and at least some oil.
2. *The New York Times*, February 13, 1980. From 1965 to 1982, Morocco received $810,973,000, Egypt received $5,404,927,000, and Sudan received $230,632,000. Source: U.S. Department of Defense, Defense Security Assistance Agency (DSAA), *Foreign Military Sales, Foreign Military Construction Sales and Military Assistance Facts as of September 30, 1982* (Washington, D.C.: DSAA, 1982), 2, 4, 32, 34, 36.
3. Tony Hodges, *Western Sahara: The Roots of a Desert War* (Westport, Conn.: Lawrence Hill, 1983), 355.
4. Leo Kamil, *Fueling the Fire: U.S. Policy and the Western Sahara Conflict* (Trenton, N.J.: Red Sea Press, 1987), 2-3.
5. The northern two-thirds of the territory, including most of its major towns and almost all valuable mineral deposits, was granted to Morocco. The southern one-third was ceded to Mauritania, which surrendered its claim in 1978 following a series of military losses to Polisario guerrillas. Morocco then seized the former Mauritanian sector, thereby claiming control of the entire territory.

6. Hodges, *Western Sahara*, 215. The Spanish government was internally divided on the question, with the United States throwing its weight behind the fascist Falangist party, which supported Morocco, against Spanish military and diplomatic officials. See Richard B. Parker, *North Africa: Regional Tensions and Strategic Concerns*, 1st ed., (New York: Praeger, 1984), 112.

7. Kamil, *Fueling the Fire*, 10.

8. Hodges, *Western Sahara*, 356.

9. Martha Wenger, "Reagan Stakes Morocco in Sahara Struggle," *MERIP Reports*, no. 105 (May 1982): 22-24.

10. *Africa News*, November 2, 1979.

11. Ibid.

12. Kamil, *Fueling the Fire*, 15.

13. Ibid., 24.

14. Tony Hodges, "At Odds with Self Determination: The United States and Western Sahara," in Gerald J. Bender, James S. Coleman, and Richard L. Sklar, eds., *African Crisis Areas and U.S. Foreign Policy* (Berkeley and Los Angeles: University of Calif. Press, 1985), 265.

15. U.S. Congress, House Committee on International Relations, Subcommittee on International Organizations, *Hearings on Human Rights in East Timor*, 95th Cong., 1st sess., June 28 and July 19, 1977, 79.

16. Daniel Patrick Moynihan, *A Dangerous Place* (Boston: Little, Brown, 1978), 247.

17. *The New York Times*, July 7, 1979.

18. Deputy Assistant Secretary of State for Near Eastern and South Asian Affairs Nicholas Veliotes testified that Morocco was violating the agreement and would likely continue to do so, but that the Carter administration still favored increased military aid. See U.S. Congress, House Committee on International Relations, Subcommittees on Africa and on International Organizations, *Hearings on the Question of Self-Determination in Western Sahara*, 95th Cong., 1st sess., October 12, 1977; U.S. Congress, House Committee on Appropriations, Subcommittee on Foreign Operations, *Hearings on Foreign Assistance and Related Agencies Appropriations for 1978*, 95th Cong., 1st Sess., March 1978.

19. U.S. Congress, House Committee on Foreign Affairs, Subcommittees on Africa International Security and Scientific Affairs, *Hearings on Proposed Arms Sales to Morocco*, 96th Cong., 2nd sess., June 24 and 29, 1980, 2-25.

20. Kamil, *Fueling the Fire*, 31.

21. Wenger, "Reagan Stakes Morocco," 24.

22. See Michael Klare, "Arms and the Shah: The Rise and Fall of Surrogate Strategy," *The Progressive* 43, no. 8 (August 1979): 15-21.

23. However, former United Nations Ambassador Andrew Young was outspoken in his opposition to U.S. policy: Less than six months after his resignation, he met with Polisario leaders in Algeria and spoke before a large crowd of Sahrawi refugees declaring; "The American people do not know what a great people you are. I will try to help the American people understand you, to know your cause, and to love you....You will be free, and victory will be yours." (*West Africa*, February 18, 1980, 333.

24. According to Assistant Secretary of State for Near Eastern and South Asian Affairs, Harold H. Saunders, the Carter administration believed that "an outright military victory over Morocco by Morocco's adversaries would constitute a serious setback to major U.S. interests in this area." See U.S. Congress, House Committee on Foreign Affairs, Subcommittees on African and International Security and Scientific Affairs, *Hearings on Proposed Arms Sales to Morocco*, 96th Cong., 2d sess., January 24 and 29, 1989, 3.

25. George Houser, "Blood on the Sahara," *The Progressive* 44, no. 12 (December 1980): 50.

26. *The Washington Post*, January 17, 1980.

27. *Philadelphia Inquirer*, January 19, 1982.

28. *The Washington Post*, November 5, 1981.

29. *The New York Times*, February 1, 1983.

30. *Philadelphia Inquirer*, January 18, 1982.

31. Tony Hodges, "At Odds with Self-Determination," in Bender, Coleman, and Sklar, eds., *African Crisis Areas*, 268.

32. Claudia Wright, "Showdown in the Sahara," *Inquiry*, April 12, 1982, 24.

33. *Philadelphia Inquirer*, January 18, 1982.

34. Wright, "Showdown in the Sahara," 24.

35. *The Washington Post*, November 5, 1981.

36. *The Wall Street Journal*, December 4, 1981.

37. Wright, "Showdown in the Sahara," 24.

38. *The New York Times*, February 13, 1982.

39. *Philadelphia Inquirer*, January 18, 1982.

40. Tony Hodges, "At Odds with Self-Determination," in Bender, Coleman, and Sklar, eds., *African Crisis Areas*, 270.

41. Interview with Steve Weissman, staff of House Subcommittee on Africa, March 25, 1988, and National Public Radio news broadcasts.

42. U.S. Congress, House Committee on Foreign Affairs, *Report on International Security and Development Cooperation Act of 1990*, 96th Cong., 2d sess., April 16, 1980, 15.

43. Claudia Wright, *In These Times*, July 28, 1982.

44. *The New York Times*, February 1, 1983.

45. Wright, *In These Times*, July 28, 1982.

46. *Philadelphia Inquirer*, January 19, 1982.

47. Hodges, *Western Sahara*, 360.

48. John Damis, *U.S. Arab Relations: The Moroccan Dimension* (Washington, D.C.: National Countil on U.S.-Arab Relations, 1986), 10-17.

49. U.S. Congress, House Committee on Foreign Affairs, *U.S. Policy Toward the Conflict in the Western Sahara*, Report of a Staff Study Mission to Morocco, Algeria, the Western Sahara, and France, August 25-September 6, 1982, 97th Cong., 2d sess., 11.

50. *Christian Science Monitor*, May 20, 1982.

51. American Committee on Africa, *The Reagan Administration and the Struggle for Self-Determination in Western Sahara* (New York: American Committee on Africa, 1981).

52. *The New York Times*, July 22, 1982.

53. Wright, *In These Times*, July 28, 1982.

54. Ibid.

55. Some of this money was diverted once again in the spring of 1983, when the relatively quiet situation in the Western Sahara allowed the administration to funnel the aid to support government forces in El Salvador.

56. U.S. Department of Commerce, Bureau of the Census, *Statistical Abstract of the United States, 1988* (Washington, D.C.: Government Printing Office, 1987) 321, 766.

57. DSAA and Department of State, *Congressional Presentation for Security Assistance Programs, Fiscal Year 1991* (Washington, D.C.: DSAA and Department of State, 1990), 11.

58. Ibid.

59. Interview with Steve Weissman, March 25, 1988.

60. The Moroccans charged that such sophisticated weapons could have only been operated by Cubans or East Germans, though such a claim is highly debatable. Nor have the Moroccans submitted any proof that SAM-6s were used at all; reporters were denied access to the flight

recording devices to determine the altitude at which the planes were shot down, which would provide clues as to the kind of weapons that were used. Charges by the United States that SAM-6s were used by the Polisario inside Morocco were later retracted.

61. *The New York Times*, August 20, 1979.

62. Some go so far to suggest that King Hassan places over half of his army in the Western Sahara to keep them out of the country and occupied with other matters so they will not try to overthrow him again, as they attempted in 1971 and 1972.

63. David J. Dean, *The Air Force Role in Low-Intensity Conflict* (Maxwell AFB, Ala.: Air University Press, 1986), 45.

64. Ibid., 41.

65. Ibid.

66. Hodges, "At Odds with Self-Determination," in Bender, Coleman, and Sklar, eds., *African Crisis Areas*, 269.

67. Ibid.

68. U.S. Congress, House Committee on Foreign Affairs, *U.S. Policy Toward the Conflict*, 5.

69. Ibid., 9.

70. According to House Subcommittee on Africa staffmember Steve Weissman, Morocco currently uses 34 percent of its export earnings on debt service. (From a presentation at American University on March 4, 1988.)

71. U.S. Congress, House Committee on Foreign Affairs, Subcommittees on Africa and on International Security and Scientific Affairs, *Hearings on Arms Sales in North Africa*, 5.

72. *The New York Times*, February 1, 1983.

73. Ibid.

74. Ibid.

75. U.S. Congress, House Committee on Foreign Affairs, *Report on the International Security and Development Cooperation Act of 1980*, 96th Cong., 2d sess., April 16, 1980, 15.

76. *Washington Star*, November 6, 1979.

77. *Africa News*, January-February 1980.

78. U.S. Congress, House Committee on Foreign Affairs, Subcommittees on Africa and International Security and Scientific Affairs, *Hearings on Proposed Arm Sale to Morocco*, 96th Cong., 2d sess., January 24, 1980, 3.

79. Kamil, *Fueling the Fire*, 79.

80. U.S. Congress, House Committee on Foreign Affairs, *U.S. Policy Toward the Conflict*, 11.

81. Ibid., 18.

82. Ibid., 12.

83. Ibid.

84. Hodges, *Western Sahara*, 315.

85. Stephen Solarz, "Arms for Morocco?" *Foreign Affairs* 58, no. 2, (Winter 1979-80): 295-96.

86. U.S. Congress, House Committee on International Relations, Subcommittees on Africa and on International Organizations, *Hearings on the Question of Self-Determination in Western Sahara*, 95th Cong., 1st sess., October 12, 1977, 19.

87. Note the World Court decision as well as French historian Maurice Barbier's study *Voyages au Sahara Occidental* (Paris: L'Harmattan, 1986). This assessment is confirmed by the author's interview with the Sahrawi scholar Mohammed Abdel Khadeh at the Dahkla Welaya in Algeria on June 21, 1987.

88. Arabel I. Kossow, "Soviet and Radical Arab Designs on the Sahara," *Armed Forces Journal International* (June 1980): 22.

89. *The Middle East*, December 1979, 42, and interviews with Polisario officials in June 1987.

90. Daniel Volman, *A Continent Besieged: Foreign Military Activities in Africa Since 1975* (Washington, D.C.: Institute for Policy Studies, 1980), 5-10.

91. Daniel Volman, *Memorandum on Proposed U.S. Arms Sales to Morocco* (Washington, D.C.: Institute for Policy Studies, 1979), 3-4, citing *The Military Balance 1979-1980* (London: International Institute for Strategic Studies, 1979).

92. Based on the interviews and observations during author's visit to the military zones to the south of Tindouf, Algeria, in June 1987.

93. *The New York Times*, July 7, 1978.

94. *Baltimore Sun*, October 31, 1979.

95. See, for example, Ian Butterfield, *Morocco: An Ally in Jeopardy*, Heritage Foundation Background Briefing no. 185, May 18, 1982 (Washington, D.C.: Heritage Foundation, 1982).

96. U.S. Congress, House Committee on Foreign Affairs, Subcommittees on Africa and on International Security and Scientific Affairs, *Hearings on Arms Sales in North Africa*, 9.

97. Moroccan troops are so thinly concentrated that the Polisario have been able to take teams of European journalists onto the wall at night

without detection.   An offer by some Polisario soldiers to similarly escort this author to the wall was politely declined.

98. *The New York Times*, February 13, 1980.

99. *Baltimore Sun*, October 31, 1979.

100. Hodges, "At Odds with Self-Determination," in Bender, Coleman, and Sklar, eds., *African Crisis Areas*, 274.

101. *The Washington Post*, October 29, 1979.

102. *U.S. News and World Report*, March 1, 1982.

103. *Africa*, April 1980.

104. Amnesty International, *Amnesty International Report 1989* (New York: Amnesty International, 1989), 271-72.

105. Background Interview, June 1990.

106. See U.S. Department of State, Bureau of Human Rights and Humanitarian Affairs, *Country Reports on Human Rights Practices for 1989* (Washington, D.C.: Government Printing Office, 1989), 1492-1507.

107. *The New York Times*, May 1, 1979.

108. *Philadelphia Inquirer*, January 19, 1982.

109. *U.S. News and World Report*, March 1, 1982.

110. *The Middle East*, February 1980, 63.

111. American Committee on Africa, *The Reagan Administration*.

112. Ibid.

113. Ibid.

114. Wright, "Showdown in the Sahara," 22.

115. *Philadelphia Inquirer*, January 18, 1982.

116. U.S. Congress, House Committee on Foreign Affairs, Subcommittees on Africa and on International Security and Scientific Affairs, *Hearings on Arms Sales in North Africa*, 43.

117. Solarz, "Arms for Morocco," 295-96.

118. Penny Gibbins, "Immobile Autocracy," *The Middle East*, February 1990, 23.

119. *Africa Confidential*, July 1, 1981.

120. Polisario Front, *Second Congress Plan of Action, Dossier, Sahara Occidental, Recontre et Development* (January-February 1976).

121. Polisario Front, *Third Congress*, (January-February) quoted in Maurice Barbier, *Le Conflit du Sahara Occidental* (Paris: L'Harmattan, 1982), 205.

122. For a detailed description of Polisario's internal governing structure, see Stephen Zunes, "Participating Democracy in the Western Sahara: A Study of Polisario Self-Governance," *Scandinavian Journal*

for Development Alternatives 7, no. 2 (October 1988): 141-56.

123. Hodges, "At Odds with Self-Determination," in Bender, Coleman, and Sklar, eds., *African Crisis Areas*, 261.

124. Congressional testimony quoted in Kamil, *Fueling the Fire*, 57.

125. Ibid., 31-32.

126. *The Middle East*, April 1980, 58-59. See also Yahia Zoubir's chapter (Chapter 1) in this book.

127. Hodges, *Western Sahara*, 354.

128. *The New York Times*, July 23, 1986.

129. *Africa News*, June 15, 1979.

130. Tony Hodges, "After the Treaty of Oujda," *Africa Report* 29 (November-December 1984): 29-30.

131. Hodges, *Western Sahara*, 326-27. Also see *Africa Confidential*, July 15, 1981, for Qaddafi's comments on Western Sahara during a visit to Mauritania.

132. Hodges, "After the Treaty of Oujda," 30-31.

133. *The New York Times*, October 22, 1981.

134. Parker, *North Africa*, 109-110.

135. Ibid., 109.

136. Quoted in Hodges, "At Odds with Self-Determination", in Bender, Coleman, and Sklar, eds., *African Crisis Areas*, 261.

137. *The Washington Post*, April 10, 1981.

138. *Multinational Monitor*, November 1980.

139. *The Middle East*, November 1978, 149.

140. Closing off a potential source for the Soviet Union would not make any sense, either, since the Soviet Union is the world's second largest phosphate producer, and their trade relations with Morocco are excellent. Statistics from Tony Hodges, "At Odds with Self-Determination," in Bender, Coleman, and Sklar, eds., *African Crisis Areas*, 260.

141. See Klare, "Arms and the Shah," 15-21.

142. Klare, "Arms and the Shah," 17.

143. Hodges, *Western Sahara*, 360-61.

144. Harold D. Nelson, ed., *Morocco: A Country Study* (Washington, D.C.: Government Printing Office, 1985), 300.

145. Hodges, *Western Sahara*, 250-51.

146. Wenger, "Reagan Stakes Morocco," 25.

147. *West Africa*, February 18, 1980.

148. *Africa Confidential*, August 25, 1982.

149. Kamil, *Fueling the Fire*, 7. [Editor's Note: Kamil provides no data for this claim].

150. Wright, "Showdown in the Sahara," 25.

151. Ibid.

152. *New African*, May 1979.

153. *Africa Report*, January 2, 1980.

154. Werner Ruf, "The Role of World Powers: Colonialist Transformations and King Hassan's Rule," in Richard Lawless and Laila Monahan, eds., *War and Refugees: The Western Sahara Conflict* (London and New York: Pinter Publishers, 1987), 94.

155. Wright, *In These Times*, July 28, 1982.

156. Parker, *North Africa*, 159

157. *Christian Science Monitor*, December 6, 1977.

158. Werner Ruf, "The Role of World Powers," in Lawless and Monahan, eds., *War and Refugees*, 68, has implied that these brigades were carefully selected so that certain officers who were seen as a potential threat to the king would get killed.

159. *The Washington Post*, November 3, 1982.

160. Ironically, some of the strongest U.S. supporters of Morocco have come from mainstream Jewish organizations, which have lobbied for increased U.S. support of King Hassan, who is seen as an Arab "moderate." In addition to his relatively nonbelligerent attitude toward Israel, he has also been more tolerant than most Arab rulers toward his country's relatively large Jewish community. David Ginsberg, a prominent liberal attorney with close ties with several Jewish members of Congress, has been particularly active in encouraging U.S. assistance. Brooklyn Congressman Stephen Solarz, once one of King Hassan's strongest critics on Capital Hill, has reportedly toned down his efforts because of pressure from Sephardic Jewish constituents.

161. Kamil, *Fueling the Fire*, 82-83. See also *The New York Times*, February 1, 1983.

162. Wright, *In These Times*, July 28, 1982.

163. Ibid.

164. *The Washington Post*, May 28, 1982.

165. John Damis, *Conflict in Northwest Africa: The Western Sahara Dispute*, (Stanford, Calif.: Hoover Institution Press, 1983), 127.

166. *Philadelphia Inquirer*, January 18, 1982.

167. In earlier articles, this author argued that another possible explanation for U.S. support of Morocco is the fear that a Polisario victory could establish a dangerous precedent for U.S. interests in the

Middle East and elsewhere. (See my articles "The United States and Morocco: The Sahara War and Regional Interests," in *Arab Studies Quarterly*, no. 4 (Fall 1987): 422-41; and "Nationalism and Non-alignment: The 'Non-Ideology' of the Polisario," in *Africa Today* 34, no. 3 (Fall 1987): 33-46). I have since concluded that this argument is probably too conspiratorial, since I have found nothing but circumstantial evidence to support the theory. The quid pro quo between the United States and Morocco, as well as the Reagan administration's Cold War myopia concerning Third World liberation movements, likely constitute a sufficient explanation of their own.

168. U.S. Congress, House Committee on Foreign Affairs, *U.S. Policy Toward the Conflict*, 5.

169. Charles Redman, *Department of State Press Briefing*, December 12, 1988.

170. See Yahia Zoubir and Daniel Volman, "Solution Needed for Western Sahara," *New African*, June 1989, 38.

171. Background interviews with U.S. officials in New York and Rabat, May-June 1990.

4

U.S. Strategic Interests and the War in the Western Sahara

Richard B. Parker

The war for control of the Western Sahara involves two northwest African states, Morocco and Algeria.[1] The United States has sought to maintain friendly relations with each. Although little noted by the U.S. news media, the conflict in the former Spanish Sahara has been a serious drain on Morocco's limited resources and has undermined regional stability and the cohesion of the Organization of African Unity (OAU). Most important to the United States, the survival of the Moroccan regime is intimately tied to the outcome of the Saharan war, and failure to reach a peaceful solution to the conflict will have dangerous consequences for King Hassan. The war has also complicated U.S. relations with Algeria, and for fifteen years it posed a theoretical risk that the Soviet Union would be able to exploit the conflict to further its own influence in a region that could provide significant support to Soviet naval operations in the western Mediterranean and the Atlantic Ocean. That risk has faded with the new era in U.S.-Soviet relations.

The United States' chief interests in Morocco are political and military. King Hassan is seen in Washington as a moderate Arab leader who has been helpful to the United States in several areas of common concern: initiating the contacts between Israel and Egypt that led to the Camp David Accords in 1978, supporting UNITA guerrillas led by Jonas Savimbi in Angola, dispatching troops to Zaire in 1977 and 1978 to support the government of General Mobutu Sese Seko against insurgents in the Shaba Province, holding a public meeting with Israeli Prime Minister Shimon Peres in July 1986, and, under an agreement signed in Washington in May 1982, providing access to Moroccan base facilities to be used by American forces as staging areas in the event of deployment to the Middle East.

U.S. economic relations with Morocco remain limited. Investment there was estimated in the summer of 1990 to be about $160 million compared to $60 million in 1970. This is up from the estimated $50 million in 1984, but given the decline in the value of the U.S. dollar since 1970, it does not represent much real change from that period. In 1988, Moroccan imports from and exports to the United States were valued at only $391 million.[2]

The United States' political relationship with Algeria, on the other hand, was for years complicated by the radical role that Algeria played in the Non-Aligned Movement and in various other international bodies. President Chadli Bendjedid, who was inaugurated in February 1979, has followed more moderate foreign and domestic policies than his predecessor, President Houari Boumedienne, and has indicated a strong interest in improved relations. U.S.-Algerian relations have improved a great deal over the past ten years as a result and can today be described as friendly.

Economic relations between the two countries are substantial. The United States is a leading purchaser of Algerian oil and gas. Algeria, in turn, is a major purchaser of American agricultural products. Trade in both directions was valued at $2,599 million in 1988.[3]

Nevertheless, the United States government has never had a large-scale political or economic involvement in northwest Africa and the region has not been one of priority in the minds of American policymakers since World War II. The region is not defined as vital to the security of the United States and, although considered part of the Middle East for bureaucratic and administrative reasons, the perceived importance of Morocco and Algeria to the United States is clearly of a different order than that of the Middle East. The nature, as opposed to the scale, of U.S. interests in the region is similar, however. The role of Morocco in Pentagon planning for the U.S. Central Command makes it militarily important to the United States. Although the U.S. obsession with the Soviet threat to the Persian Gulf has declined dramatically, the Iraqi invasion of Kuwait emphasized the importance of maintaining military allies in the region. Similarly, while northwest African petroleum resources are much less important than those of the Persian Gulf, any disruption of the flow of oil and natural gas to Western Europe would threaten Western interests, including those of the United States. Fundamental U.S. interests in maintaining access to energy supplies clearly apply to northwest Africa as well as to the Middle East.

In general terms, for the last fifteen years there have been two perspectives in Washington on how the United States should protect its interests throughout the world. The first is the *globalist* view, which holds that local conflicts are primarily the result of the international rivalry between the United States and the Soviet Union, and that all other causes are secondary. This is now fading as the Soviet menace wanes, but it is not dead yet. The other perspective is the *regionalist* view, which holds that these conflicts are primarily the result of local issues that are linked to the U.S.-Soviet competition only to the extent that the involvement of those powers becomes part of the problem.

U.S. policy in the Middle East and Africa since the mid-1970s clearly demonstrates this basic dichotomy in foreign policy perspectives. Thus, President Carter took what was essentially a regionalist approach to the Middle East and Africa until the Soviet invasion of Afghanistan in December 1979. The latter occurred at a time of increasing concern about Soviet military superiority in both conventional and nuclear weaponry, a concern encouraged by conservative foreign policy organizations and by critics of the administration's reaction to the Iranian hostage crisis. Carter responded in January 1980 by declaring that the United States would use all means necessary, including the use of military force, to prevent any outside power from taking over the oil resources of the Persian Gulf, a pledge that became known as the Carter Doctrine. This constituted a major shift in direction away from the regionalist approach. It was a globalist declaration, reflecting a new obsession with the possibility of a Soviet march to the Persian Gulf, which would, among other things, make it possible for the Soviet Union to blackmail Western Europe by threatening to cut off oil supplies.

The globalist perspective was even more dominant during the early years of the Reagan administration, leading to a marked disinterest in continuing the Camp David process, one of the chief accomplishments of those who adopted a regionalist perspective. This disinterest in regionalist approaches reached its height during Alexander Haig's term as secretary of state, when Washington sought to organize a "strategic consensus" of Israelis and Arabs to counter Soviet influence in the Middle East and virtually ignored the conflict between Israel and its Arab neighbors. Israel's invasion of Lebanon in the summer of 1982, however, rudely awakened the Reagan administration to the importance of that conflict and the strategic consensus dissolved as a U.S. initiative to resolve the Arab-Israel conflict was launched by George Shultz, the new secretary of state.

This initiative led to the Reagan plan of September 1, 1982, which was basically a regionalist initiative. But, by the fall of 1983, the Reagan administration began talking again of a strategic alliance with Israel, and administration statements describing Syria as a Soviet surrogate indicated the resurgence of the globalist approach. The eruption of the Palestinian *Intifada* (uprising) in December 1987 forced the Reagan administration to shift back to a regionalist approach, which led to the initiation of direct talks with the Palestine Liberation Organization (PLO) in December 1988.

This alternation of regionalist and globalist approaches demonstrates the limitations of both perspectives. Following either one to the exclusion of the other leads to misperceptions and mistakes. What is required is a balanced approach that takes local factors into account without neglecting global ones. U.S. policy in northwest Africa over most of the past fifteen years has generally followed the globalist approach, viewing Morocco as an ally against the Soviets and their presumed clients, the Libyans. Algeria, on the other hand, was viewed as, at best, neutral, and while the reasons for its neutrality were understood, from the globalist perspective the object of U.S. policy is to block Soviet influence, and the globalists usually saw support for Morocco as more effective in this respect than friendship with Algeria. These perceptions and their implications for U.S. policy are now changing, but how much remains to be seen.

A basic premise of U.S. policy is that King Hassan is a source of political stability in Morocco and that the United States would prefer him to any likely replacement. Although King Hassan faces significant internal opposition, he has ruled Morocco in a manner that has maintained order with an amount of political repression that is considered moderate by Third World standards. If he were to be overthrown, it would probably be by a military coup d'état, possibly supported by a popular uprising, because only the armed forces have the power to seize control in Morocco. (The changes that took place in Eastern Europe in 1989 have shown that such assumptions need to be taken with reserve). There is no indication that such an event is likely, but if it were to occur, the United States could not be indifferent to it. The United States would probably be able to maintain friendly relations with a military government in Morocco if it were dominated by senior, essentially conservative officers now in command of the Royal Moroccan Armed Forces. But if a group of radical junior officers took over, they might well be unwilling to cooperate with the United States. In fact, they might want to distance themselves as much as possible from the United States.

From my perspective, based on thirty years of diplomatic experience, it appears that the United States has overidentified itself with Morocco, not so much in the level of its economic and military assistance programs, but in the pervasive perception in Washington that King Hassan is an Arab ally, and that he serves as a surrogate for the United States by protecting U.S. interests throughout Africa and the Middle East. Even if there were no war in the Western Sahara and no regional rivalry between Morocco and Algeria, this degree of identification with a local political leader is an error. It complicates U.S. relations with Algeria and could eventually undermine the security of King Hassan himself, because Washington's commitment to his regime allows his domestic opponents to label him as a U.S. stooge.

The United States tends to view its relations with foreign states in personal terms, to see them as relations with individual heads of state, and to support any foreign leader who is seen as pro-United States, while opposing all those who are perceived as pro-USSR. If a diplomat falls victim to this tendency, he is said to have "*localitis*," meaning that he has lost his judgment of the political orientation of the local leader. When the administration as a whole gives way to this tendency, it is called *overidentification* if the leader is judged positively, and *obsession* if the judgment is negative.

In either case, the tendency is dangerous. If the United States overidentifies with a particular ruler, this can reduce the ruler's political legitimacy, and it usually leads to unrealistic expectations on both sides, which in turn leads to distrust and disharmony. The United States, for example, tends to expect Arab rulers to change their positions on the Arab-Israeli conflict simply because it wants them to do so and they are supposed to be friends. Such expectations are based on the illusion that because the ruler in question is pro-U.S., he will accept U.S. definitions of the common good and blindly follow U.S. policy.

It would be more realistic to discard labels such as "pro-U.S." and realize that King Hassan's primary responsibility is to his own people and country; that he is pro-Moroccan and pro-Hassan and not pro-anyone else. He may be willing to shift his policies to accommodate the United States on certain issues, but if he ignored Morocco's basic national interests to satisfy the demands of the United States, deliberately or not, he would be betraying his people, and the monarchy would not endure. He would be perceived as having abandoned the interests of his own country in favor of those of a foreign power. And if an overidentified local leader such as King Hassan loses, so does the foreign power that has supported him. The identification of local leaders as U.S. clients leads to their overthrow and damages U.S. interests, as the United States discovered in Iraq and Lebanon in 1958, Libya in 1969, Iran in 1979, Egypt in 1981, and Lebanon in 1984.

Overidentification also encourages local leaders to have unrealistic expectations of U.S. support for their own objectives. What Hassan expects from his relationship with the United States is support for Morocco's military occupation of the Western Sahara as well as support in broader issues, such as the conflict with Spain over colonial enclaves in northern Morocco. Hassan has not sought a security umbrella from the United States, but he probably believes that his military cooperation with Washington ensures that Morocco will receive at least some support of the sort given by the United States to Arab states in the Persian Gulf in the unlikely event of an invasion by one of his neighbors. Given Congressional constraints on the use of U.S. troops overseas and the post-Vietnam War attitude of the U.S. public toward military operations abroad, however, there would be little or no political support in the United States for a military intervention in Morocco even in the unlikely event of an Algerian or Libyan attack. Nor would there be support for the use of military force in an attempt to affect the outcome of a domestic political power struggle in Morocco or anywhere else in northwest Africa, however tempting it might be to try to do so. The United States' long-term interests in the region lie with its people and its governments, not with any particular ruler.

Fortunately, the unrealistic nature of the expectations of both sides were revealed in 1984, when Hassan signed a unity agreement with Qaddafi, the United State's *bête noire* in North Africa. This was a rude shock to Washington, and Washington's hostile reaction seems to have been an equally rude shock to Hassan. Both sides were better able to appreciate the limitations of their relationship as a result, and the United States has since returned at least part way to its traditional policy of friendly relations based on mutual respect for national interests, without any expectations that King Hassan will act as an ally or as a surrogate. An effective U.S. policy would accept that the United States must deal with the government in power but would recognize that while governments may change, the United States' interest in a friendly Morocco will not.

In contrast to relations with Morocco, the problem with U.S.

relations with Algeria has traditionally been one of underidentification. While the United States has important economic interests in Algeria, much larger than its economic interests in Morocco, political relations between the United States and Algeria have been complicated in the past by major differences in foreign policy. These differences have been ameliorated considerably under the Bendjedid government and both sides have taken positions that are considerably more pragmatic. In particular, the United States government has come to realize that although the foreign policy position of Algeria may be closer to that of the Soviet Union than to that of the United States, Algeria has had no illusions about Soviet motives, and does not take orders from the Soviets. As with Morocco, Algeria's foreign policy is based on its national interests. Although Algeria has purchased large quantities of military equipment from the Soviet Union, it has been careful to avoid becoming dependent on Soviet-produced weaponry and has deliberately diversified its sources of arms by purchasing military equipment from both the United States and France. Second, the Algerian economy is oriented toward trade with the United States and France. The bulk of Algeria's imports come from the West rather than from the Soviet Union and Algeria has made it clear that it is eager to expand economic links with the noncommunist world. Finally, Algeria has demonstrated that it can play a positive role in the Middle East, from the U.S. point of view, as it did, for instance, when it acted as a mediator between the United States and Iran during the hostage crisis.

Over the past eight years, the United States has moved from an attitude that was, at best, cool toward Algeria and that contrasted strongly with its rather warm attitude toward Morocco, to a position that is more nearly balanced. The Western Sahara conflict, however, remains an issue in which the United States is clearly on the side of the Moroccans. In the second half of 1988 and early 1989, there were hopeful signs that the parties were moving toward a peaceful settlement. These hopes were dashed, at least temporarily, by King Hassan's uncomplimentary public remarks following a meeting with Polisario representatives in Marrakech in January 1989. But in mid-1991 there is hope again that the UN-sponsored referendum in the Western Sahara will actually take place and that there will be a settlement. Regrettably, there is not a great deal that the United States can do to promote a negotiated settlement of the war before the combatants are willing to make peace, and once they are willing there is no need for mediation by the United States. Past meetings between King Hassan and President Bendjedid and, subsequently, between the King and representatives of the Polisario Front, demonstrate that the parties involved can resolve the conflict themselves if they wish to do so, and it would be preferable if the impetus came from the countries directly involved, rather than from outside parties.

Under the present circumstances, the United States should adopt a two-track policy: (1) It should make it clear to the Moroccans and others that its close relations with Morocco do not mean that the war in the Western Sahara is a U.S. war or that it endorses Morocco's claim to sovereignty over the disputed territory; (2) simultaneously, it should look for a way to encourage both Morocco and the Polisario Front to make the concessions necessary to reach an agreement on a referendum to determine the future status of the Western Sahara, despite the fact that U.S. influence and leverage are limited.

On the first track, the United States should minimize or eliminate its military involvement in the Saharan war and it should avoid actions and statements that can be interpreted as biased toward the Moroccan position. In addition, the United States should publicly restate its position that the status of the Western Sahara remains unresolved and that it does not recognize Moroccan sovereignty over the territory.

On the second track, the United States should continue to support, and encourage others to support, United Nations' effort to organize a referendum. A referendum would permit a definitive and peaceful settlement of the war and it has been accepted publicly by Morocco, Algeria, and the Polisario Front. Negotiating the differences between the parties over the modalities of the referendum proposal is simpler than starting all over again with another initiative. The UN referendum plan may not contain all the ingredients required for a peaceful settlement of the war, but it does represent the most reasonable proposal offered so far, and it has the broadest international support.

Some have recommended that the United States employ its assistance programs and its economic policies to push the parties toward a settlement. The main problem with this idea is that the United States does not provide aid to Algeria or the Polisario Front and consequently enjoys no leverage over them. Economic policy also does not endow the United States with leverage over Algeria because, in the final analysis, the Algerians can turn to alternative markets and because U.S. economic interests would suffer as much damage as Algeria's from any effort to exert economic pressures on Algeria.

On the other hand, U.S. economic relations with Morocco are too limited to provide the United States with significant leverage over the latter either.   U.S. military assistance is much more important to Morocco, but past efforts to use military aid as an instrument to force King Hassan to a more flexible position have failed and are unlikely to work in the future, because Morocco can turn to alternative sources of military assistance from Western European countries, particularly France.   Even if this were not the case, King Hassan would still resist U.S. efforts to use military aid as a lever because surrender to such pressure would undermine his political legitimacy and provoke domestic opposition.   The unpalatable truth of the matter is that military aid programs almost never provide the United States with an effective lever over recipient governments, and the case of Morocco is no exception.

Meanwhile, U.S. military assistance is the price that the United States has to pay for access to Moroccan bases and other military facilities by the U.S. Central Command.   Unless the United States is willing to do without this military cooperation, there does not appear to be any viable alternative to the continuation of U.S. arms sales and other military assistance.   The level of this assistance, however, should be determined by Morocco's legitimate defense requirements, not by what Morocco needs to maintain its military occupation of the Western Sahara.

While military and economic assistance programs offer little leverage, the United States does have other means of influencing the combatants at its disposal. U.S. political support, in the United Nations and elsewhere, can be vital to the countries concerned.   Without wielding this fact as a bludgeon, the United States can use traditional diplomatic techniques in an effective manner to encourage the parties to continue to discuss the referendum proposal. Efforts to influence them should be pursued through subtle diplomacy at the State Department, the Defense Department, and the United Nations, not by manipulating aid programs.

NOTES

1. This article is an updated reformulation of comments made in my book, *North Africa: Regional Tensions and Strategic Concerns*, revised edition (New York: Praeger, 1987).

2. International Monetary Fund, *Direction of Trade Statistics: Yearbook 1989* (Washington, D.C.: International Monetary Fund, 1989), 281.
3. Ibid., 78.

5

Moscow, the Maghreb, and Conflict in the Western Sahara
Yahia H. Zoubir

Unlike the United States, the Soviet Union has pursued a more consistent, albeit opportunistic and pragmatic, policy toward the Maghreb. For decades, Moscow has attempted to maintain stable and favorable relations with the central Maghrebi states (Algeria, Morocco, and Tunisia). The Soviets have succeeded in preserving good ties with Morocco and Algeria despite occasional disagreements on international political issues. Furthermore, the conflict in the Western Sahara has created less problems for Moscow than it did for Washington, whose "overidentification" with Morocco--to use Ambassador Richard Parker's term--led to strains with Algeria, at least until the early 1980s. This chapter examines Soviet relations with Algeria and Morocco and how Moscow has dealt with the conflict in the Western Sahara.

As this essay will show, although Moscow has consistently portrayed itself as the natural champion of national liberation movements in the Third World and has indeed extended material and military support to many nationalist movements seeking independence from colonial rule, no such commitment was ever made to the Polisario Front. The USSR has done very little to help the Sahrawi nationalist movement, which has been at war with Morocco since late 1975.

MOSCOW AND ORIGINS OF THE WESTERN SAHARA CONFLICT

When the Western Sahara was still under Spain's colonial rule, the Soviets did not hesitate to denounce the Spanish Foreign Legion for "keeping the people in El Ayoun and the underpaid nomad workers in the rich phosphates deposits of Bu-Craa under control."[1] Consequently, Polisario's military attacks against Spanish garrisons met with Soviet approval.[2] This occurred at a time when Soviet trade relations with Morocco were growing at a fast pace. Not only did the Soviet Union provide about 60 percent of Morocco's needs for oil, but it also was negotiating one of its most important barter deals ever reached with a Third World country, whereby the Soviets could exploit a new phosphate mine in Meskala, thus allowing the USSR to obtain a yearly supply of 10 million tons of phosphates beginning in 1990.[3]

Not surprisingly, when the Western Sahara again became an important issue, the Soviets sided automatically with Morocco. For instance, during a speech he gave in Berlin in October 1974, Leonid Brezhnev declared that "the struggle of Western Africa [the Western Sahara] against Spanish domination has entered a decisive stage." Although he mentioned Algeria, Mauritania, and Tunisia as supporting the struggle, Brezhnev singled out Morocco as "the leader of the struggle."[4] Moscow's problems, however, began a year later when the question of the Western Sahara and its future led to tensions among the Maghrebi states. The Soviets had no real perspective except to say that "the countries of the Arab Maghreb have no united viewpoint" on the future of the territory after Spanish withdrawal. Soviet commentators concurred that it was "rather difficult" to reach a consensus before Spain's withdrawal from the territory and that "it was difficult to consult the indigenous inhabitants of the so-called Spanish Sahara, and in the final analysis it is the opinion of the inhabitants which will be decisive."[5]

The USSR accused the Western press of instigating the differences among the Maghrebi nations on the question. The Soviet Union, having already cast its support to Morocco against Spain, now attempted to protect its relationship with Algeria. Soviet reports insisted that Algeria had no irredentist claims over the Western Sahara. In their view, Algeria's support for the liberation of the Western Sahara was devoid of any selfish objectives. "Algeria was not promoting its own interests, any more than they [Algerians] had done so in giving aid to other colonial peoples' struggles."[6]

Following the high tension prevailing in the region, Moscow's objective was to avoid a direct military confrontation between the two Maghrebi giants, namely Algeria and Morocco, over the future of the former colony. The Kremlin was confronted with a serious dilemma.

On the one hand, it was anxious to conclude the important phosphate agreement with Morocco; on the other hand, it sought Algeria's support during the crisis in Angola. Therefore, from a Soviet perspective, the best alternative consisted of a peaceful resolution of the issue in order to prevent Moscow from having to take sides should Morocco and Algeria decide to choose a military solution. Whatever their predilections, the Soviets avoided antagonizing either side.

Before the conflict took serious proportions, the Soviets showed some sympathy for Morocco's claims over the territory. In Summer 1975, for example, during his visit to Moscow, the head of the Socialist Union of Popular Forces (USFP) delegation, Al-Yazzi declared the following:

Our delegation described the current situation in our country, and discussed in particular the problem of the Spanish Sahara. The Moroccan people almost unanimously want to recover it and to struggle against foreign domination in the Sahara and in the political enclaves in Northern Morocco. *We have found a great deal of understanding on the part of our Soviet comrades, as well as fairly active and fraternal support in this anti-colonial struggle*, which obviously falls within the framework of the struggle against imperialism, colonialism and neo-colonialism.[7]

As long as the conflict was one between Morocco and Spain, the Soviets found it easy to side with the former. But when it became clear that Morocco and Algeria were heading for a direct confrontation, the Soviets started to readjust their policy and adopted a much more cautious approach that took into account Algeria's position. Moscow began to insist on its neutrality in the conflict. In October 1975, for instance, the commentator of Moscow radio protested against reports in the Moroccan *Istiqlal* party's newspaper, *L'Opinion*, for "spreading anti-Soviet lies in connection with developments in Western Sahara." He emphatically added that "the Soviet people have for many years shown friendship and respect for all the peoples of the Maghreb....The only thing the Soviet people want is the destruction of colonialism in all parts of the world, especially in Western Sahara."[8]

The almost defensive character of the Soviet attitude, however, took a different turn following the development of the situation in Angola. In late October 1975, the Moscow-backed Popular Movement for the Liberation of Angola (MPLA) in Angola was confronted with a more effective military threat when South Africa invaded in support of

UNITA. In view of the new situation, the Soviets launched a major airlift to come to the rescue of their ally.[9] Like most African countries, Algeria, too, supported the MPLA, and therefore authorized the Soviets to make stopovers at the Algiers airport.[10] Although support for the MPLA was an independent decision, Algerians were able to extract an important concession from the Soviets on the Western Sahara as a trade-off for the use of the Algiers airport. The Soviet representative at the United Nations Security Council, Yacob Malik, stated on November 3 that "the people of Western Sahara have the full right to determine their future."[11] The statement, however, did not signify a shift in relations with Morocco. In fact, Soviet commentaries in Moscow did not mark any radical departure from the previous position on the Sahara issue. One reason, of course, was Moscow's hope to finalize the phosphates negotiations with Morocco. Their hope was in vain, for the king called the deal off following the Soviet statement at the UN Security Council.

The Soviets voted favorably for UN resolutions on the former Spanish colony. Yet, they never extended any material backing to the Polisario Front. In fact, there is evidence that the Soviet leadership pleaded with the Algerian government to calm the situation. There are also indications that the Soviets, at least initially, vehemently opposed the transfer by the Algerians of Soviet military equipment to the Sahrawi combatants. Only after tough negotiations with Algerian officials did the Soviets finally agree--quite reluctantly--to allow Soviet equipment to be supplied to Polisario.[12]

Despite their obvious efforts not to be involved in the conflict, the Soviets were nonetheless accused of having had a greater role than they had admitted.[13] Whatever the accusations, there has been absolutely no indication or proof that the Soviets have ever directly supplied arms to the Polisario.[14]

The USSR has always been annoyed by any kind of allegations concerning its role in the Western Sahara conflict. This can be attributed to the special importance that the Kingdom of Morocco occupies in its calculations. In 1976, it was particularly distressed by the French report referred to earlier, that Soviet weapons were delivered to Sahrawi nationalists rather than to the MPLA in Angola.

We are grieved...[by these reports]. The Soviet Union and Morocco are linked by long-standing friendship and cooperation. Soviet and Moroccan statesmen have more than once stressed that this friendship and its development was serving the interests of both countries and their peoples. At the end of last year, King Hassan II said that he wished to maintain this friendship forever.[15]

Moscow's position has remained consistent. First, the Soviets have sought to avoid a military confrontation between Algeria and Morocco. They were really alarmed when brief military clashes took place in January and February 1976. Second, they have supported UN resolutions concerning the Western Sahara. Third, they have endorsed efforts to find a political, negotiated, solution to the conflict.

The Kremlin's neutrality in the conflict can hardly be doubted. When the Sahrawi Arab Democratic Republic (SADR) was proclaimed on February 27, 1976, Soviet media reported the event without comment except to say that "the majority of the OAU states were in favor of recognizing it."[16] Despite their initial expectation of support from Moscow, Polisario leaders were soon disillusioned with the Soviet attitude toward their cause. Fifteen years after the proclamation of the state, the SADR and Polisario have not obtained diplomatic recognition from the USSR, or any East European country (except Yugoslavia) nor have they received direct military assistance.

Although Polisario, as a nationalist movement, has not received support from the USSR, Moscow has occasionally acknowledged its existence either through official statements[17] or simply by voting in favor of UN resolutions (e.g., UN General Assembly in November 1979) that recognize the legitimacy of the Sahrawi struggle and the Polisario Front as the sole and lawful representative of the Sahrawi people.[18]

Moscow's position vis-à-vis the conflict in the Western Sahara, with a few variations, has been consistent. But what are the main reasons that have led the Soviets to adopt such a consistent position? Undoubtedly, Soviet policy toward the conflict in the Western Sahara and toward the Polisario Front is a function of the relationship that Moscow has cultivated with Morocco on the one hand and with Algeria on the other. Therefore, a review of the USSR's relationship with these two countries is necessary in order to elucidate the reasons for the Kremlin's behavior toward the conflict.

SOVIET-MOROCCAN RELATIONS

The Russians expressed an interest in North Africa well before the establishment of the USSR in 1917. Trade relations were established under the rule of Catherine the Great, who had friendly rapport with the Moroccan Sultan Mohamed Ben Abdallah in the 1780s. In 1890, a Russian consulate was opened in Tangier. During the Morccan crises of 1905 and 1911, Czarist Russia expressed its interest in playing a greater role. The Maghreb attracted Soviet attention immediately after World War II. In fact, the Soviets attempted to obtain from the Allies permission to establish bases in Libya and Morocco.[19]

In the late 1940s and early 1950s, the Soviets were so worried about the growing presence of the United States in Tangier (where the United States was about to establish a radio network and a transmitter station) that they threatened to set up a bank through which they would channel funds to the Moroccan nationalists.[20] During Morocco's struggle for independence in the 1950s, the Soviet Union and its European allies voted consistently for United Nations General Assembly resolutions favoring Morocco's independence.[21]

When Morocco became independent in 1956, the Soviets were quick to establish links with the country. A trade protocol was signed in 1957. The various contacts led to the establishment of diplomatic relations in September 1958. The Soviets were quite impressed with King Mohamed V's militant neutralism in foreign policy.

In November 1960, Soviet MiGs were delivered to the Moroccan Royal Air Force. Additional weapons were received by Morocco in 1961 and 1962, despite King Hassan II's (Mohamed V's son and successor) more pro-Western leanings. When Algeria and Morocco started a border war in Fall 1963, Soviet weapons proved effective in initially routing the Algerian armed forces, which were not yet organized as a modern army. Furthermore, Algeria had received only a small portion of the weaponry ordered from Moscow.[22] Although the Soviets generally sided with revolutionary Algeria, they adopted a neutral position. The USSR stopped sending weapons to Morocco, but resumed delivery (via Czechoslovakia) once the conflict had ended.[23]

In 1961, it had been announced that King Mohamed V and Nikita Khrushchev would exchange official visits. But the king's sudden death made such projects impossible. However, Anastas Mikoyan, vice president of the Soviet Council of Ministers, visited Morocco in January 1962. In November 1964, Leonid Brezhnev, then president of the

Supreme Soviet, paid a visit to the kingdom on his way to Conakry, Guinea. Finally, in October 1966, King Hassan made an official visit to the Soviet Union.[24]

Morocco, indisputably, was, and still is, perceived by the Kremlin as an important country. This explains why although they were closer to Algeria, the Soviets blamed the border conflict between the two countries in 1963 on the Western powers rather than on Morocco alone.[25]

Soviet-Moroccan relations continued to flourish in the 1960s despite the monarchy's repression of the leftist forces in the country. In fact, after his trip to Moscow in Fall 1966, King Hassan secured further military and economic assistance agreements with the Soviet Union. The Soviets certainly realized that their interests with Morocco were important enough to maintain good relations with the monarchy. The seemingly neutralist policy concerning the two ideological blocs pursued by the king, and Moscow's desire to diminish U.S. influence as well as to strengthen its own strategic interests in Morocco, provided the necessary justifications for the Soviets to expand their cooperation with a "reactionary regime." From a Moroccan perspective, ties with the Soviet Union helped the kingdom put pressure on the West at a time when Franco-Moroccan relations were at a low ebb due to the abduction in Paris of King Hassan's opponent, the popular leftist leader, Mahdi Ben Barka, by Moroccan officials and to other political and economic problems between the two countries.

In the 1970s, the Soviet-Moroccan trade relations grew considerably. Following the signing of the phosphates deal in March 1978, Morocco became--and still is--the USSR's major trading partner in Africa.[26] As suggested earlier, the deal could have been agreed to earlier had it not been for Moscow's strong statement in favor of the Sahrawis at the United Nations in late 1975. Nevertheless, the Soviets were able to renew the negotiations on the phosphates in 1977.[27]

The phosphates deal, dubbed by King Hassan as the *contrat du siècle* (deal of the century) is of considerable importance to the Soviets. Although the USSR is the second largest world producer of phosphates, it still needs another source of supply for its partners in the Council for Mutual Economic Assistance (CMEA or COMECON). The Soviet Union itself requires enormous quantities of phosphates. Therefore, the multibillion dollar, thirty-year contract with Morocco (which holds about 70 percent of the world reserves of phosphates) was negotiated in order to ensure a continuous supply to the Soviet Union. Other important trade agreements exist between the Soviet Union and the Kingdom of Morocco, mainly in the field of fisheries, chemicals, energy, and agriculture.

In a way, the phosphates deal has led to a quasi-dependency of the USSR on Morocco, at least as far as the supply of this raw material is concerned. One of the political consequences of the deal has been the USSR's refusal to extend any direct material support to the Sahrawi nationalists. It has also prevented Moscow from attacking the Moroccan monarchy's actions on behalf of the Western powers (e.g., Morocco's role in Zaire during the Shaba crises of 1977 and 1978; and the king's role in bringing the Israelis and Egyptians together). Both countries are aware of each other's importance. The Soviets show great respect for Morocco and the king. Despite the latter's often blunt anticommunist statements, the Soviets have never portrayed him as an agent of global imperialism or made any personal attacks similar to the ones leveled against Egyptian President Anwar Sadat.

The economic dimension is only one among several factors in the special relationship between the USSR and Morocco. Perhaps the most important Soviet consideration is the kingdom's vital geostrategic location. Keeping the Strait of Gibraltar open for the Soviet navy is obviously part of Soviet calculations. In addition, from the Soviet's ideological point of view, Morocco presents prerevolutionary features. Therefore, maintaining a presence in the country is crucial.

In the 1980s, the relationship between the two countries grew stronger despite the simultaneous rapprochement between Rabat and Washington. Due to the nature of the regime, Rabat's diplomatic positions have always been more congenial with the United States than with the USSR. Nonetheless, the Soviets did betray their uneasiness about the closer ties between Morocco and the United States, which developed at a faster pace when the Reagan administration took office. What concerned the Soviets was not so much U.S. indirect involvement in the Western Sahara conflict, but the growing strategic links between Morocco and the United States (e.g., the creation of a joint military commission in 1982 and the U.S. acquisition of transit rights at the former U.S. military facility in Morocco, which could be used by the U.S. Central Command, formerly known as Rapid Deployment Force). Paradoxically, however, it was the United States' growing involvement on the side of Morocco that led the Soviets to exercise even more caution in order to (1) avoid any direct confrontation with the United States over the Western Sahara; (2) prevent internationalization of the conflict; and (3) avoid giving

Morocco any excuse to move closer to the Western camp. This policy has been quite successful, for relations with Morocco remained stable and in the long-run, the Western Sahara conflict remains a regional issue that could be solved through a negotiated settlement.

SOVIET-ALGERIAN RELATIONS

Although the Algerian government may have resented the USSR's lukewarm support for the Sahrawi cause, Algeria's relationship with the Soviet Union never deteriorated because of Moscow's position on the Western Sahara.

Algeria holds a crucial position in Soviet policy in the Maghreb. Not only do the stances of Algiers and Moscow often converge on major political issues, but the Soviets also appreciate Algeria's role in Third World affairs. Since its independence in 1962, Algeria has been able to build its reputation as a stable revolutionary socialist state whose pragmatism has allowed it to establish good relations with both blocs. Algeria's credibility in the Non-Aligned Movement (NAM) as well as in the Organization of African Unity (OAU) constitutes an additional advantage for the Soviet Union. Due to their staunch nationalism, forged during one of the bloodiest anticolonial wars, Algerian policymakers have always made it clear that their relatively close relationship with the Soviets remains one of equal partners, with conflicting national interests. Algerians define their ties with Moscow as part of their nonalignment, but also as a counterweight to their relationship with France and the United States.

During the war of national liberation, Algerian National Liberation Front (FLN) received little support--or at least less than might have been expected--from the Soviet Union. So long as the relationship with French President Charles de Gaulle was good, the Soviets took no overt position on the Algerian question, although they voted for UN resolutions favorable to the Algerian nationalists. Only when it became obvious that France was to remain part of the Western alliance did the Soviets provide moral and indirect material support. The People's Republic of China's more forthcoming and more sincere--at least from an Algerian perspective--aid to the FLN compelled the Soviets to provide (via Eastern Europe) material assistance to the national liberation movement.[28] In spite of their ambiguous position during the revolutionary period, Algeria remained grateful to the socialist countries for their backing and continued to perceive them as natural allies against the West.

Algeria's independence in 1962 received a warm welcome in Moscow, which, in September 1963, extended a $100 million loan to the newly independent nation.[29] However, what brought the two countries closer was the military relationship. In the same way that Egyptian President Gamel Abdel Nasser formed stronger ties with the Soviet Union, Algeria moved closer to the USSR as a result of U.S. policy toward the region. After independence, the United States, like France, turned down Algeria's requests for arms.[30] Furthermore, the consequence of the alleged U.S. logistical backing of Morocco--despite claims of neutrality during the latter's border conflict with Algeria--compelled the Algerians to look for another source of weaponry at a time when it was converting its guerrilla forces into a modern army.[31]

For domestic as well as international reasons, the relationship between the USSR and Algeria grew closer. By 1964, the Soviets had described Algeria as a "socialist nation." This special relationship, however, was temporarily put in jeopardy by the June 1965 military coup that overthrew Algeria's first president, Ahmed Ben Bella, from whom the Soviets had hoped a great deal. President Houari Boumedienne's anticommunism disquieted Moscow for some time. But because of its dependency on Soviet weaponry and its desire to balance its relationships, Algeria was quick to indicate that it valued its friendly ties with the USSR. Economic relations between the two countries were, however, dismal compared to Algeria's exchanges with the capitalist world, a situation that still exists today.

Regardless of its military and political ties with the USSR, the Algerian government categorically refused to grant military bases or facilities to the Soviets. Nonetheless, the two countries maintained close relations in the late 1960s and in the 1970s due to developments in the Middle East, Africa, and the Maghreb itself. One of the main factors that led to the rapprochement between the two countries was the perceived building of an axis between Washington, Rabat, and Paris during the crisis in Zaire in 1977 and 1978. Furthermore, the Camp David Accords, on the one hand, and Saudi Arabia's financial aid to Morocco, on the other hand, frightened Algerian policymakers. This is probably what led Boumedienne to seek a strategic alliance between progressive Arab states and the Soviet Union.[32] The move was also of a tactical nature, for Boumediene wanted to extract a quid pro quo from the Soviets to support Algerians on the Western Sahara, particularly in the event of a war with Morocco.

President Boumedienne died in December 1978 without the Soviets having changed their position on the Western Sahara. They still refused to recognize the SADR or to condemn Morocco's policies in the occupied territory. Nonetheless, relations with Algeria remained as good as before. The Soviets did not reduce their arms sales to Algeria as a result of the latter's support of the Polisario Front. Boumedienne's successor, President Chadli Bendjedid, seems to have understood how little support should be expected from the Soviets on the Western Sahara.

In the 1980s, Soviet-Algerian relations remained quite good. In the military field, a considerable amount of Soviet weaponry was sold to Algeria. Undoubtedly, although the Soviets took a cautious position on the conflict in the Western Sahara in order to manage their own relationship with Morocco, the Soviets supplied enough weaponry to Algeria to deter Morocco from engaging in a direct military confrontation with Algeria. Furthermore, the Soviet Union has been quite careful not to give Algeria reasons to pursue a pro-Western orientation. Algeria, under Bendjedid, focused its attention much more on the NAM and Africa, whose support was needed to resolve the conflict in the Western Sahara.

Bendjedid's trip to Moscow in 1981 came at a time when U.S.-Algerian relations, which had considerably warmed up after Algeria's role in freeing the U.S. hostages in Iran, fell to a low point following the Reagan administration's decision to supply weapons to Morocco.[33] Despite the U.S. decision, however, Benjedid's trip to Moscow did not indicate any shift in Algeria's nonaligned stance. In fact, there is evidence that there were disagreements between the two countries. Algeria, for instance, refused to support Moscow's call for a Middle East international peace conference,[34] despite Moscow's assurance that it supported the Sahrawis' rights to self-determination.[35] From an Algerian point of view, this assurance was obviously not enough. For the Soviets, jeopardizing ties with Morocco over the Western Sahara was not worthwhile, mainly at a time when economic relations with Morocco were flourishing. The Soviets made it plain that their relations with Morocco were valuable despite "some problems which our relations sometimes experience," and that "mutually beneficial Soviet-Moroccan contacts and relations have been developing" despite the attempts of "certain circles outside and inside Morocco" to undermine them.[36] But the Soviet Union did, however, continue to reiterate its support for the OAU and UN position on the Western Sahara.

The Algerian president's historic trip to the United States in April 1985 was quite worrisome to the Soviets. The Soviet press abstained from any comment of its own on the trip, preferring to use commentaries by the Algerian media that indicated that "'significant disagreements' came to light during the discussion of the wide range of international problems."[37]   Although the Algerians exploited the thawing relations between Algiers and Washington to trouble the Moroccans, the event might also have been used to increase Algeria's leverage over the Soviets in obtaining more sophisticated military hardware.

President Bendjedid's visit to Moscow in March 1986 led to a convergence of views between the two governments on many international issues (e.g., stability in the Mediterranean and a Middle East international peace conference). However, what was conspicuously missing in Mikhail Gorbachev's speech at the dinner honoring Bendjedid was any direct reference to the Western Sahara. Gorbachev only emphasized "the right of the peoples to decide their destinies independently" and that "[regional] problems should be resolved without imperialist intervention under conditions of respect for the independence and lawful aspirations of the peoples."[38]

THE SOVIET UNION AND THE WESTERN SAHARA CONFLICT UNDER GORBACHEV

Throughout the 1980s Moscow continued to maintain its neutral position based on UN resolutions regarding the Western Sahara conflict. The Moroccan government and political parties have highly appreciated Moscow's position. In 1984, for instance, the conservative newspaper *Al-'Alam* expressed its satisfaction at Soviet attitude toward the conflict: "There is no doubt that national public opinion has welcomed this positive attitude of the Soviet Union toward the question of the integrity of Moroccan soil."[39]

In 1985, the head of a Soviet delegation of veterans visiting Morocco denied accusations that the Polisario Front received any sophisticated weapons from the Soviet Union. Major General Grachev insisted that the USSR had no links with the Polisario and that Moscow did not recognize the SADR.[40]

In 1986, the Soviet ambassador to Morocco declared unequivocally that "the Soviet Union recognizes neither the Polisario nor the SADR."[41]

In June 1987, during the visit to the Kingdom of Morocco, Arnold Ryuytel, vice chairman of the Supreme Soviet Presidium and chairman of the Estonian Supreme Soviet, declared that "settling the Sahara problem should be done within the framework of good neighborly relations to preserve peace in the region."[42]   The Soviet official expressed Moscow's satisfaction about the meeting between President Bendjedid and King Hassan II that had taken place the previous month.

King Hassan seemed so pleased with the Soviet position that he returned the favor by emphasizing the important role that the Soviet Union must play in a Middle East peace process. He has insisted that peace in the Middle East cannot be maintained without the USSR's involvement.[43]   This may stem from Soviet qualified support for Moroccan claims. It is quite likely that, privately, the Soviets may have supported some of Morocco's pretensions over the Western Sahara. Hence their success in reviving the phosphates deal in 1977. In fact, in February 1987, a communiqué issued at the end of a visit by Soviet journalists stated that "the Soviet side expressed understanding for Moroccan efforts to *preserve territorial rights* and peacefully recover the enclaves still under Spanish occupation."[44]

Nonetheless, it should be pointed out that despite their ambivalent position toward the conflict in the Western Sahara in order not to antagonize Morocco or to get dragged into the conflict, the Soviets have consistently supported a peaceful settlement. In fact, perhaps because of *Glasnost* ("openness"), the Soviet press--unlike in the past--has recently discussed the Western Sahara in more depth.[45] Moreover, they have been more emphatic about the elimination of the conflict. Andrei Gromyko, chairman of the Presidium of the Council of Ministers, told Moroccan prime minister Ahmed Osman during his visit to the Kremlin that

the Soviet Union has an interest in getting rid of tension in Northwest Africa and ensuring that peace prevails...[R]elations are improving between Morocco and Algeria, and that is precisely the path which the two states can follow in the future with benefit for both.[46]

In line with OAU and UN resolutions, as well as with Algeria's position, Gromyko was satisfied that "Morocco's line is directed at conducting business at the negotiating table."[47]   More importantly, Gromyko said, "If the plan for preparing a referendum and eliminating differences between the opposing sides does not hold, one surely does not need to grab a dagger, does one?"[48] This obviously implied that there should be a cease-fire.   There also seems to have been disagreements as to how the problem should be solved, because the report stated that "the conversation passed in a spirit of frankness and friendship," which is usually the diplomatic way of saying that the parties did not share the same views. One explanation is that at a time when Morocco and Polisario agreed on the UN secretary-general's peace plan, Moroccan officials were still talking about a "confirmatory referendum." As bluntly stated by Moulay Alaoui, minister of state, responsible for Western Sahara affairs, "Referendum on Western Sahara is only an episode, a detail. The important thing is that the Sahara is Moroccan."[49] Osman's mission to the Kremlin may have been to convince the Soviets of the same arguments. The Soviets were reluctant to accept such views for fear of alienating the Algerians, who made it plain that they reject a *fait accompli* on the Western Sahara. They might also have been genuinely concerned that such a scenario would bring back the status quo ante.

Surprisingly, since Fall 1988, the Soviets have expressed less ambivalent views about the conflict in the Western Sahara, at least as far as the press is concerned. Following the meetings between King Hassan and Polisario representatives, Soviet Foreign Ministry spokesman Gennadi Gerassimov expressed the satisfaction of his government in these terms:

The Soviet side notes with satisfaction the first signs of headway in resolving the protracted Western Sahara conflict and supports the peace efforts by the U.N. Secretary General and the Organization of African Unity....The U.S.S.R. considers that the Marrakech discussions became possible largely thanks to an improvement of the general situation in the Maghreb. They testify to a trend now gathering momentum in the world, toward liquidating regional pockets of tensions, which is a direct consequence of the assertion of the principles of the new political thinking in international relations. The Soviet Union, advocating a settlement of Western Sahara problem via dialogue on the basis of the balance of interests, can only welcome such a development.[50]

Nonetheless, the press, although expressing optimism, noted an important point: "Despite the agreement [UN peace proposal], however, we cannot close our eyes to persisting contradictions stemming, for example, from the presence of Moroccan troops in the territory and from Moroccan administration during the voting period."[51] This is precisely the point that the Algerian government and the Polisario have insisted upon. If the press still reflects the views of Soviet policymakers, this statement might indicate a tilt toward Algeria's position and an effort to bait Polisario into improving its relations with the USSR. If the referendum is favorable to the SADR, the Soviets would obviously like to be on good terms with the new independent state. Another reason might be to demonstrate to Algeria the USSR's credibility as a friend at a time when Algeria is suspected of following a more pro-Western direction. The USSR could not but have been suspicious of the strong support given by the United States and France to Bendjedid's regime during the tragic October 1988 riots in Algeria.

SOVIET POLICY IN THE MAGHREB:
PRAGMATISM, OPPORTUNISM, AND BALANCE

Soviet policy toward the conflict in the Western Sahara raises a fundamental question: Why has Moscow not given support to a genuine nationalist movement? As shown above, to argue that Soviet economic considerations in Morocco are the primary reason would be simplistic, for one can also argue that the Soviets have even greater political and military interests with Algeria and that logically they should have supported Polisario. The problem, therefore, is more complex.

First, the Kingdom of Morocco occupies a geostrategic position that could hardly be exaggerated.[52] Although at the present time the United States is the major beneficiary of this location, this might not remain so forever. If a radical regime were to take control in Morocco, its alliances could shift. The monarchical regime in Morocco, despite its seeming stability, is fragile. Cyclical economic crises and military coup attempts have often threatened the survival of the regime. Therefore, although it prefers to continue dealing with the monarchy, Moscow may be hopeful that a new regime in Morocco would be less pro-Western in orientation and better disposed toward the USSR.

Second, although it is not clear who will succeed King Hassan, the Soviets' cautious attitude toward the conflict in the Western Sahara has guaranteed Moscow a good position with any future regime, for even the legal opposition, especially the left, is as irredentist as the monarchy. The Soviets have been well aware that openly backing the Polisario Front would lead to a possible expulsion from Morocco.[53]

Third, the Soviets have been concerned not to give the conflict an East-West dimension. As a matter of fact, the Sahrawis themselves have been careful not to describe their struggle in ideological terms. Furthermore, from an ideological point of view, Sahrawi nationalism is unattractive to Moscow. Even though Polisario has emphasized its "opposition to imperialism, colonialism, and exploitation" and pledges to establish a socialist society, it categorically rejects Marxism-Leninism even as an inspiration. The movement's guidelines for socialism are drawn from Islamic tenets.[54] The Soviets are well aware that they would have little influence over the ideological and political direction of the Polisario. Moreover, the relationship between Polisario and the Soviet Union has been marked by serious incidents, such as the Sahrawi guerrillas' attacks on Soviet and East European vessels caught fishing off the Western Sahara coast.[55] Even more damaging has been the continued supply of spare parts to Morocco directly from the USSR or from its East European allies.[56]

Undoubtedly, there is evidence of Soviet sympathy, albeit discreet, for Polisario. But the Sahrawis' misfortune is that they are fighting a regime that, despite its conservative nature, is of great value to Moscow. Not only does Morocco play a leading role in the Arab world, but it also serves as a showcase of Soviet relations with conservative regimes. In a period when Moscow has been cultivating good rapport with conservative governments, it would surely be a self-defeating policy to support a guerrilla movement, regardless of the worthiness of its cause.

The Soviets have therefore succeeded in maintaining good ties with Morocco without upsetting their close relationship with Algeria. The success of this policy stems from their refusal to give direct military and political support to the Polisario Front and their even-handed relations with Morocco and Algeria. In order not to antagonize Algeria--and by extension the members of the NAM and OAU--they have consistently voted in favor of UN resolutions that support the Sahrawis' right to self-determination. Furthermore, the Soviets have continued their close military cooperation with Algeria and maintained good political and economic ties. On the other hand, they have expanded their economic relations with Morocco, an expansion that was made possible thanks to a cautious attitude that consisted in not going beyond support for UN resolutions. Morocco could not feel alienated, for the king himself has often declared that he would abide by such resolutions on a referendum. Finally, the Soviets have avoided entering into a dispute with the Polisario Front. By adopting a neutral attitude and by giving indirect political support at the United Nations, they have succeeded in giving the impression of a state that continues to support national liberation causes. In fact, it would not be surprising that should the Western Sahara become an independent state, the Soviets would remind the Sahrawis, as they did the Algerians after their independence, that although they did not give them direct military support, Soviet weaponry and political backing in international forums were instrumental in bringing them independence. Such a policy proved successful in the past. From the Soviet Union's perspective, it may work again.

Given that among the legal opposition parties inside Morocco there is consensus on the Western Sahara issue, the Soviets have had little room for maneuver with their traditional friends, the PPS and the USFP. Should the opposition in Morocco change its position, and assuming that this change will have consequential results, the Soviets may also shift their position. Or, even if the opposition does not change its position on the Western Sahara, and should it come to power, the Soviets would surely be more satisfied with a friendly, "progressive" Morocco than an uncertain independent Western Sahara.[57]

CONCLUSION

The conflict in the Western Sahara has given Moscow less difficulty than have other regional conflicts in the Third World. This is due mostly to the Soviet Union's pragmatic and cautious policy. Undoubtedly, credit should be given to the regional actors (Algerians, Moroccans, and Sahrawis) for avoiding elevating the issue to an East-West confrontation. But, the USSR's careful approach to the conflict has had a consequential impact. Moscow adopted a consistent position that has been strengthened since Gorbachev came to power. The Soviets have put a greater emphasis on peaceful means of resolving regional and international conflicts. Although the war in the Western

Sahara never reached the same degree of attention as did Afghanistan, Namibia, or Kamputchea, the Soviets have become increasingly forceful in their statements concerning a resolution of the conflict in the Maghreb. They have given full support to UN initiatives with respect to holding a referendum in the Western Sahara.[58] The statement made by the USSR Foreign Ministry spokesman on October 27, 1989, deserves to be quoted at length:

> Our position on the Western Sahara problem is well-known. There is no alternative to a political settlement of the conflict. We in the Soviet Union have welcomed processes of integration that gain momentum in the Arab Maghreb and supported the U.N. and O.A.U. plan to resolve the Western Sahara problem as well as their peace-keeping efforts.
>
> In this connection, the consensus reached by the U.N. General Assembly for the first time in many years during the vote on the Western Sahara draft resolution was viewed in Moscow as a welcomed development. In our opinion, this amounts to a new step toward undoing the Western Sahara knot on the basis of a balance of interests of all parties involved.
>
> Lately, we have repeatedly expressed our satisfaction with the positive changes that have manifested themselves in the quest for a solution to the problem. Unanimous support by the General Assembly's Fourth Committee for the draft resolution, as well as the consent of principle by Morocco and the Polisario Front, as underscored in the document, to a U.N. and O.A.U.-proposed referendum on self-determination for the people of Western Sahara, give us greater hope that a political settlement is within reach.
>
> We believe that realism, responsibility and a constructive approach demonstrated by the parties to the conflict in Western Sahara will make it possible to overcome the remaining differences and achieve a just settlement of this long-standing problem which would facilitate the progress toward lasting peace in the region. Approval of the resolution has shown that positive and generally acceptable agreements to resolve most complex regional problems can be reached now that principles of new political thinking and a nonconfrontational and constructive dialogue assert themselves in the United Nations.[59]

Unquestionably, the Soviets must have also appreciated the United States' constructive position on the Western Sahara at the United Nations.

Even though Moscow's presence and influence in the Maghreb are limited, the Soviets do nonetheless play a relatively important role. Their political and military ties with Algerià and their considerable trade relations with Morocco are important enough to allow them to exert a modicum of influence on the course of the conflict, at least through their arms supplies or in international forums.[60]

Despite the fact that the changes occurring in the Soviet Union and within Algeria itself will inevitably have an impact on Soviet-Algerian relations on the one hand, and Soviet-Moroccan relations, on the other, Moscow can be expected to maintain the same policy as before vis-à-vis the Western Sahara conflict. The Soviets would undoubtedly like to see it end peacefully and definitively. Although, as demonstrated during the Gulf War, its role as a superpower has greatly diminished, the Soviet Union remains a powerful member of the United Nations Security Council. Consequently, should the question of the Western Sahara be put on the agenda at the UN, the Soviets, in order not to be accused of apply "double standards," will push more resolutely for a political solution.

NOTES

1. Moscow Radio (in English for Africa), January 22, 1974, reported in *U.S.S.R. and the Third World* 4, no. 2 (January 14-March 3, 1974): 103.

2. Ibid., 104. It should be noted that in Spring 1973 King Hassan asked for and obtained Moscow's moral support against Spain's involvement in the region. See Virginia Thompson and Richard Adloff, *The Western Saharans: Background to Conflict* (London: Croom Helm, 1980), 163.

3. *Financial Times*, May 7, 1974.

4. Moscow Radio, October 10, 1974, reported in *U.S.S.R. and The Third World* 4, nos. 7, 8 (September 9-October 13, 1974): 429.

5. Moscow Radio (in Arabic and French for North Africa), May 28, 1975, reported in *U.S.S.R. and the Third World* 5, no. 5 (May 13-July 6, 1975): 260.

6. Moscow Radio, June 6, 1975, reported in *U.S.S.R. and the Third World* 5, no. 5 (May 13-July 6, 1975): 260.

7. Moscow Radio (in French for the Maghreb), August 14, 1975, reported in *U.S.S.R. and the Third World* 5, nos. 6-8 (July 7-December 31, 1975): 419-20 (my emphasis).

8. Ibid., 425.

9. Jiri Valenta, "Soviet Decision-Making on the Intervention in Angola," in David E. Albright, ed., *Communism in Africa* (Bloomington: Indiana University Press, 1980), 112-13.

10. David Albright, "Moscow's African Policy in the 1970s", in David E. Albright, ed., *Communism in Africa* (Bloomington: Indiana University Press, 1980), 58.

11. *Pravda*, November 4, 1975.

12. Harold Nelson, ed., *Algeria: A Country Study* (Washington, D.C.: The American University, 1979), 285.

13. See, for instance, Paris Radio (January 5, 1976), reported in *U.S.S.R. and the Third World* 6, no. 1 (January 1-March 31, 1976): 69.

14. Stephen Solarz, "Arms for Morocco?" *Foreign Affairs* 58, no. 2 (Winter 1979/80); John Damis, *Conflict in Northwest Africa: The Western Sahara Dispute* (Stanford, Calif.:   Hoover Institution Press, 1983), 130.

15. *U.S.S.R. and the Third World* 6, no. 1 (January 1-March 31, 1976): 51.

16. *Pravda*, March 1, 1976.

17. See, for instance, the declaration of the soviet ambassador to Senegal, *Le Monde*, November 5, 1977.

18. See Moris Rothberg, *The U.S.S.R. and Africa: New Dimensions of Soviet Global Power* (Miami: Advanced International Institute/University of Miami, 1980), 70.   See also the discussion by Soviet scholars in A. Chredor and A. Podtsérob, *Les Relations U.R.S.S.-Algérie*, (Moscow: Editions du Progrès, 1986), 200 ff.

19. For a more detailed historical background, see Mohieddine Hadhri, *L'URSS et le Maghreb.   De la Révolution d'Octobre à l'Indépendance de l'Algérie, 1917-1962* (Paris: Editions de l'Harmattan, 1985) and T. L. Musatova, "Sviazi Rossii i Marokko v XIX v ("Russian-Morocco Links in the 19th Century"), *Narody Azii I Afriki (Peoples of Asia and Africa)*, no. 1 (January-February 1987).

20. Luella J. Hall, *The United States and Morocco, 1776-1956* (Metuchen, New Jersey: The Scarecrow Press, 1971), 1036.

21. J. Brignon, et al., *Histoire du Maroc* (Paris and Casablanca: Hatier, 1967), 404.

22. John Waterbury, "The Soviet Union and North Africa," in Ivo Lederer and Wayne Vucinich, eds., *The Soviet Union and the Middle East* (Stanford, Calif.: Hoover Institution Press, 1974), 100; Bruce Porter, *The U.S.S.R. and the Third World Conflicts* (New York: Cambridge University Press, 1984), 61.

23. Porter, *The U.S.S.R. and the Third World Conflicts*, 61.

24. On the different official visits, see Jean-Paul Constant, *Les Relations Maroco-Soviètiques, 1956-1971* (Paris: Librairie générale de Droit et de Jurisprudence, 1973).

25. *Pravda*, October 17, 1963, in *Current Digest of the Soviet Press* (hereafter *CDSP*) 15, no. 42 (November 13, 1963): 23.

26. "Morocco: Soviet-American Rivalry," *Africa Confidential* 19, (October 1978): 5; *Middle East Economic Digest* (hereafter *MEED*), March 17, 1978, 32.

27. Despite the freeze on the deal, trade relations continued to flourish. In 1975, the USSR had become the main market for Moroccan citrus and the second oil supplier to Morocco. In the period 1972-76, trade between the two countries increased by 110 percent. See Elsa Assidon, *Sahara Occidental: Un Enjeu pour le Nord-Ouest Africain* (Paris: Maspéro, 1978), 112.

28. For further information, see Yahia H. Zoubir, "The United States, the Soviet Union, and the Decolonization of the Maghreb, 1945-1962," Paper presented at the Middle East Studies Association Annual Convention, San Antonio, Texas, November 10-13, 1990.

29. David and Marina Ottaway, *Algeria: The Politics of a Socialist Revolution* (Berkeley: University of California Press, 1970), 158.

30. William B. Quandt, "Can We Do Business With Radical Nationalists? Algeria: Yes," *Foreign Policy*, no. 7, (Summer 1972): 114-15.

31. Ibid.; Ottaway, *Algeria*, 158.

32. See Rashid Khalidi, *Soviet Middle East Policy in the Wake of Camp David* (Beirut: IPS, 1979), 22-24.

33. *The Washington Post*, March 25, 1981.

34. Robert O. Freedman, *Soviet Foreign Policy Toward the Middle East Since 1970*, 3rd ed. (New York: Praeger 1982), 402. Algeria finally acquiesced to the Soviet appeal for holding such a conference in October 1982. See *Foreign Bulletin Information Service/Soviet Union* (hereafter *FBIS/SOV*), October 18, 1982.

35. A. Ustanov, "U.S.S.R.-Algeria--A Common Approach," *The New Times*, no. 25 (1981): 7, made only an indirect allusion to the Sahrawi conflict, without mentioning it by name.

36. *FBIS/SOV*, March 3, 1981, H1.

37. *FBIS/SOV*, April 26, 1985, H2.

38. *FBIS/SOV*, March 27, 1986, H4.

39. "Soviet Support, Western Sahara, and Morocco: Well Placed Support," *Al-'Alam*, reprinted in *FBIS/Middle East and Africa*, (hereafter *FBIS/MEA*), February 2, 1984, Q3.

40. *FBIS/MEA*, March 28, 1985, Q1.

41. *Jeune Afrique*, August 13-20, 1986.

42. *FBIS/Near East and South Asia*, (hereafter *FBIS/NES*), June 15, 1987, F2.

43. *FBIS/SOV*, April 22, 1987 (my emphasis).

44. *FBIS/MEA*, February 24, 1987, Q3.

45. Moscow Tass International Service, reprinted in *FBIS/SOV* September 8, 1988, 21; Moscow Tass in English, reprinted in *FBIS/SOV*, September 13, 1988; *Izvestia*, January 12, 1989, reprinted in *CDSP* 41, no. 2 (1989): 23.

46. *FBIS/SOV*, September 8, 1988, 21.

47. Ibid.

48. Ibid., 22.

49. New Conference, Paris International Service in French, September 8, 1988, reprinted in *FBIS/NES*, September 8, 1988, 20.

50. Moscow Tass in English, January 11, 1989, reprinted in *FBIS/SOV*, January 12, 1989, 7.

51. *Izvestia*, January 12, 1989, reprinted in *CDSP* 41, no. 2 (1989): 23.

52. See George Joffe, "Strategic significance of the Maghreb," *Navy International* (July 1981): 388-91. For a Soviet viewpoint, see Verniamin Mashin, "For Stability in the Mediterranean," *International Affairs* (Moscow), no. 6 (June 1987): 93-94.

53. In 1975, when the Soviet Union expressed public support for Algeria's position on the Western Sahara, the king severed relations with East Germany, possibly as a warning to the Kremlin.

54. See Tony Hodges, "The Western Sahara File," *Third World Quarterly* 6, no. 1 (January 1984): 87.

55. *The New York Times*, July 23, 1986; *West Africa*, December 15, 1986.

56. *Defense and Foreign Affairs* 12, no. 48 (December 15-21, 1986): 1; See also, *West Africa*, December 15, 1986, 26-27. The parts are generally used to upgrade Soviet T-54 tanks purchased by Morocco in the 1960s to a level suitable for use in the Western Sahara conflict.

57. This would be a similar situation to what took place in Ethiopia. The USSR abandoned the Eritrean cause once Ethiopia followed a pro-Soviet direction. On this question, see Hélène Carrère d'Encausse, *Ni Paix, Ni Guerre* (Paris: Editions Flammarion, 1987), 76.

58. *West Africa*, October 22-26, 1989, 1724.

59. Union of Soviet Socialist Republics, Permanent Mission to the United Nations, *Press Release*, no. 201, New York, November 1, 1989. Following the adoption of Resolution 658 by the UN Security Council in June 1990, the Soviets praised the role that the UN was now playing in the resolution of regional conflicts. See full statement by USSR Foreign Ministry spokesman in *Izvestia*, July 1, 1990, reprinted in *FBIS/SOV*, July 6, 1990, 7-8.

60. For further details, see Yahia H. Zoubir, "L'URSS dans le Grand Maghreb: une stratégie équilibrée at une approche pragmatique," in Bassma Kodmani-Darwish and May Chartouni-Dubarry, eds., *Maghreb: Les Années de Transition* (Paris: Institut Français des Relations Internationales/ Masson, 1990), 342-60 and Yahia H. Zoubir, "The United States, the Soviet Union, and the Maghreb: Prospects for the Future," *The Maghreb Review* 15, no. 3-4 (Winter 1990/91).

6

The Western Sahara:
International Legal Issues

Beth A. Payne

Over the past four decades the world has witnessed the successful and often peaceful decolonization of over a billion people with few exceptions--one of the most noted being the Western Sahara. The annexation of the Western Sahara by Morocco in 1975, in violation of established international legal principles, has been described as a "decolonization disaster"[1] and "the gravest setback that the Human Rights movement has suffered in respect of the 'right' of self-determination."[2]

Although the Western Sahara was one of the last African countries to submit to colonialism, it remains one of the last to be decolonized. Twenty-four years after the United Nations first called for the decolonization of the Western Sahara,[3] Sahrawis are still waiting to exercise their right of self-determination. Approximately half of the territory's original population live in refugee camps in Algeria. Within the territory, Moroccan forces and an armed liberation organization--the Frente Popular para la Liberación de Saguia el Hamra y Río de Oro (the Polisario Front)--are fighting a prolonged war of attrition for control of the territory.

Morocco's annexation of the Western Sahara, despite established legal norms prohibiting such actions, raises important questions regarding the power of international law. The United States' extensive military assistance to Morocco for use in the Western Sahara also raises disturbing questions regarding the United States' obligation to ensure and respect the UN Charter and principles of international law.[4]

SELF DETERMINATION UNDER CUSTOMARY
INTERNATIONAL LAW

Polisario argues that the inhabitants of the Western Sahara have a legal right of self-determination that was violated initially by Spanish colonization, and later by Morocco's annexation of the Western Sahara in 1975. King Hassan of Morocco, however, claims a right of sovereignty over the Western Sahara, asserting that Morocco's historical control of the territory demands its reintegration with Morocco. Under customary international law, the Sahrawis' right of self-determination takes precedence over King Hassan's claim of historical sovereignty. Thus, Morocco must respect the Sahrawi's right to freely determine the status of the Western Sahara. In reaching this conclusion, this chapter will discuss whether a right of self-determination exists under customary international law, and if so, whether the inhabitants of the Western Sahara can claim this right; and if the Sahrawis do have a right of self-determination, whether Morocco has violated the Sahrawis' right, and has, therefore, violated customary international law.

Since the first demand for self-determination in 1865,[5] the principle has evolved from a political and moral principle to a legal right under customary international law. The principle of self-determination gained international prominence during World War I when President Woodrow Wilson stated that, with respect to German colonies, "there shall be no annexations...peoples are not to be handed from one sovereignty to another...peoples may now be dominated and governed only by their own consent."[6] Despite Western states' acceptance of self-determination as a governing principle in the determination of European states, they rejected its relevance with respect to the colonies of Africa and Asia.

However, colonies soon began to demand the same rights as those applied to Western states. The right of self-determination was invoked by a colony for the first time when the Pan-African Congress convened in 1919 in Paris and coined the slogan "Africa for Africans." In the early 1920s Egyptian nationalists also demanded independence in the name of self-determination.[7]

After World War II, European nations again relied on the principle of self-determination in resolving territorial disputes. Winston Churchill and Franklin D. Roosevelt committed themselves to the principle of self-determination--phrased as the right of people to choose the sovereignty under which they wished to live--in their first statement of allied principles in the Atlantic Charter in August 1941.[8] Again, the European powers did not intend to apply the principle to their colonies, and resisted efforts by the United States to incorporate the principle of self-determination into the UN Charter.

Eventually, the international community accepted the right of self-determination as a governing principle and included it in all major UN resolutions and conventions, including the UN Charter.[9] Article 1(2) of the charter states that one of its purposes is "to develop friendly relations among nations based on respect for the principle of equal rights and self-determination of peoples." The charter also requires members of the UN who have "assumed responsibilities for the administration of territories whose peoples have not yet attained a full measure of self-government" to recognize that "the interests of the inhabitants of these territories are paramount." The inclusion of the right of self-determination in the UN Charter was welcomed by Africans who were increasingly asserting a right of national self-determination and liberation from colonial rule in the late 1940s and the 1950s.[10]

The right of self-determination has remained an important principle in the decolonization of Africa. The Organization of African Unity (OAU) Charter stresses the "inalienable right of all people to control their own destiny." The charter adopted language much stronger than the UN Charter, stating that its purpose is to "eradicate all forms of colonialism from Africa" toward a goal of "total emancipation of the African territories which are still dependent."

While the principle of self-determination was initially vague, an accepted definition has evolved over time. In 1960, the UN General Assembly (UNGA) passed the "Declaration of the Granting of Independence to Colonial Countries and Peoples," which defines the right to self-determination provided for under the UN Charter. The declaration states that "the subjection of peoples to alien subjugation, domination, and exploitation constitutes a denial of fundamental human rights" and is "contrary to the Charter of the UN." The declaration further called for the cessation of "all armed action or repressive measures of all kinds directed against dependent people." The declaration also outlined three methods in which a nonself-governing territory can reach a full measure of self-government:

1. emergence as a sovereign independent state;
2. free association with an independent state; or
3. integration with an independent state.

While the provision allows a territory to freely associate or integrate with a second state, the choice must be the "result of a free and voluntary choice by the peoples of the territory concerned expressed through informed and democratic processes."[11]   Additionally, if the nonself-governing state chooses to integrate with a second state, the first state retains the freedom to modify the status of the territory.

In 1966, the UNGA passed two important human rights covenants that recognized self-determination as a right of "all peoples."   The "International Covenant on Economic, Social, and Cultural Rights" states that all people have a right to "freely determine their political status and freely pursue their economic, social, and cultural development" and parties to the covenant "shall promote the realization of the right of self-determination."[12]   This language is repeated in the "International Covenant on Civil and Political Rights."[13]

In 1971, Western powers recognized self-determination as a legal right and its denial as a violation of the UN Charter.   The UNGA unanimously adopted the "Declaration of Principles of International Law Concerning Friendly Relations and Cooperation Among States in Accordance with the Charter of the UN," which confirms that the principle of self-determination constitutes a "significant contribution to contemporary international law."[14]

There have been few instances since the passage of the "Declaration of the Granting of Independence to Colonial Countries and Peoples" where a colonial power has rejected a request by the UN to supervise a self-determination election or referendum.[15]   Additionally, states that have annexed bordering colonies have not rejected the principle of self-determination outright, but have attempted to argue that either self-determination has in fact occurred or that they are justified in denying the right based on other legal claims.   States' recognition of a legal obligation to grant a colony's right of self-determination, and their attempt to justify a denial of this right rather than reject the principle outright, is strong evidence that the principle has evolved into customary international law.

In the decolonization of East Timor, while Indonesia ignored a UN demand for Indonesia's withdrawal from the territory, it did not reject the principle of self-determination per se.   Instead, Indonesia argued that the integration of East Timor with Indonesia was the will of the East Timorese people, and that historical ties between Indonesia and the territory established East Timor as an integral part of Indonesia. Indonesia further argued that East Timor was not economically viable and required assistance from a more economically stable state. The United Nations rejected these arguments and both the UNGA and the Security Council affirmed East Timor's right to self-determination.[16]

King Hassan also had not rejected the principle of self-determination per se, but argued that Saharans' have already exercised their right of self-determination through a vote of sixty-five members of the *Djemma*, the old Sahrawi local governing body, in support of integration with Morocco. However, the United Nations did not recognize the vote as valid because sixty-seven members of the Djemma, an absolute majority of its 102 members, had previously signed the Proclamation of Guelta Zemmour formally dissolving the body and declaring their support for Polisario.[17]

The question of self-determination of Eritrea is distinct from East Timor and Western Sahara. Eritrea's struggle for self-determination arose ten years after the territory had been united with Ethiopia as an autonomous unit within an Ethiopian "federation." Eritrea's claim arises from Ethiopia's abolition of Eritra's autonomous status, and therefore, centers on the question of whether a territory that chooses to become integrated with a second territory retains a right of self-determination. The question of Eritrea's initial right of self-determination was settled peacefully without significant opposition.[18]

By the 1980s, most noted legal scholars had recognized self-determination as a legal right under customary international law with respect to colonized nations.[19] A minority of scholars have rejected self-determination as a legal right because they view it as a challenge to the established order that will provoke anarchy. However, this claim is invalid, because the recognition of self-determination as a legal right will, in fact, decrease violence. Rigo Sureda argues that the presupposition of strife between nations is not of itself a consequence of the principle of self-determination but the "reflection of a desire to resist it."[20] If the states involved were prepared to accept a result based on a legal determination of self-determination, then there is no reason to presuppose violence will ensure. For example, in the decolonization of Belize, the UN rejected Guatemala's claim to the territory and called for self-determination for the Belize people. Although Guatemala protested the eventual declaration of independence by Belize and its admission into the UN, it took no military action in opposition to Belize's independence.[21]

Others argue that self-determination is too vague and thus creates potential for misuse.[22] However, the difficulty in defining a principle does not preclude it from becoming a standard of international law. Judge Elihu Lauterpacht argues that "although it may be admitted that the effective implementation of a rule is somewhat reduced by the lack of precision, there is no logical reason to say that the rule, therefore, does not exist; for the existence of a rule of law, strictly speaking, is independent of the exactness of its definition."[23]

While most scholars accept self-determination as a legal principle, the definition of "peoples" who are entitled to a legal right has been heavily debated. However, a distinction has been drawn between states under colonial control and minorities calling for secession from an existing state. A resolution passed in conjunction with the "Declaration on the Granting of Independence to Colonial Countries and Peoples," titled "The Principles Which Should Guide Members in Determining Whether or Not an Obligation Exists," made such a distinction. It established detailed guidelines for determining whether a right of self-determination exists. The principles require two elements before one can presume an existing right of self-determination:

1. a geographical, and ethnic or cultural distinctness of a territory; and
2. elements of an administrative, political, juridical, economic, or historical nature that affect the territory concerned in a manner that arbitrarily places the latter in a position or status of subordination.

While legal scholars have differed on the extension of the definition of "peoples" entitled to self-determination to include secessionist movements, they have generally agreed that people under foreign domination fall within the category of those having a right of self-determination. Umozurike Oji Umozurike defines "self" as "a collection of individuals having a legitimate interest that is primarily political, but may also be economic, cultural, or any other kind."[24] W. Ofuatey-Kodjoe defines "self" as a self-conscious politically coherent community that is under the political subjugation of another community.[25] Benyamin Neuberger believes that the emergence of a national self occurs--at least in the formative stages--through a process of differentiation from the opposing group.[26] The common requirement in all these theories of "self" and "peoples" is that a community must exist that is geographically, culturally, and politically distinct from a second dominating entity.

THE RIGHTS OF SAHRAWIS TO
SELF-DETERMINATION

Under the definitions of "people" set forth above, the inhabitants of the Western Sahara would clearly qualify as a people entitled to self-determination under international law. Historically, Sahrawis have led a lifestyle very distinct from that of Moroccans and a number of common features characterize the territory. Tony Hodges, the leading expert on the Sahrawi culture, has concluded that despite the dispersal of Sahrawis across several countries, "a marked sense of kinship remained among the members of tribes and factions separated by political frontiers."[27] The camel-herding nomads' Sahrawi language-- the Hassaniya dialect of Arabic--distinguishes them from the sedentary, Tashelhit-speaking Berbers in Morocco. Unlike Morocco, the Western Sahara's economy is based on pastoral nomadism and commerce. Sahrawi religious customs dispense with the use of mosques and regard religion as an essentially personal issue. Some Sahrawis view the Alawite traditions of Morocco, where King Hassan is both temporal and spiritual leader, as somewhat shocking.[28] A host of other cultural features, ranging from poetry to diet to clothes, distinguish Sahrawis from Moroccans.[29]

The growth of a nationalist movement in the Western Sahara is also evidence of a distinct political self. After a first attempt to establish an urban-based Sahrawi political movement failed in 1970, Sahrawi students in Rabat began discussing the formation of a new liberation movement.[30] The Moroccan administration was not sympathetic to the new movement and Moroccan officials often harassed Sahrawi student leaders. In March and May 1972, anti-Spanish demonstrations by Sahrawi students and youth in Tan-Tan were broken up by the police and a number of the demonstrators were briefly detained. The group, wary of Morocco's response to the new movement, concluded that a "Sahrawi liberation movement on Moroccan territory would carry serious political risks."[31]

On May 10, 1973, Polisario was born.[32] Its first Congress issued a manifesto announcing that the front had been founded as the "unique expression of the masses, posing for revolutionary violence and the armed struggle as the means by which the Sahrawi Arab African people can recover its total liberty and foil the maneuvers of Spanish colonialism." During its founding year, both Morocco and Algeria rejected Polisario's request for assistance. This forced self-reliance was instrumental in the development of Polisario and Sahrawi identity. Thus, while the Polisario did not initially call for full independence of the Western Sahara, at their second Congress, held on August 25-31, 1974, the Front unambiguously came out in favor of full independence.[33] The 1975 UN Mission to the Western Sahara concluded that "the population, or at least almost all those persons encountered by the UN Mission, was categorically for independence."[34]

Sahrawi support for Polisario grew after Morocco's annexation of the Western Sahara and Polisario's declaration of the Sahrawi Arab Democratic Republic (SADR). Polisario has created a national, as opposed to a purely tribal, sense of political consciousness, and achieved an extraordinary degree of independent organizational competence.[35] Journalists and veteran observers of African liberation movements who have visited the Tindouf camps and traveled with Polisario units in the Western Sahara have concluded that the Polisario is overwhelmingly based on the indigenous Western Sahara population. George M. Houser of the American Committee on Africa, testifying before House Committee hearings, confirmed that Polisario was a "popularly supported, democratic movement."[36]

Realpolitik theorists argue that since great states will seek to engulf smaller neighbors, small states should not be granted independence, despite a right of self-determination.[37] This argument, however, has no legal basis; the right of self-determination has never been denied because a state is small. Alfred Cobban, a leading expert on self-determination, argues that the "solution [to the question of state viability] is not the abolition of small states. The forces which have enabled small states to survive . . . have not ceased to operate."[38] In their study on *Size and Democracy*, Robert Dahl and Edward Tufte came to the conclusion that there is no correlation between size, economic viability, and political survival.[39]

The Western Sahara is an example of a small state that would be economically viable and would not have great difficulty supporting its modest population. Exploitation of the territory's large phosphate resources alone would give the Western Sahara one of the highest levels of per capita income on the African continent. It is estimated that the Western Sahara has phosphate reserves of approximately 1.6 to 1.7 billion tons, with a 31 percent pure quality, one of the highest levels in the world.[40] The 1975 UN Mission to the territory concluded that if the phosphate mines were fully developed, they alone would "furnish a per capita revenue equal to that of some developed countries in

Europe."[41] Other mineral resources, that had only been partly explored in 1975, include possibilities of iron deposits, petroleum, and an extensive continental shelf reaching to the Canary Islands rich in fishing resources.

The success of Saharan refugee camps is also evidence that the Western Sahara would be a viable political entity. The Sahrawi refugee camps have been described as the "most democratic, unified and well-functioning political system that exists in Africa today."[42] The SADR, Polisario, and its relief organization, the Sahrawi Red Crescent,[43] operate within the Sahrawi camps without restriction, for the Algerian government has temporarily ceded jurisdiction of the camps to the SADR until a settlement of the conflict has been reached.[44]

The UN and the OAU have recognized the Sahrawis' right of self-determination under international law, and to date seventy-five nations have recognized SADR as a nation-state. The UN first acknowledged the Sahrawis' right of self-determination in 1965, when the UNGA adopted a resolution requesting Spain to take all necessary measures for the liberation of the Spanish Sahara from colonial domination.[45] After Morocco's annexation of the territory, the UN reaffirmed the "inalienable right of the people of the Spanish Sahara to self-determination" and called for a cease-fire and a referendum in the territory.[46]

Initially, the OAU was reluctant to address the Western Sahara question, due to conflicting considerations and Morocco's influence in Africa. While most African governments were opposed to Morocco's rejection of their most hallowed principles--the right of self-determination and the sanctity of the frontiers inherited from colonialism--many African governments were influenced by Moroccan threats to withdraw from the OAU if it adopted resolutions openly critical of its role in the Western Sahara.[47] After years of debate and numerous resolutions on the conflict, the OAU recognized SADR as a member-state in 1983.[48] The OAU also passed a resolution that year naming Morocco and Polisario as the parties to the conflict for the first time and urging the Moroccan government and Polisario to undertake direct negotiations toward a "cease-fire to create the necessary condition for a peaceful and fair referendum of self-determination of the people of the Western Sahara. . . under the auspices of the UN and the OAU."[49] SADR took its seat on the OAU without serious challenge in November 1984, causing Morocco to withdraw from the organization.[50]

Morocco claims to have established sovereignty over the Western Sahara before Spanish colonization, and as a result, claims a legal right to reintegration of the territory into Morocco based on the principle of territorial integrity. Morocco argues that Article 2(4) of the UN Charter, which states that all parties to the charter shall refrain from the threat or use of force against the "territorial integrity" of any state, supports their claim. The Declaration of the Granting of Independence to Colonial Countries also ensures that "any attempt aimed at the partial or total disruption of the national unity and the territorial integrity of a country is incompatible with the purposes and principles of the UN Charter." Morocco asserts that, based on the principle of national unity and territorial integrity, decolonization may come about only through the reintegration of a province with the mother country from which it was detached.[51]

The superiority of Morocco's historical claim over the Sahrawis' right of self-determination must be rejected under international law. First, the International Court of Justice (ICJ), responding to a UNGA request for an advisory opinion on the question of whether there were legal ties between the Western Sahara and Morocco, concluded that the "information before the Court does not establish any tie of territorial sovereignty between the territory of Western Sahara and the Kingdom of Morocco."[52] While there were some indications of a legal tie of allegiance between the sultan and some nomadic peoples of the territory, the ties were insufficient to find a tie of territorial sovereignty. The ICJ also reaffirmed the right of the population of the Western Sahara to self-determination, stating that this right was not prejudiced by the court's decision.[53]

While ICJ advisory opinions are not binding on any state, they are the most authoritative source of customary international law. If the ICJ concludes that a given position has become a rule of customary international law, that holding, while not binding precedent in theory, is the "law" for all practical purposes. Thus, the ICJ's rejection of Morocco's legal claims is strong, if not definitive, evidence that Morocco has no legal right to sovereignty over the Western Sahara.

Additionally, the UN has rejected a state's claims of territorial integrity when they conflict with a legal right of self-determination. In the decolonization of Belize, the UN gave Belize's right of self-determination priority over Guatemala's claim to territorial integrity.[54] The UNGA asserted the right of self-determination in East Timor, despite Indonesia's claim to the territory. Finally, the UNGA has rejected Morocco's claim of sovereignty in favor of the Sahrawis' right of self-determination.

The right of the peoples living under colonial domination to self-determination is clearly established as customary international law. In addition, colonized peoples' right of self-determination takes precedence over a second state's claim of historical territorial sovereignty and provides that such peoples must freely and voluntarily determine their governing status. The Sahrawis' right of self-determination is widely recognized by the international community, including seventy-five countries, the UNGA, and the OAU. Morocco's claim of historical sovereignty, therefore, must fail when juxtaposed with the Sahrawis' right of self-determination. Thus, Morocco's annexation and continued administration of the Western Sahara violates customary international law.

UNITED STATES ARMS SALES: DOMESTIC AND INTERNATIONAL LEGAL ISSUES

During the 1970s, the United States Congress, in an attempt to link human rights with foreign policy decisions, inserted provisions into various foreign assistance legislation denying assistance to gross violators of human rights. The Foreign Military Assistance Act, the primary bilateral foreign assistance legislation, contains several human rights provisions, its most notable being §502B. Provision §502B prohibits U.S. military assistance to governments that engage in a "consistent pattern of gross violations of internationally recognized human rights." Assistance can only be provided in such situations if "extraordinary circumstances exist warranting provision of such assistance." Initially, the provision only expressed the will of Congress. However, when the Nixon administration consistently failed to apply the provision, Congress amended §502B so as to make the provision mandatory.

The four key elements in determining whether §502B prohibits U.S. military assistance to Morocco are

1. whether Morocco is in violation of "internationally recognized rights";
2. whether there is a "consistent pattern" of such violations;
3. whether the violations are of a "gross" proportion; and

4. if the answers to 1-3 are in the affirmative, whether "extraordinary circumstances" exist warranting the provision of military assistance to Morocco.

The definition of internationally recognized human rights contained in §502B(d)(1) provides specific examples of gross violations; however, the use of the word "includes" suggests that the list was not intended to be all-encompassing and that other violations would also warrant the application of §502B.   Since self-determination is an internationally recognized human right, a violation of this right would be covered by the act.

Second, the act requires a consistent pattern of violations. Unlike many human rights violations that can be identified by specific actions, the denial of self-determination must be viewed as an ongoing violation until one's right of self-determination is freely exercised.

Morocco first violated the Sahrawis' right of self-determination by annexing the territory and seizing control of its main population centers. This initial violation is continuous and will end only when the Sahrawis freely and voluntarily determine the status of their territory. A violation of self-determination is not an isolated incident, but affects the entire citizenry of a state. Thus, Morocco's continued military presence in the territory, which prevents Sahrawis from exercising their right of self-determination, constitutes a "consistent pattern" under §502B.

Section 502B also requires that violations be of "gross" proportions. Both UNGA resolutions[55] and noted legal scholars have recognized the right of self-determination as a fundamental human right upon which the exercise of all other human rights depends. Therefore, its denial would constitute a gross violation of human rights. Furthermore, in addition to Morocco's violation of Sahrawis' right of self-determination, human rights groups and reporters have documented serious rights abuses committed by Moroccan officials and directed at Sahrawis and Polisario sympathizers in the Western Sahara.

Moroccan officials have been accused of committing torture, detaining Sahrawis for prolonged periods without charges and trial, and orchestrating the disappearances of Sahrawis and Polisario supporters.

These actions are clearly prohibited by Article 7 of the International Covenant on Civil and Political Rights, which states that "no one shall be subjected to torture or to cruel, inhuman or degrading treatment or punishment."   Article 7 is nonderogable under any circumstances, including armed conflicts (Art. 4(2)). These actions are also prohibited by Article 3 common to the four Geneva Conventions, which prohibits "violence to life and person, in particular murder of all kinds, mutilation, cruel treatment and torture." Common Article 3 is widely accepted as customary law and is, therefore, binding on Morocco.[56] These rights are also specifically included in §502B as examples of gross violations of human rights.

When Morocco annexed the Western Sahara in 1976, nearly half of the Sahrawi population fled into the desert. Even though the fleeing refugees were civilians, the Moroccan troops poisoned the wells and repeatedly bombed refugee encampments with napalm.[57] Western journalists testified to soldiers slitting the stomachs of pregnant women or the throats of babies while their parents watched and of the wholesale disappearance of young men.[58] A number of Sahrawi refugees testified to having witnessed torture, the killing of relatives, or rape of their mothers.[59]

Independent legal organizations have confirmed journalists' accounts of human rights violations by Moroccan officials in the Western Sahara. In February 1976, the International Federation of Human Rights reported that "soldiers of the two occupying countries have butchered (*égorgé*) hundreds and perhaps thousands of Sahrawis, including children and old people who refused to publicly acknowledge the King of Morocco. . . some have seen their children killed in front of them by way of intimidation. . . women described to us how they have been tortured. . . and how soldiers had cut off young men's fingers to make them unable to fight." The report concluded that "to look, speak or dress like a Sahrawi is to be open to arrest; meetings, even festivities such as weddings risk police intervention."[60]

The Minority Rights Groups reported that "Sahrawis were made to live in camps around the military posts, to act as human shields against Polisario raids. A curfew was declared and movement was restricted. Sahrawi-owned vehicles had to be painted red and white so that if their owners fled, they would be easily recognized in the open desert."[61] This use of civilians to shield military targets violates customary principles of distinction and civilian immunity enshrined in UNGA Resolution 2444 (13), January 12, 1969, adopted by unanimous vote. The United States has expressly recognized these general principles "as declaratory of existing customary international law."[62]

In 1977, Amnesty International reported that the Moroccan army made arbitrary arrests on a massive scale within the Western Sahara. Detention camps were established in the territory, not only for prisoners of war, but also for members of the civilian population suspected of sympathizing with Polisario. Amnesty International estimated the number held as between 100 and 150; however, because Moroccan authorities maintain great secrecy about the names and number of those detained, there may have been several hundred members of the local population held in army camps.[63]

Human rights violations in the Western Sahara have continued since Morocco's initial annexation of the territory. Sahrawis who have remained in the occupied territories, where Moroccan military personnel outnumber the Sahrawi civilians, live under a state of siege. Those known or suspected to be supporters of Polisario, or even sympathetic to Polisario, have been kept under strict surveillance. In many cases they are subject to arrest, interrogation, imprisonment, and torture.[64]

In addition to repressive military measures, King Hassan has initiated a program of "Moroccanization" of the population of the Western Sahara. Spanish may not be taught in the occupied territory. Hassaniya, the Sahrawi dialect, is forbidden, and Sahrawi pupils in school must wear Moroccan-style clothing.[65] Hassan has also encouraged the settlement by Moroccan citizens in the Western Sahara, resulting in the immigration of tens of thousands of Moroccans into the main urban centers.[66]

Morocco has continuously denied Sahrawis their right of self-determination, and has violated numerous articles of the Universal Declaration of Human Rights, the International Covenant on Civil and Political Rights, and rules of customary international law. Such violations, in addition to Morocco's denial of the Sahrawis' right of self-determination, constitute consistent and gross violations of internationally recognized human rights.

Therefore, under §502B, the United States can provide military assistance to Morocco for use in the Western Sahara only if "extraordinary circumstances" exist warranting the provision of such assistance. The Reagan administration provided various arguments to justify continued military assistance to Morocco for use in the Western Sahara. First, Morocco and the United States have common foreign policy objectives. Morocco is said to have played an active and constructive role in the Middle East peace process, facilitating better communication between Arabs and the United States.[67] Second, in May 1982, the United States and Morocco signed an access and transit agreement,[68] which would help the United States defend the Persian Gulf in certain contingencies.[69] Third, the United States and Morocco have developed joint economic and military commissions.[70] While the United States' interests are legitimate, they do not constitute "extraordinary circumstances" justifying military assistance under §502B.

First, the administration has not shown how the denial of military assistance only for use in the Western Sahara, as opposed to defensive weaponry, would jeopardize their stated interests. Morocco would still have access to defensive weaponry, as well as economic assistance. The United States would only limit Morocco's use of weaponry in a manner more consistent with its obligations under international and domestic law. Second, the access and transit agreement is not critical to United States strategic interests. The Congressional Budget Office analyzed the strategic value of the access agreement and concluded that the facilities were important merely as a backup to other bases. The other bases could meet all of the airlift requirement for rapid deployment forces going into the Persian Gulf. Additionally, the Moroccan air bases are subject to limitations, in that they could not be used against friendly Arab countries.[71] The administration has concluded that unconditional military assistance would maintain "a close relationship with a friendly Morocco" that "is important to [United States] security".[72]

The Reagan administration argued that the United States was faced with a clear and present danger from the Soviet Union and its allies and proxies; thus, the United States should respond with more, not less, security assistance to its friends. Additionally, repressive allies of the United States, by definition, are thought to be better than communists because they would eventually move toward democracy; therefore, they are not engaging in a consistent pattern of gross violations of human rights.[73] However, this analysis is flawed in that it ignores §502B entirely, which specifically requires that extraordinary circumstances actually exist that justify continued military assistance. The Reagan administration's reasoning would, in fact, justify military aid to any ally, regardless of their human rights record; thus, it is clearly inconsistent with §502B. Since "extraordinary circumstances" that would justify military assistance to Morocco for use in the Western Sahara do not exist, the provision of military assistance to Morocco for use in the Western Sahara is prohibited under §502B.

An argument can also be made that the United States, by aiding Morocco in its annexation and occupation of the Western Sahara, has breached its obligations under the UN Charter. Article 55 of the charter states that member-states of the UN "shall promote universal respect for, and observance of, human rights and fundamental freedoms. . . based on respect for the principle of equal rights and self-determination of peoples." Members pledged to take joint and separate action in cooperation with the UN for the achievement of these purposes. While states are obligated to do no more than "promote" self-determination, the charter would prohibit states from taking any action in direct conflict with the promotion of self-determination.

The UNGA, recognizing states' obligation to promote self-determination under the UN Charter, unanimously passed the "Declaration on Friendly Relations and Cooperation Among States." The declaration emphasizes the duty of all states to "promote, through joint and separate action, the realization of the principle of equal rights and self-determination of peoples." The declaration determined that "subjection of people to alien subjugation, domination and exploitation constitutes a violation of the principle, as well as a denial of fundamental human rights, and is contrary to the Charter of the UN." It further states that "every state has the duty to refrain from any forcible action which deprives peoples. . . of their right to self-determination."[74]

States' obligations under the UN Charter and the declaration suggest a corresponding duty of one state not to support another state that is engaged in gross violations of people's internationally recognized right of self-determination.[75] Thus, there is a strong argument that the United States has violated the UN Charter by providing military assistance to Morocco, with the knowledge that such assistance will be used to deny Sahrawis their right of self-determination.

In enacting §502B of the Foreign Military Assistance Act, the United States recognized its obligations under the UN Charter to restrict military assistance to those countries that commit gross violations of human rights. The act itself includes language acknowledging the United States' international obligations, with §502B(a)(1) providing that

> the United States shall, in accordance with its international obligations as set forth in the Charter of the UN. . . promote and encourage increased respect for human rights and fundamental freedoms. . . . Accordingly, a principal goal of the foreign policy of the United States shall be to promote the increased observance of internationally recognized rights by all countries.[76]

U.S. military assistance to Morocco for use in the Western Sahara is a violation of United States domestic law, and arguably international law. The inhabitants of the Western Sahara have an internationally recognized right of self-determination, which Morocco has violated by annexing and occupying the territory. U.S. military assistance has been used by Morocco to successfully maintain control over the major portions of the Western Sahara, in defiance of calls by the UN and OAU for Morocco to comply with principles of international law. The United States, by knowingly assisting Morocco, has become an aider and abetter to Morocco's violations and has breached the UN Charter.

CONCLUSION

The United States' failure to uphold domestic and international law has had a devastating long-term impact on international affairs. In the words of international lawyer Thomas Franck, "Unhindered, successful violation of law undermines the law itself, and in consequence, the regime of good order which it was intended to uphold.[77] The United States' support for Morocco's annexation of Western Sahara and willingness to ignore United Nation resolutions sent a signal to military powers that serious violations of international law and even invasions of smaller neighboring countries would be ignored if politically advantageous.

In 1990, Iraq tested the waters by stating its intention to invade Kuwait and assumed from the United States ambassador's indifference that an invasion of Kuwait was unlikely to provoke a negative American response.   However, Iraq misjudged the importance to the Bush administration of economic and other interests in Kuwait, which generated a very different response than Morocco's annexation of Western Sahara. The United States justified its military action to expel Iraq from Kuwait, costing billions of dollars and thousands of lives, by citing the importance of enforcing international legal principles and maintaining "world order." This "world order," however, will never be stable unless the United States is consistent in enforcing international law throughout the world. The United States has a duty to abide by the same international principles it so strongly supported in expelling Iraq from Kuwait and withdrawing its military support from Morocco.

Morocco's annexation of the Western Sahara is a clear violation of international law.   Morocco's successful violation of accepted international norms undermines the international legal system and encourages other countries to disregard legal norms that are against their self-interest.   The United States' active participation in Morocco's actions is not only a violation of its domestic laws, but may also be a violation of international law.   Thus, the United States has weakened the impact of its own law, and has jeopardized the role of international customary law.   While the United States government has legitimate interests in maintaining friendly relations with Morocco, these interests are outweighed by the importance of maintaining international and domestic order.

NOTES

A special thanks to Robert Rhoda and Susan Gorman-Shaw for their invaluable assistance.

1. Tony Hodges, "Introduction," in Richard Lawless and Laila Monahan, eds., *War and Refugees: The Western Sahara Conflict* (London and New York: Pinter Publishers, 1987), 3.
2. James Joyce, *The New Politics of Human Rights* (London: Macmillan, 1978), 165.
3. UN General Assembly, 20th sess., Official Records, supplement 14, resolution 2071 (20), A/6014, 1965.
4. In order to pay the estimated $2 million per day it costs Morocco to maintain the war in Western Sahara, Morocco has relied on military assistance from France, Egypt, Saudi Arabia, Spain, Israel, South Africa, and the United States.   Werner Ruf, "The Role of World Powers," in Lawless and Monahan, eds., *War and Refugees*, 81. See also David Seddon, "Morocco at War," in Lawless and Monahan, eds., *War and Refugees*; "Morocco: Military Pact With Spain," *Africa Report*, January-February 1985, 44.
5. Benyamin Neuberger, *National Self-Determination in Postcolonial Africa*, (Boulder, Colo.: Lynne Rienner Publishers, 1986), 5.
6. Osita Eze, *Human Rights in Africa: Some Selected Problems* (Lagos: Macmillan, 1984), 71.
7. Neuberger, *National Self-Determination*, 5.
8. Eze, *Human Rights*, 74.
9. Neuberger, *National Self-Determination*, 5.
10. Ibid., 5.

11. UN General Assembly, 15th sess., Official Records, supplement 16, resolution 1514 (15), A/4684, 1960, 66.

12. UN General Assembly, 21st sess., Official Records, supplement 16, resolution 2200A (21), A/6316, 1966, 49.

13. Ibid.

14. UN General Assembly, 25th sess., Official Records, supplement 28, resolution 2625 (25), A/8028, 1971, 121.

15. Thomas Franck, "The Stealing of the Sahara," *American Journal of International Law* 70, no. 4, (1976): 701; Eze, *Human Rights*, 70.

16. UN General Assembly, 30th sess., Official Records, 4th committee (2188th meeting) (30), A/C.4/S.R.2188, 1975, 407, 412; UN Security Council, 30th sess., Official Records, resolution 384 (30), S/Res/384, 1975, 10.

17. Tony Hodges, *Historical Dictionary of Western Sahara*, (Metuchen, New Jersey: Scarecrow Press, 1982), 101-4.

18. "Eritrea's Claim to Self-determination," *The Review*, June 1981, 8.

19. Umozurike Oji Umozurike, *Self-Determination in International Law* (Hamden, Conn.: Shoestring Press, 1972); Robert Vance, "Recognition as an Affirmative Step in the Decolonization Process: The Case of Western Sahara," *Yale Journal of World Public Order* 7 (1980): 45; Malcolm Shaw, *International Law* (Cambridge, Mass.: Grotius, 1986), 158; Malcolm Shaw, *Title to Territory in Africa: International Legal Issues* (New York: Oxford University Press, 1986), 91.

20. Rigo Sureda, *The Evolution of the Right of Self-Determination: A Study of United Nations Practice* (Geneva: Sijthoff-Leiden, 1973), 26.

21. "The Decolonization of Belize: Self-Determination v. Territorial Integrity," *Virginia Journal of International Law* 22 (1982), 849.

22. Alfred Cobban, *The Nation State and National Self-Determination* (London: Collins, 1969), 103.

23. Ibid.

24. Umozurike, *Self-Determination*, 195.

25. Ibid., 156.

26. Neuberger, *National Self-Determination*, 20.

27. Tony Hodges, "The Origins of Sahrawi Nationalism," in Lawless and Monahan, eds., *War and Refugees*, 51.

28. *West Africa*, June 13, 1988, 1060.

29. Ibid.

30. Hodges, "The Origins of Sahrawi Nationalism," in Lawless and Monahan, eds., *War and Refugees*, 51.

31. Ibid., 53.

32. Ibid.

33. Ibid., 54.

34. UN General Assembly, 30th sess., Official Records, supplement 23, *Report to the Special Committee on the Situation With Regard to the Implementation of the Declaration on the Granting of Independence to Colonial Countries and People*, A/10023/Rev. 1, 1975, 7.

35. Stephen Solarz, "Arms for Morocco?" *Foreign Affairs* 58, no. 2 (Winter 1979-80): 278.

36. U.S. Congress, House Committee on International Relations, Subcommittees on Africa and on International Organizations, *Hearings on U.S. Policy and the Conflict in the Western Sahara*, 96th Cong., 1st sess., June 23-24, 1979, 47.

37. Ibid., 103.

38. Ibid., 18; Rupert Emerson, "Self-determination," *American Journal of International Law* 65, (1971), 459-69.

39. Robert Dahl and Edward Tufte, *Size and Democracy* (Stanford, Calif.: Stanford University Press, 1973), 132.

40. Kwasi Sarfo, *United States Policy Towards Local and Regional Conflicts in Africa: Anatomy of Globalist and Regionalist Perspectives* (New York: Rockefeller College of Public Affairs, 1985), 133.

41. UN General Assembly, 30th sess., Official Records, supplement 23, *Report of the United Nations Visiting Mission to Spanish Sahara*, A/10023/Add.5, 1975, 52.

42. Stephen Zunes, "Nationalism and Non-Alignment: The Non-Ideology of the Polisario," *Africa Today* 34, no. 3 (Fall 1987): 33.

43. Hodges, *Historical Dictionary*, 495.

44. James Firebrace, "The Sahrawi Refugees: Lesson and Prospects," in Lawless and Monahan, eds., *War and Refugees*, 168; Calude Bontems, "The Government of the Sahrawi Arab Democratic Republic," *Third World Quarterly* 9, no. 1 (1987), 168.

45. UN General Assembly, 30th sess., Official Records, supplement 14, resolution 2072 (30), A/6014, 1965.

46. UN General Assembly, 30th sess., Official Records, supplement 34, resolution 3458 (30), A/10034, 1975, 116-17.

47. Hodges, *Historical Dictionary*, 261.

48. John Damis, "The O.A.U. and Western Sahara," in Yassin El-Ayouty and I. William Zartman, eds., *The O.A.U. After Twenty Years* (New York: Praeger, 1984), 276.

49. Organization of African Unity Assembly, 19th sess., resolution 104 (19), AHG/Res.104, 1983, cited in Damis, "The O.A.U. and Western

Sahara," in El-Ayouty and Zartman, eds., *The O.A.U. After Twenty Years*, 294.

50. David Seddon, "Morocco at War," in Lawless and Monahan, eds., *War and Refugees*, 111. For a summary of the struggle by SADR for its seat on the OAU, see Jeffrey M. Schulman, "Wars of Liberation and the International System: Western Sahara--A Case in Point," in Irving L. Markovitz, ed., *Studies in Power and Class in Africa* (New York: Oxford University Press, 1987), 67-87. For a more thorough discussion of the series of OAU resolutions, see Tony Hodges, "The Western Sahara File," *Third World Quarterly* 6 (1984): 107.

51. International Court of Justice, *Advisory Opinion on Western Sahara* (The Hague: International Court of Justice, 1975), 46.

52. Ibid., 85.

53. Ibid., 85. For an in-depth analysis of the ICJ decision see Franck, "The Stealing of the Sahara"; Vance, "Recognition"; "International Court of Justice Does Not Find 'Legal Ties' of Such a Nature to Affect Self-Determination in the Decolonization Process of Western Sahara," *Texas International Law Journal* 11 (1976): 354; "Sovereignty Over Unoccupied Territories--the Western Sahara Decision," *Case Western Reserve Journal of International Law* 9 (1977): 135; "Questions Concerning Western Sahara: Advisory Opinion of the International Court of Justice, October 16, 1975," *International Lawyer* 10 (1976): 199.

54. UN General Assembly, 35th sess., Official Records, supplement 48, resolution 3520 (35), A/35/48, 1981, 214.

55. UN General Assembly, 15th sess., Official Records, supplement 16, resolution 1514 (15), A/4684, 1960, 66: UN General Assembly, 21st sess., Official Records, supplement 16, resolution 2200A (21), A/6316, 1966; UN General Assembly, 25th sess., Official Records, supplement 28, resolution 2625 (25), A/8028, 1970, 121; UN General Assembly, 30th sess., Official Records, 4th committee (2188th meeting) (30), A/C.4/S.R 2188, 1975, 407, 412; UN Security Council, 30th sess., Official Records, resolution 384 (30), S/Res/384, 1975, 10.

56. "Humanitarian Law Conference," *American University Journal of International Law and Policy* 2 (1987); see pages 471-97 for the remarks of James E. Bond, W. Fenrick, Hans-Peter Gasser, Waldemar Solf, and Burrus Carnahan.

57. See Anne Lippert, "The Sahara Refugees: Origins and Organization," in Lawless and Monahan, eds., *War and Refugees*, 151; John Mercer, *The Sahrawis of Western Sahara*, (London: Minority

Rights Groups, 1979), 27.

58. U.S. Congress, House Committee on International Relations, Subcommittees on Africa and on International Organizations, *Hearings on the Question of Self-Determination in Western Sahara*, 95th Cong., 1st sess., October 5, 1977, 5, 22.

59. Lippert, "Saharan Refugees," in Lawless and Monahan, eds., *War and Refugees*, 51.

60. Mercer, *The Sahrawis*, 9-10.

61. Ibid., 18.

62. Letter of September 22, 1968, from the General Counsel, U.S. Department of Defense, to Senator Edward Kennedy regarding war-related problems in Indo-China, in Arthur Rovine, "Contemporary Practice of the United States Relating to International Law," *American Journal of International Law* 67 (1973): 122-25. See also the commentary on Protocol II, commenting that the diplomatic conference did not share others' view that there is any effective body of customary international law applicable to noninternational armed conflict. Michael Both, Karl Joseph Partsch, and Waldemar A. Solf, *New Rules for Victims of Armed Conflict--Commentary on the Two 1977 Protocols Additional to the Geneva Conventions of 1949* (Dordrecht, Netherlands: Martinus Nijhoff, 1982), 671.

63. Amnesty International, *Morocco: Amnesty International Briefing, October 1977* (New York: Amnesty International, 1977), 10. See also Amnesty International, *Amnesty International Report, 1989*, 271-72, and Amnesty International, *Morocco: Human Rights Violations in Garde á Vue Detention* (New York: Amnesty International, 1990).

64. Seddon, "Morocco at War," in Lawless and Monahan, eds., *War and Refugees*, 16.

65. Lippert, "Saharan Refugees," in Lawless and Monahan, eds., *War and Refugees*, 53.

66. Mark Tessler, *Continuity and Change in Moroccan Politics Part II: New Troubles and Deepening Doubts*, Universities Field Staff International Report, no. 2 (1984), 5. See also, *Department of State Country Reports*, (Washington, D.C.: Department of State, 1986), 1248.

67. U.S. Congress, House Committee on Foreign Affairs, Subcommittees on Africa and on International Security and Scientific Affairs, *Hearings on U.S. Policy Toward the Conflict in the Western Sahara*, 98th Cong., 1st sess., March 15, 1983, 12.

68. Ibid., 11.

69. Ibid., 12.

70. Ibid., 10.

71. Ibid., 23.

72. Ibid., 12.

73. See David P. Forsythe, "Congress and Human Rights in U.S. Foreign Policy: The Fate of General Legislation," *Human Rights Quarterly* 9 (1987): 382.

74. UN General Assembly, 25th sess., Official Records, supplement 28, resolution 2625 (25), A/8028, 1970.

75. See Stephen B. Cohen, "Conditioning Security Assistance on Human Rights Practices," *American Journal of International Law* 76 (1982): 76.

76. United States Code, Title 22 §2304(1), 1988 ed., 496.

77. Thomas Franck, "Theory and Practice of Decolonization," in Lawless and Monahan, eds., *War and Refugees*, 3.

7

The Role of Foreign Military Assistance in the Western Saharan War

Daniel Volman

The conflict in the Western Sahara was the product of local and regional forces, particularly the irredentist policies of the government of King Hassan of Morocco and the emergence of the Sahrawi nationalist movement, the Polisario Front, in the former Spanish Sahara. But since the outbreak of the war in 1975, both sides have received substantial military assistance from foreign powers, including the Soviet Union, Algeria, Libya, Saudi Arabia, France, and the United States. The aim of this chapter is to evaluate the impact of arms sales and other forms of foreign military assistance on the conduct of the war and on the behavior of the two combatant forces.

In military terms, the war in the Western Sahara has proceeded through four distinct phases.[1] The first phase began with the Moroccan invasion of the territory in November 1975 and lasted until July 1979. This initial phase of the war was characterized by attacks by mobile Polisario Front guerrillas against the fixed positions of Moroccan troops stationed in the major urban centers. The second phase began in August 1979 when Morocco began using large mechanized army units and its growing air power to take the offensive against Polisario Front forces throughout the territory. This phase lasted until October 1981, when the Polisario Front initiated the third phase of the war by introducing sophisticated antiaircraft missiles to neutralize Moroccan superiority in the air during the second battle of Guelta Zemmour. This resulted in a decisive Polisario Front victory at Guelta Zemmour and led to a period of Moroccan military paralysis that lasted from October to December 1981. During this third phase of the war, Moroccan forces were virtually inactive and Polisario Front troops enjoyed free movement throughout the Western Sahara. By January 1982, the Moroccan armed forces had recovered from their paralysis, resumed offensive military operations, and began constructing a system of earthen walls to protect their positions. The fourth phase of the war, from January 1982 to the present day, has been characterized by a military stalemate in which neither combatant has been able to gain a significant military advantage.

As this brief outline suggests, weapons systems and other kinds of military hardware have had a significant effect on the course of the war. But arms were not the only significant military assistance sold by foreign powers to Morocco and the Polisario Front over the past fifteen years. Foreign powers also provided military training outside the region and sent military personnel into the region to train and assist local forces in the use of sophisticated foreign-supplied weapons systems. In addition, foreign powers played an important financial role in the war by providing a large proportion of the funds required to pay for the arms and other forms of military assistance that Morocco and the Polisario Front have received. The following section examines the impact of the military assistance sold by the United States, France, and the Soviet Union on the two combatants and also on Algeria, which provided substantial support to the Polisario Front.

AMERICAN MILITARY ASSISTANCE

Since the war began in 1975, the United States has sold more than $750 million worth of military assistance to Morocco through the Foreign Military Sales (FMS) program and an additional $150 million worth through the Commercial Sales program.[2] This represents about one-fourth of the total foreign military assistance that Morocco has purchased over the past fifteen years. The most visible types of U.S. weaponry sold to Morocco for use in the Saharan conflict were six F-5A and fourteen F-5E jet fighter aircraft. These aircraft were designed primarily to intercept enemy aircraft, not to attack troops on the ground, and were intended for export to Third World countries to defend them against the air forces of aggressive neighbors. Furthermore, they were designed for use against forces that did not possess air defense systems such as the SA-6 surface-to-air missile launcher, which is produced by the Soviet Union and which first appeared in the Polisario Front inventory in 1981.

Thus, the F-5 is not equipped with radar warning receivers that would signal an impending missile threat from Polisario Front forces on the ground. The F-5s, therefore, have generally been ineffective for assaulting Polisario ground forces and have proven highly vulnerable to Polisario missile attacks, which have brought down about a dozen of these aircraft. As a result, according to Lieutenant Colonel David Dean of the U.S. Air Force, the author of a unique study of the military aspects of the Saharan conflict, Moroccan F-5s "are used only minimally in the war zone."[3]

The United States has also sold Morocco six OV-10 propeller-driven counterinsurgency aircraft. Although these planes were designed for ground attack, unlike the F-5, they were intended for use against lightly armed guerrilla forces and were used extensively in South Vietnam. However, the OV-10 is "too slow and too vulnerable to SA-7 attacks to use in the war zone" and "have never been used for combat missions."[4]

The U.S.-supplied aircraft that have played the most significant role in the Saharan conflict have actually been the C-130 transport plane and the KC-130 aerial tanker plane. During the early years of the war, before the construction of the Moroccan defensive walls in the Western Sahara, Polisario Front attacks made it nearly impossible for Morocco to move troops and military equipment on the ground. But the "Royal Moroccan Air Force accomplished this important, and often overlooked, mission of supplying Moroccan ground forces in the cities and remote garrisons with its fleet of C-130 cargo planes."[5] As a result, Morocco was able to maintain its forces in the Western Sahara during the early years of the war and to build the defensive walls that made it possible for Morocco to gain control over approximately two-thirds of the territory by 1982.

In 1980, the Royal Moroccan Air Force also began using one of its squadron of fifteen C-130 cargo planes as an airborne reconnaissance and command center. This plane is equipped with side-looking airborne radar for surveillance and defense against missile attacks and, when refueled in the air by the two KC-130 tanker planes that Morocco has purchased, can remain airborne for long periods of time, detecting Polisario Front forces on the ground and directing ground attacks by Moroccan combat aircraft.[6]

Early in 1982, the United States also began selling the Royal Moroccan Air Force cluster bomb units, an extremely powerful and lethal antipersonnel weapon, for use against the lightly armored forces of the Polisario Front.[7]   At the same time, the U.S. Air Force dispatched a three-man U.S. training team to the Moroccan F-5 base at Meknes for two months to provide training and to evaluate the performance of the Moroccan F-5s in the war.[8] The United States also made what Dean describes as "a concerted effort to locate the position of SA-6s operated by the Polisario." At "considerable expense, US forces obtained specific intelligence data" on the location of Polisario missiles and provided it to the Moroccan government. But, "Morocco did not use efficient procedures to disseminate the information properly" and "frequently the timely intelligence obtained by the United States did not reach the south in time to do any good."[9]

In addition, the United States has sold Morocco a sophisticated ground-surveillance and air-defense radar systems manufactured by the Westinghouse Corporation. This included the construction of the Royal Moroccan Air Force's command center at Salé, which is connected to radar stations throughout the country, and the installation of a network of radar and ground sensors along the Moroccan earthen walls in the Western Sahara to detect Polisario forces and to direct artillery fire against Polisario positions.[10]

The Royal Moroccan Army has also purchased substantial quantities of U.S. military assistance. These have included 420 M-113 armored personnel carriers, 60 Vulcan 20mm self-propelled air-defense guns, 37 Chaparral surface-to-air missile batteries, and 55 towed and self-propelled 155mm howitzers.[11]   And in 1982, at the time that Secretary of State Alexander Haig was engaged in creating a "strategic consensus" that would bring Israel and friendly Arab states together in an effort to reduce Soviet influence in the Middle East and North Africa, the United States also sent a team of 20 U.S. Army counterinsurgency experts to Morocco to train a special battalion-sized unit which could be employed in commando-style attacks on Polisario Front SA-6 units.[12]

In addition to military equipment and in-country military training, the United States has provided training at military installations in the United States for more than 1,500 Moroccan troops through the International Military Education and Training Program at a cost to the Moroccans of more than $17 million.[13] This program provided training in combat flying and the use of other advanced U.S.-supplied military hardware, counterinsurgency tactics, and military command and control.

The impact of this U.S. weaponry and other kinds of military assistance on the military capabilities of the Royal Moroccan Armed Forces and on the conduct of the war has been mixed. As noted above,

U.S.-produced combat aircraft have proven to be of limited effectiveness in the Saharan conflict because of the way they are designed and equipped and because of their vulnerability to Polisario Front SA-6 missiles. Other assistance, such as the Royal Moroccan Air Force command center, the cluster bomb units, and intelligence information on the location of Polisario Front SA-6 units, has had a limited impact because of the inability of the Royal Moroccan Armed Forces to use this assistance in a timely or efficient manner. For example, the tightly controlled and highly centralized nature of the Moroccan military establishment has prevented the quick dissemination of the U.S. intelligence reports to combat units that could use them. And the cluster bombs have been wasted in poorly-coordinated operations that have had negligible military value.[14]

On the other hand, other kinds of U.S. military assistance have significantly increased the capabilities of the Moroccan armed forces. The C-130s provided Morocco with an essential capability to transport men and equipment during the early years of the war and, when equipped with electronic surveillance and control systems, improved the ability of the Royal Moroccan Air Force to coordinate air strikes against Polisario Front forces, particularly using French-produced Mirage jet fighters designed for ground attack operations and equipped with radar warning receivers and electronic countermeasures to defend against SA-6 missiles. On the ground, U.S.-produced radar surveillance and fire-control systems have been used effectively in combination with tanks, armored vehicles, heavy artillery, and other ground weaponry to detect and assault Polisario Front forces involved in attacks on the Moroccan positions along the earthen walls.

The economic impact of U.S. military assistance to Morocco was also mixed. The United States did provide more than $475 million in Foreign Military Financing credits and more than $200 million in nonrepayable Military Assistance Program Merger Fund grants to Morocco between 1975 and 1990 for the purchase of U.S. military equipment.[15]   But these credits and grants covered only about nine-tenths of the total cost to Morocco of U.S.-supplied military assistance and, of course, the Foreign Military Sales credits have to be repaid with interest, thus reducing spending on economic development and social services and adding to Morocco's debt burden. Repayments, interest, and the costs of sales that were not financed through the credit program were funded either by Morocco itself, adding further to the country's economic problems, or by the government of Saudi Arabia, which has given up to $1 billion to the Moroccan government annually in nonrepayable financial aid.[16] Although U.S. and Saudi grants have softened some of the financial impact of the war on Morocco, the costs of obtaining military assistance from the United States and also from France have still had a substantial economic impact on Morocco. And in 1988, frustrated by Morocco's failure to achieve any significant military or diplomatic successes, the Saudis cut off their subsidy for Moroccan military spending.[17]

FRENCH MILITARY ASSISTANCE

France has been the other main source of military assistance to Morocco. Since the war began, France has sold more than $2 billion worth of weaponry and other kinds of military equipment to the Royal Moroccan Armed Forces, roughly half of the total foreign military assistance that Morocco has received over the past fifteen years.[18] As in the case of U.S. assistance, the most visible types of military equipment that Morocco bought from France consisted of sophisticated jet aircraft, specifically twenty-four F-1CH and fifteen of the more advanced F-1EH Mirage fighters. Designed for ground attack operations and equipped with radar warning receivers and electronic countermeasures to defend against SA-6 missiles, these aircraft have proven relatively effective in attacks against Polisario Front forces operating in the Western Sahara.[19] France has also sold the Royal Moroccan Air Force 24 Gazelle helicopter gunships, equipped with antitank missiles and other ground attack weaponry. According to Lt. Colonel Dean, these attack helicopters have "done some credible work in the war zone flying flank reconnaissance for moving ground forces."[20]

The Royal Moroccan Army has also purchased substantial quantities of military hardware from France. This includes 30 AMX-13 light tanks, 360 VAB armored personnel carriers, more than 250 AMX-10RC, AML-90, and AML-60 armored cars, and 100 AMX-F-3 self-propelled 155mm howitzers.[21] Along with an undisclosed amount of military training provided by French military instructors in Morocco and in France, these sales of French military equipment have had an important impact on the Saharan war. In particular, the French-produced Mirage aircraft have given Morocco an essential ability to launch aerial operations against Polisario ground forces, while French-produced ground equipment have provided the Royal Moroccan Army with some of the vital mobility and firepower it needed to attack Polisario forces outside of the earthen walls in the Western Sahara.

SOVIET MILITARY ASSISTANCE

The Polisario Front, on the other hand, has received most of its military equipment from Algeria and--until it was cut off in 1983--from Libya, and these countries obtained it, in turn, from the Soviet Union.[22] The quantities and costs of the military assistance that Algeria and Libya provided to the Polisario Front were relatively small, but included such powerful weapons as SA-6 and SA-7 surface-to-air missiles, ZSU-23 self-propelled 23mm antiaircraft guns, antitank weapons, artillery, BMP-1 armored cars, and a small number of T-54 and T-55 tanks.[23] Although it is impossible to quantify the level of military assistance provided to the Polisario Front by Algeria and Libya, the delivery of these weapons beginning in 1981 made it possible for Polisario forces to defend themselves to a certain extent against Moroccan aerial attacks and to counter the firepower of Moroccan strong points along the earthen walls. Without this weaponry, it would have been much more difficult for Polisario forces to move about in the Western Sahara or to launch effective attacks on Moroccan positions along the earthen walls.

It is also necessary to consider the sale of Soviet military assistance to the government of Algeria. Since 1975, Algeria has bought nearly $8 billion worth of military assistance from the Soviet Union, along with smaller amounts of equipment from the United States and France.[24] This equipment has included 400 T-62 and T-72 tanks, 320 BTR-50, BTR-60, and BTR-152 armored personnel carriers, 920 BRDM-2, BMP-1, and BMP-2 armored cars, 65 SA-6 surface-to-air missiles, 18 SU-7 and 20 MiG-23 ground attack aircraft, 35 MiG-21 fighters, 15 MiG-23 fighters, and 18 MiG-25 fighters, 48 MiG-24 helicopter gunships, and 17 U.S.-supplied C-130 transport planes.[25] In addition, the Soviet Union has sent one thousand military personnel to Algeria to train Algerian troops and maintain Soviet-produced military equipment.[26]

Although only a minuscule proportion of this weaponry was *independently* transferred by Algeria to the Polisario Front for use in the Saharan conflict, it played a major role in the conduct of the war by ensuring that Algeria would continue to enjoy military superiority in any direct confrontation with Morocco. This made it impossible for the

Moroccan government to seriously consider assaults on Polisario Front bases located near Tindouf in southwestern Algeria, despite King Hassan's repeated threats to launch such cross-border operations. Consequently, the Algerian government was able to continue to provide military assistance and other support to the Polisario Front with little risk that this would result in a broader regional war. It is important to note, however, that Algeria had to use considerable quantities of its oil and gas revenues to finance the purchase of Soviet military assistance, which reduced its ability to use these revenues for economic development, particularly when oil and gas prices began to decline in the mid-1980s. Thus, although the direct economic impact of the Saharan war on Algeria was small, the indirect cost of maintaining military superiority over Morocco was quite large and contributed significantly to the economic problems and political unrest that Algeria is currently facing.

Internal developments with Algeria, particularly the process of democratization and economic reform, and the fact that the Soviet Union now will only sell weaponry for hard currency, are likely to reduce the acquisition by Algeria of new weapons systems from the Soviet Union and other suppliers in the future. However, this will not significantly alter the military balance between Algeria and Morocco for many years, even if Morocco is able to make large arms purchases in the future, which is not likely given Morocco's own financial problems. Nor is a reduction in Algerian arms purchases likely to reduce the ability of the Polisario Front to maintain its weapons stockpiles, especially since the types of equipment they employ are relatively inexpensive and, in any case, Algeria already has substantial quantities of these weapons in its inventory.

THE ROLE OF FOREIGN MILITARY ASSISTANCE

Having examined the impact of foreign military assistance on Morocco, the Polisario Front, and Algeria, it is necessary to consider the role that foreign military powers played in determining both the course of the Saharan war and the current military and diplomatic posture of the combatants. To begin with, the statistics on foreign military assistance in Tables 1, 2, and 3 demonstrate that neither the United States, France, nor the Soviet Union exercised much restraint in supplying military assistance, despite the economic costs imposed on the combatants and on friendly states in the region. In order to prevent the military defeat of the side they supported, foreign military powers were willing to provide them with almost any weapons and other military assistance they needed.

Table 1

Sources of Arms Deliveries to Algeria and
Morocco, 1975-1987
(Deliveries in Millions of Current Dollars)

Algeria	Total	Soviet Union	United States	France	Other
1975-1979	1,900	1,500	--	10	430
1978-1982	3,800	3,200	--	30	500
1982-1987	3,230	2,500	240	60	430
Morocco					
1975-1979	1,400	20	310	725	360
1978-1982	1,900	--	470	1,100	325
1982-1987	840	--	260	310	270

Source: U.S. Arms Control and Disarmament Agency, *World Military Expenditures and Army Transfers, 1970-1979* (Washington, D.C.: Government Printing Office, 1982); *World Military Expenditures and Arms Transfers, 1972-1982* (Washington, D.C.: Government Printing Office, 1984); and *World Military Expenditures and Arms Transfers, 1988* (Washington, D.C.: Government Printing Office, 1989).

Table 2

Annual Value of Arms Imports, 1977-1987
(Imports in Millions of Current Dollars)

	Algeria	Morocco
1977	600	300
1978	800	440
1979	550	470
1980	725	350
1981	1,200	340
1982	1,200	270
1983	675	320
1984	775	200
1985	480	110
1986	600	80
1987	700	130
Total	8,305	3,010

Source: U.S. Arms Control and Disarmament Agency, *World Military Expenditures and Arms Transfers, 1988* (Washington, D.C.: Government Printing Office, 1989).

Table 3

U.S. Arms Sales and Deliveries to Morocco, 1976-1990
(Sales and Deliveries in Thousands of Dollars)

	1976	1977	1978	1979	1980	1981
FMS Agreements	95,583	27,466	6,465	2,646	251,483	25,491
FMS Deliveries	15,827	33,730	86,173	132,116	50,827	123,761

	1982	1983	1984	1985	1986	1987
FMS Agreements	10,235	63,122	32,195	63,403	28,294	34,345
FMS Deliveries	55,776	50,123	68,628	49,446	37,048	42,951

	1988	1989	1990 (est.)	Total 1976-1989	Undelivered Balance (1990)
FMS Agreements	92,402	19,089	20,000	752,219	123,629
FMS Deliveries	74,367	33,822	---	854,595	---

Table 3
(Continued)

Source: Defense Security Assistance Agency, *Foreign Military Sales, Foreign Military Construction Sales and Military Assistance Facts* (Washington, D.C.: Defense Security Assistance Agency, 1985, 1987, 1988, and 1989); and Defense Security Assistance Agency and Department of State, *Congressional Presentation for Security Assistance Programs, Fiscal Year 1991* (Washington, D.C.: Defense Security Assistance Agency and Department of State, 1990).

This contradicts the argument presented by Stephanie G. Neuman, who has examined the international arms trade and concluded that foreign powers (specifically the two superpowers) have demonstrated great restraint in supplying major weapons systems and other military assistance to the countries involved in regional conflicts. According to Neuman, the superpowers have effectively used their control over the delivery of military assistance to "regulate the level of armed hostilities" in the Western Sahara and in other regional conflicts and this control has made it possible for foreign powers to act as a "moderating influence on the level, if not the frequency, of conventional conflict."[27]

My own examination of the evolution of the war in the Western Sahara reveals that the fluctuations in the deliveries of foreign military assistance did not reflect restraint on the part of foreign arms suppliers. Instead, changes in the levels of military assistance provided by foreign powers were the result of changes in the international situation, in the internal politics of the foreign powers involved (particularly in the United States), and in the ability of Morocco, the Polisario Front, and Algeria to pay for expensive weapons systems and to absorb them into their military arsenals.

For example, the dramatic shift in the policy of the Carter administration toward the delivery of military assistance to Morocco for use in the Western Sahara in September 1979 was primarily the result of the exaggerated and almost hysterical concern about the stability of the Moroccan government that arose in Washington immediately after the overthrow of the Shah of Iran in February 1979. Thus, in the summer of 1979, reports prepared by both the State Department and by the Central Intelligence Agency argued that King Hassan faced both a possible military coup and mounting popular opposition, and suggested that unless he won a quick victory in the Western Sahara he would probably be overthrown within five years. The shift in the arms sales policy of the Carter administration was also the result of significant changes within the administration itself, especially the resignations of the United Nations representative Andrew Young and of Secretary of State Cyrus Vance, which removed the influence of policymakers opposed to supplying military assistance to Morocco for use in the desert war. This left policy under the control of National Security Adviser Zbigniew Brzezinski and other policy makers who insisted on the necessity of supporting King Hassan.

Furthermore, the statistics on arms transfers to both Morocco and Algeria indicate that foreign powers dramatically increased their deliveries from 1978 to 1982, as both sides sought to gain a military advantage and the war escalated, and that deliveries leveled off after 1982, as each side settled into a war of attrition and foreign powers worked to maintain the military capabilities of the side they supported.

In this regard it is important to note that the relatively low proportion of military assistance provided to Morocco by the United States, compared with that provided by France, does not indicate restraint on the part of the U.S. government. Instead, it reflects the fact that the Moroccan government now prefers to buy the more effective French-produced Mirage rather than the American-produced F-5 Phantom fighter when it purchases combat aircraft, which are the most expensive type of military equipment.

Indeed, my examination of arms deliveries indicates that foreign arms suppliers were actually willing to provide Morocco and Algeria with as much weaponry as they could absorb and afford and even, in some cases, more than they wanted. For example, the Carter administration approved the sale of 24 Hughes Model 500 helicopter gunships to Morocco in 1979 and the Reagan administration approved the sale of 108 M-60 heavy tanks to Morocco in 1981, but neither sale was completed. In the first case, Morocco decided to buy Gazelle helicopter gunships from France instead, and in the second case, Morocco decided not to purchase additional tanks because of the cost and limited usefulness of tanks in the desert war.

Moreover, there is no evidence to indicate that any additional military assistance would have significantly altered the course of the war. Both combatants received as much, if not more, military assistance as they could effectively use. But this foreign military assistance did not give either combatant a significant military advantage. Instead, the unrestrained flow of foreign military assistance made it impossible for either side to achieve a military solution to the conflict, and by 1982 it had produced a complete military stalemate.

On the other hand, once a military stalemate had developed, no foreign military power showed any inclination to seek a military victory for either side. Given the military balance between Morocco and Algeria, any attempt to resolve the conflict militarily would have risked provoking a general regional war or direct military intervention by a foreign military power, and neither the United States, France, nor the Soviet Union were willing to take this risk. They were willing to escalate the war, but only up to the point where it threatened to involve them directly.

The impact of foreign military assistance, thus, has been to significantly increase the destructiveness of the Saharan war and the economic burden that the war imposed on the combatants and their regional supporters without shortening its duration or giving victory to either side. This was not the intention of the United States, France, or the Soviet Union. But all of the foreign powers involved preferred an endless war of attrition to a negotiated solution that did not favor the side they supported. Consequently, foreign military powers continued to provide greater and greater quantities of military assistance in the hope that this would persuade the other side to give up and accept an unfavorable settlement. Instead, this created a regional arms race that has continued up to the present day and that has encouraged both sides to seek to use their military resources to wrest political concessions from the other side.

Despite recent movement toward a negotiated solution to the war, including the efforts of the United Nations to mediate between the two combatants, the initiation of direct talks between the Moroccan government and the Polisario Front in January 1989, and a unilateral cease-fire declared by the Polisario Front during the month of February 1989, neither side has truly abandoned the hope that continued fighting will gain them a political advantage. Thus, in September 1988, the Polisario Front mounted a major assault on the Moroccan garrison at Oum Dreiga on the defensive wall.[28] Another lull in the fighting followed, but the failure of King Hassan to continue direct negotiations and the fact that the resumption of diplomatic relations between Algeria and Morocco did not lead to a settlement, as the Algerian government had hoped, led the Polisaro Front to end its unilateral cease-fire in September 1989. Between September and November 1989, the Polisario Front mounted intense assaults against Moroccan positions in the Guelta Zemmour, Hawza, and Amgala sectors of the Western Sahara, inflicting heavy casualties on Moroccan forces.[29] In response to these Polisario military operations, the Moroccan government is now attempting to obtain additional weaponry from the United States. In February 1989, the Bush administration announced that it was considering a Moroccan request for the sale of twenty-four (two full squadrons) advanced F-16 fighter-bombers.[30] In March 1990, the Bush administration announced that it might also sell Morocco some of the M-60 tanks that it plans to remove from Western Europe as part of the force reductions that would be part of a conventional weapons agreement between NATO and the Warsaw Pact.[31] And, in a stunning act of hypocrisy, King Hassan dispatched a symbolic unit of seventeen hundred soldiers (many of whom were part of a motorized brigade fighting in the Western Sahara) to Saudi Arabia and the United Arab Emirates in August 1990 to participate in the American-led military operation mounted in response to Iraq's occupation and annexation of *its* neighbor, Kuwait.[32] King Hassan's action is clearly intended to publicly reaffirm his loyalty to the United States in order to undercut opposition in the U.S. Congress to the role of the United States in his attempt to occupy and annex *his* neighbor, the Western Sahara, and to ensure a continued supply of American weaponry. Thus, despite action by the UN Security Council and other signs of real progress toward a diplomatic settlement, the war and the regional arms race goes on.

NOTES

1. See David J. Dean, *The Air Force Role in Low-Intensity Conflict* (Maxwell Air Force Base, Ala.: Air University Press, 1986), 41-51; and William H. Lewis, "War in The Western Sahara," in Stephanie G. Neuman and Robert E. Harkavy, eds., *The Lessons of Recent Wars in the Third World, Vol. I: Approaches and Case Studies* (Lexington, Mass.: Lexington Books, 1985), 126-31. For purposes of analysis, the minor involvement of Mauritania in the Saharan war from 1975 to 1979 will not be discussed in this chapter.

2. Defense Security Assistance Agency (DSAA), *Foreign Military Sales, Foreign Military Construction Sales, and Military Assistance Facts [hereafter FMS Facts], as of September 30, 1985* (Washington, D.C.: DSAA, 1985), 38-39; DSAA, *FMS Facts, as of September 30, 1989* (Washington, D.C.: DSAA, 1989), 46-47; and DSAA and Department of State, *Congressional Presentation for Security Assistance Programs, Fiscal Year 1991* (Washington, D.C.: DSAA and Department of State, 1990), 48.

3. Dean, *Air Force Role*, 62

4. Ibid., 61.

5. Ibid., 42.

6. Ibid., 45-47, 59.

7. Ibid., 69-70.

8. Ibid., 68.

9. Ibid., 69.

10. Ibid., 46, 57-58.

11. International Institute for Strategic Studies (IISS), *The Military Balance, 1987-1988* (London: IISS, 1987), 107-9; IISS, *The Military Balance, 1989-1990* (London: IISS, 1989), 108-10.

12. Dean, *Air Force Role*, 69.

13. DSAA, *FMS Facts, as of September 30, 1989* (Washington, D.C.: DSAA, 1989), 86-87, 94-95; DSAA and Department of State, *Congressional Presentation for Security Assistance Programs, Fiscal Year 1991*, (Washington, D.C.: DSAA and Department of State, 1990), 19.

14. Dean, *Air Force Role*, 63-64, 69-70.

15. DSSA, *FMS Facts, as of September 30, 1985*, 24-25, 47; DSAA, *FMS Facts, as of September 30, 1989*, 32-33, 57; and DSAA and Department of State, *Congressional Presentation for Security Assistance Programs, Fiscal Year 1991*, 11.

16. Dean, *Air Force Role*, 40.

17. *The Guardian*, September 28, 1988.

18. U.S. Arms Control and Disarmament Agency (ACDA), *World Military Expenditures and Arms Transfer [hereafter WME and AT], 1970-1979* (Washington, D.C.: ACDA, 1982), 127; ACDA, *WME and AT, 1972-1982* (Washington, D.C.: ACDA, 1984), 95; and ACDA, *WME and AT, 1988* (Washington: ACDA, 1989, 96.

19. Dean, *Air Force Role*, 44, 46, 62, 67-69.

20. Ibid., 61.

21. IISS, *The Military Balance, 1987-1988*, 107-9; IISS, *The Military Balance, 1989-1990*, 110.

22. Dean, *Air Force Role*, 34-38.

23. IISS, *The Military Balance, 1987-1988*, 109; IISS, *The Military Balance, 1989-1990*, 95-96.

24. ACDA, *WME and AT, 1970-1979*, 127; ACDA, *WME and AT, 1972-1982*, 95; and ACDA, *WME and AT, 1988*, 96.

25. IISS, *The Military Balance, 1987-1988*, 94-95; IISS, *The Military Balance, 1989-1990*, 95-96.

26. IISS, *The Military Balance, 1989-1990*, 45.

27. Stephanie G. Neuman, "Arms, Aid and The Superpowers," *Foreign Affairs*, 66, no. 5 (Summer 1988): 1064-65; see also Stephanie G. Neuman, "Military Assistance in Recent Wars: The Dominance of The Superpowers," Center for Strategic and International Studies Washington Papers 14, no. 122 (New York: Praeger Publishers, 1986), especially 13, 36, 51, 84-85, 102-4, 118. But Dr. Neuman's analysis is

fundamentally contradicted by the work of William H. Lewis, her collaborator and the author of the case study that she cites in her own works.   See William H. Lewis, "War in the Western Sahara," in Stephanie G. Neuman and Robert E. Harkavy, eds., *The Lessons of Recent Wars in the Third World, Volume I: Approaches and Case Studies* (Lexington, Mass.:   Lexington Books, 1985), 117-37; and William H. Lewis and Christopher Joyner, "The Runaway Arms Race in the Third World," *The Washington Post*, October 25, 1988.

28. *West Africa*, September 26-October 2, 1988, 1814.

29. *West Africa*, October 9-15, 1989, 1702; *West Africa*, October 30-November 5, 1989, 1826-27; *West Africa*, November 20-26, 1989, 1928-29; and Tom Arkell, "The desert war flares anew," *The Middle East*, November 1989, 21.

30. *The New York Times*, February 3, 1989.

31. *The Washington Post*, March 1, 1990.

32. *The Washington Post*, August 26, September 24, 1990.

8

The Greater Maghreb and the Western Sahara

Robert A. Mortimer

In her authoritative study of Algerian foreign policy, Nicole Grimaud coined the term "fraternal environment" to designate the Maghreb and the larger Arab world as arenas of Algerian diplomacy.[1] Relations among the "brothers" have often been contentious and occasionally even fratricidal, as, for example, upon the outbreak of the hostilities over the Western Sahara. Yet paradoxically, that conflict became the catalyst for a renewed push for Maghreb unity, a perennial theme in Maghrebi affairs. In searching for a Western Saharan settlement, Algeria launched a campaign for a "Greater Maghreb" that eventually produced a new regional organization, the Arab Maghreb Union (UMA). The future of the UMA is, in turn, linked to the resolution of the Saharan question.

Grimaud's category of brother countries is especially apt for Tunisia, Algeria, and Morocco, the three states most commonly designated as the Maghreb. All three came under the sway of France, albeit for different durations and under different juridical regimes. During the nationalist period, Maghrebi brothers often came to know one another in France, forming such organizations as the Association des Étudiants Musulmans de l'Afrique du Nord as early as 1927. These bonds among *colonisés* (colonized people) carried over into the relation among the dominant nationalist movements--*Neo-Destour*, *Istaqlal*, and the Algerian National Liberation Front (FLN)--which generally supported each other's aspirations for independence. The three independent states commonly refer to one another as *pays frères*, brother countries; or when state-to-state relations heat up, the reference may shift to "brother peoples."

To be sure, even among brothers harmony is never assured. I. William Zartman cites the North African proverb, "My cousins and I against the others, my brother and I against the cousins, myself against my brother."[2] Zartman sees the proverb as a good expression of the dynamics of a pluralist model of regional relations in which sovereign states compete over local issues. Boundary disputes and rivalry regarding the weaker periphery to the south (notably including the Western Sahara, Mauritania, and Chad) are characteristic of this pluralist pattern. Zartman suggests that this competition is functional in justifying each state's "separate national existence" and in establishing a "sense of rank" among them.[3] The Greater Maghreb idea, on the contrary, implies that such rivalry is dysfunctional.

Zartman views the Greater Maghreb campaign as a phase in a cycle that alternates between pluralist rivalry and integration. Each prior integration phase (the Tangier meeting of 1958, the Casablanca conference of 1961, the functional cooperation of 1964-69, and Tunisia's 1984-85 efforts to convene a pan-Maghrebi summit) has lapsed back into indifference or conflict. During the spring and summer of 1987, however, Algeria (pressed on by certain Libyan initiatives) embarked upon a major effort to transcend the pluralist pattern. This time the momentum toward regional cooperation was more sustained and successful. In February 1989 at Marakech the Maghrebi states signed a treaty creating the UMA, marking a new stage in the pursuit of regional integration. Yet since then the cycle has begun to repeat itself.

This chapter analyzes the geopolitical and diplomatic determinants of the process that produced the UMA. To be sure, economic factors like the plan for a united Western Europe by 1992 also played a role, but regional geopolitics underlay the process. The utility of the Greater Maghreb design lay precisely in its intent to transcend the classic Maghreb trio (Tunisia, Algeria, Morocco) by incorporating Mauritania, Libya, and the Western Sahara as well. In the spirit of the proverb, one might suggest that the Greater Maghreb approach seeks to bring the cousins together with the brothers, in part to deal with such "others" as the great powers and Europe, and in part to end the strife over the Western Sahara.

The evolution of regional politics in the Maghreb is one of the crucial international dimensions of the Western Saharan conflict. For more than a decade after 1975, the dispute dominated the diplomatic agenda. By the end of the 1980s, other issues assumed growing prominence, but the Saharan problem did not go away. The initiative in regional affairs began to shift from a politically volatile and economically ailing Algeria toward a relatively stable and prosperous Morocco. The victory of the Islamic Salvation Front (FIS) in Algeria's June 1990 local elections may exacerbate regional rivalries once again, completing yet another cycle of integration/disintegration. Alternatively, however, the rise of the Islamist opposition may push the ruling elites of Algeria and Morocco into closer cooperation, requiring one or the other party to give ground on the Western Sahara issue. The Greater Maghreb concept is instrumental to any strategy of Algerian-Moroccan, and hence regional, cooperation.

Analyzing the Greater Maghreb concept in 1985, I argued that it was a response to two regional foyers of unrest, the Western Sahara and Libya.[4] Algeria, primarily concerned about the first, and Tunisia, uneasy about the second, together rallied around the banner of regional community in 1983 in an attempt to influence Morocco and Libya to change their policies. Initially they succeeded only in provoking King Hassan II and Colonel Muammar Qaddafi to join forces against them, but in the longer term they set a process in motion that has continued into the 1990s.

Algeria and Tunisia took the first step in March 1983 by signing an agreement known as the Treaty of Fraternity and Concord. The treaty explicitly stipulated that it was "open to the adherence, with the agreement of the high contracting parties, of the other states of the Arab Greater Maghreb."[5] Indeed, the text of the treaty, which was not long, employed the expression "Arab Greater Maghreb" six times. Clearly the intent was to create a dynamic that would draw in the other brothers. In the months following signature of the treaty, the two governments mounted a sustained campaign to broaden the arrangement. At the end of May rumors abounded that King Hassan II would join Presidents Habib Bourguiba of Tunisia, Chadli Bendjedid of Algeria, and Khouna Ould Tayah of Mauritania in a summit meeting in Algiers. King Hassan never arrived, however, presumably because the Western Sahara issue remained a sticking point. Even so, the Tunisians in particular continued to press for a regional summit throughout the summer.

For Tunis, Moroccan entry into the fraternity treaty was highly desirable, because that would provide greater balance to the arrangement, in effect providing Tunisia with two protectors against Libyan pressures. Thus, Tunisian Prime Minister Mohammed Mzali called upon all Maghrebi leaders to transcend "narrow national entities" and upon Morocco especially to resolve the Saharan conflict by placing it "in the framework of the Arab Greater Maghreb."[6] Mzali's vision, shared by Algeria, was to finesse the Western Saharan issue by allowing both Morocco and the SADR to accede to the new treaty. The rallying cry of the Greater Maghreb was designed to entice all regional actors into a larger transnational cooperative arrangement that would make disputes over boundaries and even sovereignty irrelevant. The idea was unduly optimistic, or at the minimum premature, in 1983-84. Morocco was not seduced; on the contrary, it began to plan its liaison with Libya, the other outsider to the Algerian-Tunisian accord. By the end of 1983, the only newcomer enticed into the treaty was Mauritania. This was hardly the outcome desired by Tunisia, for it established Algiers as the center of tripartite alliance with two lesser partners. Yet at the same time, the adherence of Mauritania kept alive the idea of a larger entity and furthermore extended the membership beyond the classic Maghreb.

Although Tunisia continued to propose regional meetings throughout 1984 and 1985, the Greater Maghreb idea waned, especially once the Oujda treaty was signed in August 1984. The presence of two competing alliance axes was not congenial to discourse about regional cooperation. In the summer of 1985, Tunisian-Libyan relations became inflamed with the abrupt expulsion of some 30,000 Tunisian workers from Libya. Algeria sprang to Tunisia's support, and the lines of cleavage (Tunis-Algiers vs. Tripoli-Rabat) seemed more marked than ever. At the beginning of 1986, however, the lines blurred again, and Algeria assumed the central role in promoting the Greater Maghreb.

The turning point was the January 1986 meeting between Qaddafi and Bendjedid at In Amenas, an oasis 1,200 miles southeast of Algiers near the border with Libya. Several factors prompted this desert rendezvous. Algeria, of course, had an interest in detaching Libya from its Moroccan alliance. Libya, fearful of an Algerian-Egyptian rapprochement that would capture it pincer-like between the two well-armed states, had begun to question the utility of its Moroccan tie. The report that the CIA had hatched a plan to bring down Qaddafi with the joint assistance of Egypt and Algeria could only reinforce Libyan anxieties. The fact that Algeria indignantly denied complicity in any such plot and assured "sister Libya" of its solidarity demonstrated that Libya might consider mending its fences (not to say borders) with Algeria.[7] The two countries had long pushed common energy policies within OPEC and generally similar foreign policies until Libyan intervention in Chad and its abandonment of Polisario in favor of the Treaty of Oujda had cooled the relationship. At In Amenas, the two states agreed that they had a mutual interest in reconciliation.

Within two months, they signed an impressive array of economic cooperation projects. Algeria viewed these agreements as the indispensable infrastructure for long-term political cooperation. Libya, on the other hand, interpreted them as the springboard to an early union between the two states; indeed Qaddafi liked to insist that Algeria had agreed to a political union way back in late 1975, when he met President Houari Boumedienne at Hassi Messaoud. The divergence between these two interpretations was discernible during Algerian Premier Abdelhamid Brahimi's visit to Tripoli in March 1986. His counterpart, Abdessalem Jalloud, declared, according to the official communiqué, that the objective of the meetings was "union, in prelude to unity of the Arab Maghreb and of the Arab nation."[8] For Libya, in other words, Libyan-Algerian union was the immediate goal, to be followed by the rallying of the other Maghreb states. For Algeria, on the contrary, a more gradual process grounded in the existing fraternity treaty was the proper approach. At the same time that Brahimi was in Tripoli, Bendjedid invited Premier Mzali to Algiers to assure him of Algerian intentions. The joint communiqué on their talks stated that they had discussed "the perspectives of construction of the Arab Greater Maghreb on the basis of the principles set forth in the Treaty of Fraternity and Concord."[9] Thus, Algeria reiterated the primacy of the established treaty framework and the priority that it placed upon close consultation with Tunisia. While seeking to woo Libya away from Morocco, Algeria did not want to jeopardize its relationship with Tunisia.

Within days of Brahimi's trip to Tripoli, hostilities flared in the Gulf of Sidra between U.S. and Libyan forces. Three weeks later, U.S. planes bombed Libyan territory in a barely veiled attempt to kill or depose Qaddafi. On both occasions, Algeria immediately declared its support for the Libyan government and criticized the U.S. engagement in the region. One must recall as well that in October 1985 Israeli planes had attacked Tunisian territory in a raid against Palestinian Liberation Organization headquarters. These various military operations heightened the sense that North Africa was prey to a wave of external interventions. They intensified Algeria's desire to push ahead in the construction of a regional ensemble. Indeed in April 1986, Bendjedid intimated that a new proposal for a union of Maghreb states "could be announced in the near future and submitted to a referendum for approval."[10] In fact, a breakthrough was not imminent, but Bendjedid was gradually preparing Algerian opinion for such an eventuality.

Other developments were pushing Algeria along this course in Spring 1986. One was the ruinous state of inter-Arab affairs in the aftermath of the U.S. operations against Libya. Algeria favored convening an Arab summit to articulate a common position on this and other matters, including the Palestinian question. The Algerian press deplored the failure to organize such a summit as a sign of the "patent incapacity of those who guide the destinies of the Arab world."[11] The Algerians undertook an initiative of their own, inviting five Palestinian factions to Algiers for reconciliation talks. Disaffection from the Arab East inclined Algeria to devote more diplomatic attention to the Arab West. Reinforcing this trend was the fact that proximity talks between Morocco and the Polisario Front were taking place in April-May 1986 as well. Although nothing came of these talks, their mere existence suggested that resolution of the Western Sahara dispute was not unthinkable. The lure of the Greater Maghreb thus persisted as a possible way out of the impasse.

From Algeria's perspective, the next breakthrough was not on the Western Sahara front but rather on the Libya front, thanks to the dissolution of the Treaty of Oujda.[12] The divorce between Morocco and Libya increased the probability that Algeria could snare its southeastern neighbor in the Greater Maghreb net. Bendjedid promptly dispatched his Minister of State Benahmed Abdelghani to Tripoli in September; in October Jalloud returned the favor; then in December, Bendjedid embarked upon his first state visit to Libya. The principal item on the December agenda was not actually Algerian-Libyan relations but rather joint consultations on the continuing divisions among the Palestinians. Bendjedid's tactic was to engage Qaddafi on an issue dear to him, and enlist his support vis-à-vis Syria which was pursuing a policy hostile to the Yassar Arafat wing of the PLO. By associating Qaddafi in his own efforts to reconcile Palestinian factions, Bendjedid broadened the base of Algerian-Libyan collaboration. At the same time, Bendjedid realized that the Libyan leader was losing control over his adventure in Chad and was therefore in need of new directions in which to turn.

Ever sensitive to the interests of his Tunisian partner, Bendjedid took care to stop in Tunis on his return trip. Having forthrightly backed Tunisia during the expulsion crisis, Algeria now was seeking a reconciliation, including indemnities for the Tunisian workers expelled from Libya. Algeria was unable to deliver full resolution of these problems, but the Libyan press did cease its campaign of insults against the Tunisian regime. Bendjedid's solicitation of Bourguiba's counsel was doubly significant in that Algeria had been disappointed by the abrupt demise of the Mzali government earlier in the year. As Mzali had been the architect of the Treaty of Fraternity and Concord (and as Algeria had permitted his escape from Tunisia across the Algerian border), one might have expected a sharp deterioration of Algerian-Tunisian relations. Instead Benjedid realistically kept the lines of communication open. By the same token, the stopover conveyed to Libya that Algeria was intent on maintaining its tie with Tunis.

The Tunisian tie proved to be a critical variable when Libyan-Algerian momentum picked up again in mid-1987. The context of events was not unlike that of 1983 in that a second meeting between Bendjedid and Hassan (in May 1987) once again failed to provide a breakthrough on the Western Sahara dispute. The stalemate on the western front rekindled Algerian attention to the eastern front, which Qaddafi, now reeling from setbacks in Chad, reciprocated. For over a year, various economic and political delegations had been shuttling back and forth between Algiers and Tripoli. The former were generally led by government ministers, the latter by party officials like Mohamed Cherif Messaadia (head of the FLN) or Sadek Zouaten (head of the party's Council on Friendship and Solidarity). The pattern of visits suggested that the party apparatus under Messaadia may have been particularly favorable to the idea of a union with Libya. In June, the Libyans mounted a new push to exploit these sentiments.

A large Libyan economic delegation arrived in Algiers on June 12, 1987, for the signature of diverse agreements that instituted eight new joint ventures between the two governments. On June 14, Jalloud joined the delegation to conduct talks on a "political document regarding a union between Libya and Algeria."[13] Subsequent reports indicated that the Libyan document proposed to establish a joint presidential council, a ministerial council, and a union parliament.[14] The following week Qaddafi told a Kuwaiti newspaper that Algeria and Libya would form a federation in November. Then on June 28, Qaddafi arrived on an impromptu visit that lasted four days. One must assume that the Libyan leader pressed hard for his union proposal; the evidence suggests that Algeria--or at the minimum the FLN--was greatly tempted by his offer.

This hypothesis arises from a rather curious set of public statements. During the Qaddafi visit, the Central Committee (CC) of the FLN held one of its regularly scheduled sessions. Normally the Algerian government press publishes a resumé of such meetings quite promptly.

In this instance, however, *El-Moudjahid* did not provide an extended account of the CC's deliberations until July 18, two-and-a-half weeks after the session.   According to this belated account, the Central Committee was informed of a working document that the two delegations had settled upon. The text declared:

> The Central Committee considers that union between Libya and Algeria is imperative ("impérieuse") and answers to the logic of history, to the demands of the community of destiny and to the aspirations of large popular masses.
>   The Central Committee commends the practical steps already taken to meet the objective conditions necessary to effect this union in conformity with the will of the two brother peoples and *has decided to submit the draft document to the popular masses* for discussions and enrichment.[15]

To judge by this resolution, the Central Committee was on the brink of endorsing an Algerian-Libyan union.

The curiosity was that the CC resolution was not the only indicator available by mid-July, because the Political Bureau had met on July 16. Its resolution was published in *El-Moudjahid* on the same day as the CC resolution. The Political Bureau document implied that the leadership had retreated from the brink toward the earlier policy based upon the fraternity treaty. In reaffirming Algeria's "unshakable attachment" to the Greater Maghreb, the Political Bureau stressed the "need for a methodical procedure" grounded in "economic complementarities" and an "integrated Maghrebi economy."   The resolution went on to "underline the historic function fulfilled by the Treaty of Fraternity and Concord" as a basic point of reference in the process of constructing Maghreb unity. The sense of imminent union was absent.

There is little secret as to where it was lost. On July 7, President Bendjedid flew to Monastir, hometown of President Bourguiba, to "reflect together" about the future of the Maghreb.[16]   The Tunisians were in no hurry to charge ahead. For them a methodical approach meant first and foremost settlement of the financial dispute that arose out of the Libyan expulsion of Tunisian workers two years earlier. Bendjedid decided to respect the reservations and conditions of those Tunisian partners. Nonetheless, he may have believed that they could be met fairly promptly; according to one account, he persuaded Bourguiba to meet again with President Tayah of Mauritania and Qaddafi in order that the three treaty members could admit the fourth. The date set was August 3, Bourguiba's birthday.[17]

In fixing a date less than a month away, Bendjedid overestimated Qaddafi's willingness to compromise. The Libyan leader had set his hopes on the draft project for a federal union that the Central Committee had ostensibly approved. Indeed, Qaddafi may have calculated that the Algerians would tire of Bourguiba and rally to his own approach to Maghreb unity. In fact, despite evidence to the contrary, he rashly asserted in a September 1 speech that unity with Algeria would be proclaimed on November 1. Both Bourguiba's birthday and Algeria's revolutionary holiday passed without any such announcement.

If Bendjedid misread Libyan flexibility, Qaddafi misjudged Algeria's priorities as established by the July 16 Political Bureau meeting. The evidence suggests that Algerian policy was under debate from mid-June to mid-July. It is plausible to argue that the party secretariat led by Messaadia was favorable to the immediate union approach. The party chief had carried out numerous missions to Tripoli for Bendjedid. A union of the two North African radical states was ideologically attractive from the FLN perspective. Such a predilection appears to be reflected in the June 30 CC resolution. At the same time, Foreign Ministry officials, led by Foreign Minister Ahmed Taleb Ibrahimi, regarded the fraternity treaty framework as the most effective way to collaborate with the other states of the region (including Morocco and Libya). During the critical period between Bendjedid's trip to Monastir and the Political Bureau communiqué, all of Algeria's ambassadors abroad assembled in Algiers for a conference. It is unlikely that this group unanimously supported an immediate Algerian-Libyan federation. Likewise, other government ministers may have expressed reservations; they were the ones, after all, who had been carrying out the "methodical procedures" of functional cooperation that the Political Bureau statement stressed. The majority of the Political Bureau is made up of government ministers, not of full-time party officials. One can reasonably conclude that the Political Bureau statement of July 18 signaled a reassertion of the more pragmatic treaty (as distinguished from union) approach to constructing the Greater Maghreb. Tunisia's objections and preconditions strengthened the hand of Algerian pragmatists in the policy debate.

Subsequent developments are consistent with this interpretation. First, the assumption of power by Zine el-Abidine Ben Ali in Tunisia, in November 1987, facilitated the process of Libyan-Tunisian

reconciliation. Although the substance of the Tunisian position did not
change, the tone of Tunisian-Libyan relations improved, thus providing
Libya with a new incentive to clear up the obstacles. Tripoli agreed (as
Algeria had been urging) to settle the financial claims arising out of the
1985 crisis and reopened its border to Tunisian labor. The
post-Bourguiba government, nevertheless, reiterated the same connection
of gradualism and the necessity for Libya to respect Tunisian
sovereignty. As the new Tunisian Foreign Minister Mahmoud Mestiri
put it, "It will be necessary for Colonel Qaddafi to pledge to respect all
the provisions" of the Treaty of Fraternity and Concord, notably
nonintervention in one another's internal affairs.[18] In the context of
such mutual understanding, Tunis and Tripoli restored diplomatic
relations at the end of 1987.

    While Tunisia and Libya were thus normalizing their relations,
Algeria resumed its orchestration of the distant music. In his annual
state-of-the-nation address in mid-December 1987, President Bendjedid
placed the Greater Maghreb at the center of his foreign policy statement:

> Strengthened by the appreciable gains resulting from the Treaty
> of Fraternity and Concord, Algeria has undertaken to bring
> together the preconditions for the reinforcement and enlargement
> of this decisive stage (étape), and to open new horizons to the
> unity enterprise. The progress recorded in the process of
> normalizing Tunisian-Libyan relations is encouraging. We are
> pursuing our action with the Libyan people for the concretization
> of tangible results which can transcend conjunctural
> difficulties.[19]

A few days later, the foreign ministers of Algeria, Tunisia, and
Mauritania convened in Algiers to discuss the terms under which Libya
might eventually adhere to the treaty. Beyond the normalization of
relations (satisfied a week later), Tunisia merely wanted an
understanding that Libya would officially request its accession to the
treaty. Following Qaddafi's successive visits to Tunisia and Algeria in
February 1988, numerous signs suggested that such a request was
imminent (indeed rumor had it that a quadripartite summit would take
place on March 19, 1988, on the fifth anniversary of the original treaty).
Bendjedid revealed that he believed that he had "an agreement in
principle from all the parties" that Libya would adhere to the treaty.[20]
During Ben Ali's early March visit to Algiers, the two presidents

affirmed the "exigency of . . . enlarging and enriching the Fraternity and Concord Treaty."[21]   Yet the anniversary passed without Libya making the desired move.

Qaddafi, as it turned out, still was not on the same wavelength as the other brothers. Instead of a treaty among sovereign states, he wanted the suppression of borders and total union. Toward this end he ordered the customs station at the Libyan-Tunisian passage point to be blown up. This impetuous gesture toward a Maghreb without borders fit into Qaddafi's larger dream of an Arab union from the Atlantic to the Gulf. Where Algeria saw the Arab West as a discrete entity exercising regional autonomy vis-à-vis external powers, Libya saw the Maghreb as a potential exemplar for the entire Arab world. Algeria was obliged to conclude that, having succeeded all too well in sponsoring Libyan-Tunisian rapprochement, it had not achieved its immediate policy objective, a four-party treaty.

The fraternity treaty framework had always been designed not to exclude Morocco but to pressure it.   In an interview with U.S. journalists in February 1988, Bendjedid stated that he wished to include Morocco in the grouping and to construct a joint natural gas pipeline with Morocco on the condition that the Western Sahara dispute be resolved.[22]   One can see the parallel that had appealed to Algeria: Libya being diplomatically isolated eventually resolved its differences with Tunisia in order to join an economically and politically attractive regional cooperation arrangement; Morocco being diplomatically isolated and drained by the cost of pursuing the Saharan war would eventually likewise see the Greater Maghreb as offering a framework for a compromise settlement. Having come up short on the Libyan front, Algeria took a new look at the western front.

Despite the absence of striking results from the second Hassan-Bendjedid meeting, the two governments had continued to send emissaries back and forth quite frequently since May 1987.   Both acknowledge the cost of their respective Saharan commitments at a time of strapped national budgets.   Algeria in particular was feeling the crunch of depressed oil prices. Both saw concrete economic benefits in resuming normal relations.   At the end of March 1988, a common enemy in the form of invading locusts obliged the two countries to work together. This peril of nature served to dramatize how much Algeria and Morocco had in common and just how costly their dispute was. Yet another variable was Algeria's strong desire to organize an Arab summit on the Palestinian *Intifada* (Uprising) at which Hassan's presence would be valued. All these determinants converged in May 1988 in the conclusion that both states' interests lay in the restoration of diplomatic relations between Rabat and Algiers.

Very swiftly the brothers moved to end their twelve-year estrangement. King Hassan named a close palace confidant, a doctor and former dean of the medical school, Abdellatif Berbiche, as his ambassador to Algiers. The Algerians reciprocated by recalling Abdelhamid Mehri from the embassy in Paris to represent them in Rabat. Mehri was widely respected as a veteran of Maghrebi affairs, having attended the landmark Tangier conference on Maghreb unity thirty years earlier. Regularly scheduled flights were quickly established and a progressive reopening of the border was implemented. King Hassan accordingly agreed to attend the Algiers summit on Palestine in early June. In the midst of this spectacular reconciliation, only one area remained rather vague. Indeed, as *Jeune Afrique* observed, the paragraph on the Western Sahara in the May 16 joint communiqué was a "genuine masterpiece of ambiguity."[23] Yet the assumption had to be that both governments believed that some form of negotiated settlement was within reach under the cover of Greater Maghreb cooperation.

The Algerian-Moroccan rapprochement was a major breakthrough in the construction of the Greater Maghreb. Within a month of the decision, King Hassan sailed royally into the port of Algiers, not only to attend the pan-Arab summit but also to permit a precedent-setting Maghreb summit. On June 10, 1988, the chiefs-of-state of five nations from Mauritania to Libya met at Bendjedid's Zeralda residence to institutionalize the idea of Maghreb cooperation. They set up a commission to implement steps toward a regional market; the commission held its first session in July and established five subcommittees, each chaired by a representative of a different participating state, on security, economic, financial, and cultural matters. Over the ensuing months, the commission met several more times to prepare the Marrakech summit at which the treaty founding the UMA was signed. After six years of persistent regional geopolitical maneuvering, the Greater Maghreb finally assumed an institutional form.

Equally significant was the impetus according to the pursuit of a negotiated settlement of the Western Sahara dispute. Shortly after his visit to Algeria, King Hassan suggested that the solution to the Saharan conflict might lie in the "regionalization" of Morocco itself, a federal scheme on the model of the German federal states. He stated that he was prepared to offer considerable regional autonomy not only to the southern provinces (the Western Sahara) but throughout the kingdom in order to preserve its great diversity.[24] The king's offer of practical autonomy under Moroccan sovereignty was not the solution that Polisario ideally preferred, but it did imply a willingness to reconsider the status quo. At the same time, UN Secretary-General Javier Pérez de Cuéllar was canvassing both sides with a cease-fire/referendum proposal that Algeria saw as constructive. In the new climate of regional cooperation, the disputants were under pressure to try a conciliatory approach.

In pursuit of his mediation, the secretary-general had set September 1, 1988, as a deadline for approval of his peace plan. On August 30, the two sides announced that they accepted Pérez de Cuéllar's proposal. In fact, hostilities did not cease right away. Polisario, still backed by Algeria, insisted that the precise terms of the referendum would have to be negotiated directly with Morocco, a longstanding demand that the king had steadfastly rejected and that Pérez de Cuéllar had not specifically addressed in his plan. Just as the process appeared to be bogging down again, however, King Hassan gave another interview in which he expressed his willingness to meet "all who find themselves on the other side" in order to "be informed of their grievances" and of "what they want for this part of [Moroccan] territory."[25] In offering this conclusion, Hassan presumably calculated that Polisario, under Algerian pressure, was likewise ready to make some substantive concessions as well.

The Sahrawis sprang at this new opportunity. In the first days of 1989, a three-man Polisario delegation arrived to hold *discussions*--Moroccan officials were intent to insist that these were not negotiations--concerning the situation prevailing in the contested territory. Although both sides were discrete about the outcome of the meeting, they indicated that the talks were productive. Polisario official Bechir Mustapha Sayed predicted an accord by March. At the end of January, moreover, Polisario declared a month-long truce, subsequently extended. Its top leader, Mohamed Abdelaziz, said, "The most important thing is to arrive at an agreement with the Moroccans before the referendum."[26] This remark implied that Polisario expected further talks that could lead to consensus upon a formula (such as local autonomy within a larger regional framework) that both sides could live with for the sake of peace within the Greater Maghreb.

Yet the founding of the UMA three weeks later, the result of an irresistible momentum that had built up behind the idea of the Greater

Maghreb, still left the Western Sahara question in limbo. The fact that the treaty was signed *without* any gesture whatsoever toward SADR was clearly a point for the Moroccan side. On the Algerian side, it was assumed that cooperation in the new organization ought to be a two-way street; it expected (perhaps unrealistically) that Morocco would remain open to further direct talks with Polisario. Algeria was rudely disappointed. Instead of extending his January initiative, Hassan refused any further direct negotiation and declared that Saharan dispute was but a "grain of sand" in the larger design of the Greater Maghreb.[27]

The king apparently interpreted the signature of the UMA treaty at the royal palace in Marrakech as a vindication of Moroccan policy. The new regional organization came into being without any public guarantee on the Saharan issue. Hassan may well have reasoned that Algeria, still reeling from the effects of the October 1988 domestic crisis, was in no position to press the Sahrawi cause further.[28] This interpretation, however, neglected the dialectic that had existed from the outset between the Greater Maghreb theme and some form of negotiated settlement of the Saharan question. Thus, Hassan's failure to renew talks with Polisario virtually halted the UMA in its tracks before it got started. Everything bogged down again; neither the newborn UMA nor the fledgling peace process made any headway throughout the remainder of 1989. In September, Polisario called off its truce and some of the bloodiest battles of the entire war ensued.

Both Morocco and Algeria, one can conclude, ended up manipulating the Greater Maghreb idea in the hope of cajoling the other into concessions. Algeria gambled that the king would enter into direct talks with Polisario in order to maintain the momentum of the UMA. Morocco calculated that Algeria would place a higher value upon economic cooperation than on sticking by the Sahrawis. In this sense, each one's policy was the mirror image of the other's; thus the Saharan stalemate persisted into the 1990s, and the UMA marked time as a consequence.

Throughout the 1980s, inter-Maghrebi politics were unquestionably dominated by the Saharan conflict. Until the issue is resolved by one concession or another, it will remain more than a speck of sand in regional affairs. The fact remains that the idea of regional integration, however instrumentally it has been employed to date, entrails very large stakes for the states of North Africa. The Maghreb needs to become a "grand ensemble," as Bendjedid has been fond of saying.

The states of North Africa today confront the tremendous changes that are occurring in Europe. The countdown to a united Western European Community is well underway as 1992 draws near. A common North African market of 62 million people makes eminent good sense for all of the Maghrebis. Only by pooling their resources in a regional entity can the brothers hope to maintain any semblance of autonomy in the rapidly evolving international political economy. The Greater Maghreb theme acknowledges this emergent economic reality as much as it evokes the old dream of Maghreb brotherhood.

The Algerian diplomat Abdelmalek Benhabylès once referred to the idea of Maghreb unity as "distant music," faintly beckoning, never quite fully heard.[29] The metaphor seems apt to characterize the situation in the early 1990s: the music can be heard ambiguously emanating from somewhere behind the dunes of the Saharan problem. Far from the "grain of sand" that Hassan imagined, the Western Sahara has been a major feature of the Maghrebi landscape. The future edification of the Greater Maghreb still remains linked to an honorable settlement of the Saharan issue.[30]

From the fraternity treaty of March 1983 to the union document of February 1989, the states of North Africa all advanced proposals to reorganize the "fraternal environment" around one or another conception of Maghreb unity. Each tried to exploit the unity idea to achieve its own primary goals. The founding of the UMA raised hopes that they were moving to a common understanding of the path to regional cooperation. These hopes were not borne out, as Algeria continued to back direct talks that Morocco was unwilling to hold. As compelling as the logic of regional integration would seem, the status of the sixth brother must be resolved if the Greater Maghreb is to prosper.

NOTES

1.Nicole   Grimaud, *La politique extérieure de l'Algérie* (Paris: Karthala, 1984), 165.
2. I. William Zartman, "Foreign Relations of North Africa," in Gerald J. Bender, ed., *Annals of the American Academy of Political and Social Science* (Newbury Park, Calif.: Sage Publications, 1987), 19.
3. Ibid., 16.

4. See my "The Politics of Reassurance in Algeria," *Current History* 84, no. 502 (May 1985): 201-4, 228-29.

5. The text appears in *Annuaire de l'Afrique du Nord, 1983* (Paris: Editions du Centre National des Recherches Scientifiques, 1985), 694-95.

6. Interview with *An Nasr* (Constantine) cited in *Grand Maghreb* 29 (March 1984).

7. The report about the CIA appeared in *The Washington Post*, November 3, 1985; the Algerian reaction is reported in *Le Monde*, November 6, 1985.

8. *Le Monde*, March 25, 1986.

9. Ibid.

10. *Le Monde*, April 11, 1986.

11. *El-Moudjahid*, May 4, 1986.

12. Morocco denounced the treaty at the end of August 1986 after Qaddafi qualified Hassan's July meeting with Israeli Prime Minister Shimon Peres as treason.

13. The expression is taken from the official communiqué as reported in *Le Monde*, June 30, 1987.

14. *The Washington Post*, October 7, 1987; *Le Monde*, October 9, 1987.

15. *El-Moudjahid*, July 17-18, 1987 (my emphasis).

16. *Le Monde*, July 9, 1987.

17. *Le Monde*, November 6, 1987.

18. Ibid. See also *Le Monde*, December 30, 1987.

19. *Le Monde*, December 17, 1987.

20. *The Washington Post*, February 7, 1988.

21. *Le Monde*, March 5, 1988.

22. *The Washington Post*, February 7, 1988.

23. *Jeune Afrique*, no. 1430, June 1, 1988.

24. *Le Monde*, August 3, 1988.

25. *Le Monde*, December 27, 1988.

26. *Le Monde*, January 29-30, 1989.

27. One should note that *indirect* talks did continue under the auspices of the United Nations; Pérez de Cuéllar toured the region in June 1989 and again in March 1990, as did his special emissary, Johannes Manz, in February 1990. In July 1990, the secretary-general brought Moroccan and Polisario delegates together in Geneva for what he expected to be *direct* talks; once again, however, Morocco refused to meet face-to-face with Polisario.

28. For an analysis of the October crisis and its aftermath, see my "Algeria after the Explosion", *Current History* 89, no. 546 (April 1990): 161-64, 180-82.

29. Cited in Grimaud, *La politique extériere*, 165.

30. Shortly, before the July 1990 meeting of the UMA presidential council, Algerian Foreign Minister Sid Ahmed Ghozali indicated that the main obstacle to full development of the union was the unresolved Saharan question. *Al Sharq al Awsat* (Washington), July 10, 1990.

9

The Proposed Referendum in the Western Sahara: Background, Developments, and Prospects

Anthony G. Pazzanita

INTRODUCTION

In surveying the one-hundred-year period since the colonization of the territory known as the Western Sahara by Spain and especially since its takeover in 1975 by the Kingdom of Morocco, one fact will, upon reflection, be readily apparent. The inhabitants of the Western Sahara, the Sahrawis, have been in the unenviable position of being subjected to forms of colonialism and outside domination that have proved to be far more difficult to overcome than the forms of colonialism and outside domination imposed on other territories in the region. Morocco has refused to genuinely consult with the indigenous populations and accept their wishes regarding their future, as required by the United Nations in its well-known General Assembly Resolution 1514.[1] Indeed, the Western Sahara conflict is one of the relatively few instances in which the termination of colonial rule has not been accomplished essentially peacefully or with at least some consultations of the affected peoples by the colonial power or other neutral parties. As stated by Thomas Franck, "In the entire four-decade history of the decolonization of a billion people, there were only three exceptions to this rule of decency, reason and good order: Western New Guinea and [East] Timor . . . and the Western Sahara--a Spanish colony which was occupied by Morocco against the clearly evident wishes of its inhabitants."[2]

Herein lies the nucleus of the Western Sahara dispute: the question whether the people who inhabit the entity known as the Western Sahara will be consulted in a meaningful and internationally acceptable manner concerning their wishes. Also at issue is the present situation in the territory, Moroccan occupation of portions of the Western Sahara and the displacement of most of its people to refugee camps in Algeria. Those same inhabitants have never been consulted about their desires at any time, either during the Spanish colonial period or after the occupation of the territory by Morocco.[3] This right to be consulted, known as the right to self-determination, is firmly embedded among the general principles of international law in the contemporary world community. It has long been the subject of numerous resolutions and commentary by the United Nations and others, both as a general proposition and with regard to the Western Sahara.

Throughout the time during which former colonies were emancipated from foreign control, the preferred method for the United Nations to ascertain the wishes of the indigenous population when those opinions were the subject of controversy has been by means of a referendum or plebiscite held under the auspices of the world body. This procedure is of special significance when it is realized that it has ample precedent. It has most often been used in situations approximating that in the Western Sahara: instances in which competing claims exist with regard to all or part of the territory in question. As Thomas Franck states, "To the very limited extent that a colony was permitted to become independent either by dividing into two states . . . or by joining another nation . . . it was only after the indigenous populations concerned had been consulted in a democratic electoral process under supervision or observation of the United Nations."[4] In the Western Sahara, the cause of the current conflict is a relatively uncomplicated one: Morocco claims the entire territory,[5] while the Polisario Front, a political and military group that purports to speak for the inhabitants of the territory, claims the right of self-determination. The proposals made by various parties over the years with a view to settling the conflict, such as those made by the United Nations (UN) or the Organization of African Unity (OAU), all have referendum proposals at their heart.[6]

This chapter describes and evaluates the proposals of the UN and the OAU for a plebiscite, and examines the attitudes of Morocco, the Polisario, and various other actors toward holding such a vote. It also examines some of the practical and political problems inherent in a Western Sahara referendum scenario.

WESTERN SAHARA: EARLIER EVENTS AND
REFERENDUM PROPOSALS

The concept of a referendum in the Western Sahara long predates the events of 1974-76, which culminated in the takeover of the territory by Morocco and Mauritania and the proclamation by Polisario of the Sahrawi Arab Democratic Republic (SADR). In fact, UN referendum proposals, and the reactions to them by Spain, Morocco, and Mauritania, date back to the Spanish colonial period.

Against the backdrop of the UN's Resolution 1514 (and Resolution 1541) concerning the rights of self-determination and of preserving the territorial integrity of newly independent, or still dependent, countries, the UN passed its first resolution on the Western Sahara on December 16, 1965.[7] The resolution was directed toward Spain, the colonial power, whose inflexible diplomatic stance and particular variety of colonialism had aroused much opposition in the world community. The inhabitants of the Spanish Sahara were without even the theoretical possibility of deciding their future status, since Spain did not consider the Sahara a colony, but rather an "overseas province."[8] The UN resolution called upon Spain to take "all necessary measures" for the liberation of the Western Sahara from colonial control. It also requested Spain to enter into negotiations relative to the future of the territory, but it did not specify with whom these negotiations were to be conducted, or what their substantive content was to be.[9]

Subsequent UN resolutions focused on the desirability of holding a referendum in the Western Sahara to ascertain the wishes of the population, in line with prior UN practice. The first such resolution, passed by the General Assembly in December 1966,[10] contained rather detailed recommendations for the modalities of such a vote. United Nations Resolution 2229 requested that Spain "permit the return of all refugees, ensure that only indigenous Western Saharans could vote, and provide all the necessary facilities for a United Nations mission so that it may be able to participate actively in the organization and holding of the referendum."[11]

The resolution also requested the UN secretary-general to send a visiting mission to the Western Sahara to, "determine the extent of United Nations participation in the preparation and supervision of the referendum."[12] Similar resolutions, with essentially the same language, passed the General Assembly every year between 1967 and 1973. The UN's approach to this problem was also adopted by the Organization of

African Unity.

Despite a notably rigid posture from the outset of this diplomatic activity, the Spanish government began to accept the principle of a referendum beginning in 1967.[13] However, it kept delaying the date it would be willing to hold the plebiscite, stating disingenuously that the indigenous population was not yet ready and willing to have one.[14] Given this, it seems correct to accept John Damis' statement that "in retrospect, Madrid's support for a referendum in the Sahara can be seen as a tactic for perpetuating Spain's presence in the territory."[15] The Spanish position also pointed to a very significant problem with UN sponsorship of referenda: sufficient determination by an occupying state could block any such vote, because its acquiescence would be required for the referendum to transpire. This situation recurred later in the conflict with regard to Morocco. Both Morocco and Mauritania, which had previously articulated claims to the territory, accepted the principle of a plebiscite in the Western Sahara, but proved notably unenthusiastic about assisting in its implementation. Benyamin Neuberger said, "Morocco insisted on self-determination by plebiscite . . . as long as it thought it might lead to reunification [with Morocco],"[16] and another writer opined that Mauritania's president, Mokhtar Ould Daddah, may have sincerely believed that a free vote by the Sahrawis would have resulted in the Western Sahara's joining Mauritania.[17] These sentiments, although advanced for reasons of self-interest, were not inherently implausible at the time, given the fact that there was (at least until 1970) no mass scale, organized pro-independence nationalist movement in the territory, a void filled by the formation of Polisario in 1973.

The results of this political and diplomatic activity during the 1965-73 period illustrate some aspects of the Western Sahara dispute that remain important today. Specifically, a situation existed in which all the parties to the controversy (Morocco, Mauritania, and Spain) supported the idea of a neutrally conducted and supervised referendum, but anticipated (sincerely or not) that the result would favor their own national interests. When they feared this would not happen, support for the vote waned. The net outcome was a period of stalemate.

THE CRITICAL PERIOD: 1973-76

The period of 1973 to 1976 is of great importance in any study of the Western Sahara conflict. During this roughly three-year time frame, the territory witnessed the departure of the European colonial power, the armed takeover of the Western Sahara by Morocco and Mauritania, and the forced dispossession of the Sahrawi people under extremely harsh conditions. These years also witnessed a major decision by the International Court of Justice that affirmed the right of the Sahrawis to self-determination.[18] In addition, Polisario was founded, and the SADR was proclaimed on February 27, 1976.[19]

The number and location of the people who call themselves Sahrawis for the purpose of voting in a referendum is a major point of contention between the parties to the conflict. In 1974, the Spanish authorities conducted a census in the Western Sahara, their last before leaving the country and the last by anyone that even purported to be accurate. The census showed a total of 73,497 Saharans living within the territory.[20] This was, however, almost certainly a substantial underestimate of the true number of Sahrawis living at the time. The Spanish authorities themselves noted the reluctance of many Sahrawis to cooperate, which was understandable in light of Spain's repressive policies. Perhaps most importantly, "The census also took no account . . . of the Sahrawis living beyond Western Sahara's frontiers."[21] A substantial number of Saharans had, over previous years, migrated to surrounding countries, either for economic reasons, by reason of a nomadic way of life, or to escape the brutal Spanish-French military campaigns against them in the late 1950s.[22] One estimate puts the actual number of Sahrawis at roughly 200,000 in 1974, with about one-half living within the Western Sahara, and the other half situated elsewhere.[23] Thus, the Spanish census was riddled with shortcomings.

By 1974, Spain faced increasing pressure from the international community to relinquish its hold over the Western Sahara, and also faced the nascent armed resistance mounted against it by the newly founded Polisario. This pressure was greatly increased by Portugal's April 1974 Revolution, which was accompanied by a weakening of its resolve to remain in its own "overseas provinces." Therefore, Spain notified the UN secretary-general that it would permit a referendum to be held in the Western Sahara during the first half of 1975, eight years after the UN had first asked that it do so.[24]

Too much should not be made of this policy shift. Aside from the obvious fact that, as such, the referendum would tend to exclude any Sahrawis living outside Western Sahara, at least by implication, Spain had strived in the preceding few years to cultivate a conservative and "collaborationist" Sahrawi leadership to preserve, in the event of independence, Spanish economic and political interests. Among the instruments for this task was the *Djemma*, an adaptation of a traditional Sahrawi ruling body that was, under Spanish colonial rule, consultative and advisory and without any real power. It was dominated by traditionalists.[25]   More telling, perhaps, was the Spanish-induced founding of the *Partido de la Union Nacional Saharoui* (PUNS) in November 1974. This group espoused more conservative social and political policies than Polisario, whose activities PUNS was designed to counter, and, like the *Djemma*, was composed of mainly traditional, ethnically based elements.[26]   In these circumstances, the prospective referendum was bound to have a different meaning for Spain than it did for the UN or for the African community. To Spain's credit, however, these efforts were intended to preserve the Western Sahara as a separate territorial and political unit (albeit under Madrid's influence) and to frustrate Moroccan and Mauritanian claims to the territory.[27]

Subsequent events were to vitiate all possibility of holding a free vote, despite the ruling of the International Court of Justice (ICJ) rejecting the claims of Morocco and Mauritainia and upholding the principle of self-determination. "Within hours of the publication of the ICJ's advisory opinion, King Hassan announced that 350,000 Moroccan volunteers would march, *Koran* in hand, across the Western Sahara border to assert Morocco's territorial claim."[28]   This so-called Green March took place on November 6, 1975. To coincide with this, Morocco embarked on a military buildup in and near the disputed territory and, along with Mauritania, negotiated the Madrid Accords with Spain, which provided for a Spanish withdrawal from Western Sahara by February 1976 and the partition of the land between Morocco and Mauritania.   No mention was made of a referendum or of any representation of the Sahrawis. Duly consummated, this agreement led to the invasion of the Western Sahara by the two claimant states and the uprooting of the Sahrawis and their arduous relocation to Algeria's Tindouf region.   Immediately after Spain's withdrawal, and with Morocco and Mauritania already making military inroads into the territory, Polisario, at a ceremony at Bir Lehlou within the Western Sahara, proclaimed the SADR on February 27, 1976.[29]   It intensified its military and political campaign to regain the territory from its new occupiers.

OAU INVOLVEMENT

Although the Organization of African Unity has been concerned with the question of the Western Sahara almost since the time of the Moroccan-Mauritanian occupation and the declaration of the SADR by Polisario, it is only comparatively recently that the OAU has been intimately involved in the conflict. This period, which culminated in the SADR's seating as a full member-state in the organization in 1984 and Morocco's consequent withdrawal, is also noteworthy for the disputes it caused within the OAU concerning the SADR's membership and for the occasions when the organization faced complete collapse.[30]

The OAU initiatives required some time to take shape. At first, the organization refrained from taking any substantive position on the conflict; it merely passed resolutions expressing the belief that the matter should best be discussed and resolved at an extraordinary OAU summit, which was never held.[31] However, in July 1978, the leader of Mauritania, Mokhtar Ould Daddah, was overthrown in a coup d'état mounted by the military establishment,[32] a move that reflected widespread discontent in Mauritania with the Sahara war. This was possibly the event that forced the OAU to take greater cognizance of the situation. At the same time, the SADR was constructing, in the Tindouf region of Algeria, governing structures and relief efforts for the Sahrawis, which exhibited, then as now, a high degree of cohesiveness and organization. And for its part, Morocco refused to endorse the idea of a referendum even in principle.[33]

The first attempt to resolve the dispute within a purely OAU framework was the so-called Wise Men's Committee (*Comité des Sages*) composed of the heads of state of Mali, Nigeria, Sudan, Tanzania, and Ivory Coast, whose leaders had considerable stature both in Africa and in international forums.[34] It was tasked with investigating the Western Sahara question by means of interviews, visits, and meetings. The committee began its work in late 1978 and continued into the first half of 1979, although rancor soon divided some of the group's members with the lines of division drawn between those who were disposed towards Morocco and those whose sympathies lay more with Polisario or its principal backer, Algeria.[35] Nevertheless, the Wise Men's Committee did adopt a resolution in July 1979 that marks the formal birth of the referendum idea within the OAU. After an "immediate and general" cease-fire in the territory between the two warring parties, the Sahrawi population would be given the opportunity to exercise its right to self-determination by choosing either independence for the Western Sahara or opting for the status quo, meaning integration with the Kingdom of Morocco; that is, a choice between the two entities (Morocco and the SADR), which had competing, mutually exclusive claims to the same land. The referendum would be held in cooperation with the United Nations, which, aside from being the party that first requested a plebiscite, had more expertise in the technical and administrative aspects of referenda.

Confronted with the results of this OAU foray into conflict resolution, Morocco's King Hassan II swung into action. "Feeling the diplomatic ground slipping from under his feet,"[36] he refused to attend the OAU summit in Liberia at which the Wise Men's proposals were accepted. He also ruled out talks between Morocco and Polisario and rejected a referendum in principle. Hassan's foreign minister, M'hamed Boucetta, stated that "The Sahara is and will remain Moroccan."[37] Polisario agreed to a referendum conducted under impartial supervision, but rejected a cease-fire unless a more flexible stance was adopted by Morocco.

For many African countries, Morocco's unyielding stance engendered frustration and suspicion of Hassan's motives, which increased after Morocco occupied and annexed Tiris el-Gharbia, the portion of the Western Sahara Mauritania had earlier occupied. This unilateral act, coupled with Morocco's plans to resettle Moroccan civilians in those parts of the territory it controlled, was construed as a gesture of defiance toward the OAU. This set of policies had the effect of increasing support for SADR and Polisario. More and more African states recognized the Saharan Republic, making full membership in the OAU a real possibility.

The Wise Men's Committee dissolved itself soon after it presented its report, although not before urging the formation of an ad hoc committee of five African heads of state to supervise a plebiscite in the Western Sahara in accordance with internationally accepted guidelines. This gave further impetus to the OAU's efforts, but strong African feelings could not affect Morocco's basic attitude or the situation in the territory itself; namely, the continued Moroccan military and administrative presence. What was to differentiate this phase from previous ones was Morocco's acceptance of the principle of a referendum in mid-1981.

The ostensible change in Morocco's stance was first enunciated at the 1981 OAU summit conference in Nairobi, Kenya. In a statement read by King Hassan to the assembly of heads of state and government, he said he would accept a "controlled referendum whose modalities should give justice simultaneously to the objectives of the ad hoc committee, that is to say the committee of wise men, and to Morocco's conviction regarding the legitimacy of its rights."[38]   Having finally endorsed the principle of a free vote in the Western Sahara, some Africans saw "magnanimity" in the king's offer.   But Polisario was intensely skeptical, seeing in the proposal a ploy by Morocco to perpetuate its hold on the territory and to forestall the SADR from being admitted as an OAU member-state.[39]   Indeed, Morocco did state that the referendum, if held, would be one of "confirmation" of Moroccan sovereignty, that no option to become independent would be given to the Sahrawis, and that the refugees in the Tindouf region would be only reluctantly allowed to return and then only if they did not, either alone or in concert with Polisario, press for independence.[40]   King Hassan also refused to consider Polisario as an independent actor in the dispute, saying that "for me, the parties interested in the Saharan affair remain Morocco, Algeria, and Mauritania, to the exclusion of the Polisario, which has never existed for the African community."[41]

Despite King Hassan's possible ulterior motives, the OAU decided to give this "liberalized" policy time to be operationalized. It (1) put off consideration of OAU membership for the SADR for a second year, and (2) mandated that "Implementation Committee" made up of certain African states ensure that a free and fair plebiscite take.[42]   The report of the committee contained detailed guidelines for an impartial vote in the territory.   In addition, its contents differed from Morocco's referendum concept as elucidated during King Hassan's Nairobi overtures.   For example, voters would be offered independence as an option.   An interim administration would "work in collaboration" with the governing structures of Morocco and the Polisario for the duration of the voting process, rather than insist on Morocco's total withdrawal of its military and administrative presence from the territory, a step always demanded by Polisario.   The troops of the parties to the conflict (not named, to avoid antagonizing Morocco) would, however, be confined to their bases during the time of the referendum.[43]

The Implementation Committee maintained a high profile and level of work, issuing two more decisions on the proposed plebiscite and its modalities in February 1982 after another meeting in Nairobi.   Both documents outlined conditions and methods for the referendum in increasing detail, but did not explicitly name the Kingdom of Morocco and Polisario as parties to the conflict.[44]   As before, the pitfall preventing progress toward a referendum was Morocco's refusal to talk to Polisario, which it alleged was controlled by Algeria and was thus not an independent actor.[45]

Henceforth, questions before the OAU regarding the Western Sahara were largely ones of procedure. The complex political maneuvering that took place within the organization during this period is beyond the scope of this chapter, but it should suffice to say that the activities of the Implementation Committee to facilitate negotiations and free voting in the Western Sahara came into conflict with the increasing number of states that recognized the SADR and wanted it seated as a member of the OAU. Ranged on the other side were those African states that were more attuned to Moroccan concerns or that desired more compromises. These tensions were brought into high relief when, in February 1982, Edem Kodjo, then secretary-general of the OAU, formally admitted the SADR as a full member of the organization, pursuant to the notification provisions of Article 28 of the OAU Charter.[46] This action split the OAU roughly into pro-SADR and pro-Moroccan camps and (along with a dispute about the situation in Chad) prevented the 1982 summit conference from being held because over fifteen African states boycotted the organization in protest.[47] Morocco stated that if the SADR were seated as a member-state, it would withdraw completely from the OAU, a threat later carried out. For its part, Polisario "voluntarily and temporarily" absented itself from OAU proceedings, allowing the 1983 summit in Addis Ababa, Ethiopia, to take place. This helped stave off the organization's total breakdown.[48]

Morocco's intransigence may have proved to be its undoing, however. The issue of SADR membership could not be delayed indefinitely; to do so would gravely jeopardize the OAU. Many more African states grew disenchanted with King Hassan's refusal to negotiate with Polisario and end a struggle that hindered the ability of the organization to address Africa's other extremely serious problems. Also not overlooked was the continued Moroccan extension of the defensive earthen barriers or walls in the territory: at about this time, Morocco began extending them to Guelta Zemmour in the east-central sector of the Sahara, strongly indicating that King Hassan meant to keep the territory permanently. So pressure on the OAU grew to explicitly name the parties to the conflict and finalize the membership issue, and so defend the organization's most cherished principles: territorial integrity (even if this meant accepting artificially drawn borders), self-determination, and the proposition that disputes in Africa should be addressed peacefully.[49]

The year 1984 was to be a pivotal one in the history of the Western Sahara conflict. Frustrated by Morocco's refusal to genuinely cooperate with the Implementation Committee, and building upon the pathbreaking Resolution 104, passed in Addis Ababa in 1983,[50] other members of the OAU brought matters to a head. Other states refused to join Morocco in another protest boycott of the OAU, so the organization was able to hold its twentieth annual summit conference, again in Addis Ababa, on November 12-15, 1984, at which the SADR finally took its seat as a full OAU member without substantial opposition.[51] The organization has subsequently indicated that it considers the membership issue closed.

This undoubted diplomatic victory for Polisario, however, came at a rather heavy price. Morocco made good on its earlier threat to quit the OAU.[52] Thus, the organization was quickly deprived of the presence of one of the parties to the dispute, as well as losing a member-state that was important in its own right. Nigeria, showing its frustration with the lack of Implementation Committee progress, recognized the SADR just before the 1984 Addis Ababa summit,[53] and concurrently withdrew from the committee as an added sign of its impatience, rendering it moribund. With this, the most active period of OAU involvement in the Western Sahara conflict came to an end. If nothing else, this phase brought into sharp focus the varying interpretations placed upon the organization's referendum work, with the international community supporting the neutral administration of such a vote, while Morocco, from the evidence, leaned towards the plebiscite idea only if it could somehow be made to legitimize its presence in the Western Sahara.

Although OAU involvement in the Western Sahara conflict diminished after 1984, the years from 1985 witnessed a revitalized United Nations role in attempting to find a solution to the Sahara imbroglio, building upon the OAU's referendum plans but also facing some of the same problems that bedeviled that organization's efforts in the early 1980s.

EVENTS TO 1988 AND ANALYSIS OF THE REFERENDUM PROPOSALS

The first half of 1985 passed without appreciable diplomatic activity at any level relative to the Western Sahara dispute, but activity began to revive in September 1985 when, at the foreign ministers' conference of the Non-Aligned Movement held in Launda, Angola, a resolution was adopted supporting the OAU's stance on the Western Sahara and endorsing the language of Resolution 104, which called for direct talks between Morocco and Polisario, and which explicitly named both of them as parties to the dispute. This underscored Morocco's isolation on this issue, since it remained adamant in its refusal to speak with representatives of the Sahrawi group. Meanwhile, at the July 1985 OAU summit, SADR's president Mohamed Abdelaziz, was elected one of the organization's vice presidents.[54]

Confronted with this state of affairs, King Hassan may have come to see the United Nations, with its lower level of activity on the Western Sahara since the events of 1975-76, as his last hope to recoup some of his lost prestige and credibility. Morocco had apparently urged the UN to consider sidestepping Resolution 104 and adopting a referendum plan that would not require direct negotiations with Polisario.[55] This effort failed. In December 1985, the UN General Assembly adopted Resolution 40/50, which put the world body firmly on record as endorsing the OAU approach of direct negotiations, a cease-fire and interim administration in the Western Sahara, and a referendum in the territory "without any administrative or military constraints."[56] Morocco, by now seeing its strategy in disarray, withdrew from the UN's Fourth (Decolonization) Committee. Polisario characterized all of this Moroccan activity as an attempt to circumvent the will of the OAU through the use of the United Nations.[57] But if this was Morocco's intention, it backfired, for the subsequent period was marked by a higher level of UN activity and by an even greater degree of congruence between its approach and that of the OAU.

The United Nations Secretary-General, Javier Pérez de Cuéllar, embarked in late 1985 and early 1986 on a serious effort to reconcile the parties by means of visits to northwest Africa and by indirect discussions. This was accomplished by means of "proximity talks," in which representatives of Polisario and Morocco presented their respective views to the secretary-general, who then relayed them to the other party; this spared them the necessity of meeting face-to-face.[58] It was hoped that these indirect negotiations would evolve into direct talks and lead to a cease-fire and preparations for a plebiscite.

Although the sincerity of the UN's intentions could not be doubted, it took only a short time for this "good offices" endeavor to falter because of Morocco's insistent refusal to meet directly with Polisario. King Hassan, in a letter sent to Pérez de Cuéllar at about the time of the proximity talks, reaffirmed his country's unyielding stand on the Sahara issue. Also, Polisario reiterated its demand for a total administrative and military pullout by Morocco prior to any referendum. The talks progressed no further.[59] A meeting of King Hassan and other Moroccan officials with Pérez de Cuéllar during his visit to Rabat in July 1986 also accomplished nothing.

In spite of these setbacks, sentiment within the UN was simply too strong to abandon these latest "confidence-building" measures. As a result, the UN's efforts entered their latest phase, which began on October 31, 1986, when the General Assembly passed Resolution 41/16,[60] which, aside from reendorsing the referendum concept, asked the secretary-general to continue "to follow the situation in Western Sahara closely with a view to the implementation of the present resolution."[61] Later, it was decided jointly by the UN and the OAU to send a "technical mission" to all the states and territories of the region in the latter part of 1987 to assist in preparing for a cease-fire and plebiscite. Morocco accepted the presence of the mission, having been assured that it would engage in no political activity.[62] President Abdelaziz was skeptical due to Morocco's continued rigid stance on direct negotiations, and was tiring of the seemingly endless rounds of diplomatic activity with no substantive results for the Sahrawis. Abdelaziz stressed the need for the withdrawal of the Moroccan presence in Western Sahara "as a precondition to the organization of the referendum."[63]

After making its preparations, the UN-OAU technical mission visited the region during the months of November and December 1987, meeting with many individuals and gathering much information. According to press reports, the mission dwelt upon the military and political situation in the territory and modalities for the proposed referendum.[64] To facilitate its safety and activities, Polisario unilaterally declared a temporary truce in the territory through early January 1988 as a gesture of good faith.[65] The technical mission's final report was not made public.

While visits of outside actors to the territory and the compilation of military and other information regarding the conflict are of considerable importance, the continued maintenance of the political and military status quo in the territory by Morocco means that the most that could reasonably be expected of the technical mission was that it would generate more publicity about the dispute and keep Western Sahara in full view of the international community as an unresolved self-determination issue. It is thus helpful at this point to set forth and analyze some of the features of the proposed plebiscite, and to examine some of the problems that may present themselves in its execution.

THE FACTORS IN HOLDING A REFERENDUM

The threshold question of a general and complete cease-fire in Western Sahara prior to and during the referendum should be addressed first. While the actual institution and maintenance of a cessation of hostilities at the time of the plebiscite are contingent upon the so-far nonexistent cooperation--or at least tacit agreement--of Morocco and Polisario, this phase presents difficulties in that it will require resources, both human and material, to supervise the cease-fire and to prevent and mitigate violations by any of the parties. This will be in addition to the personnel and logistical support needed to implement and oversee other aspects of the referendum. As John Damis has commented, "From whatever source and however large the peace-keeping force, the Western Sahara's vast territory and long, unguarded frontiers present enormous logistical problems."[66]

Although largely correct in an overall sense, this assessment overlooks the fact that only a portion of the Western Sahara will be critically situated with regard to the cease-fire and the referendum process. All or most of the Sahrawi voters will probably be located in or near the population centers of the territory, which are rather few in number; many remote parts of the Western Sahara will probably not require a level of policing necessary to prevent harm to the Sahrawis. An astute combination of strategically placed human observers, technical monitoring devices under international control, and the confinement of the armed forces of both sides to areas remote from the voting, will help ensure that cease-fire violations, if they do transpire, will be quickly and easily detected and exposed before any part of the population of the territory is put at risk.

Given this imperative, the supervision of a cease-fire in the Western Sahara during the period in question will substantially tax the resources of the United Nations and the OAU. The best solution to this problem would be to draw the monitoring force and observers from both organizations. Any approach falling short of this will increase the chances that the interim administration will be overstrained or disrupted, giving either party to the conflict reason to disown the results of the referendum. John Damis observes that "if the OAU proves incapable of providing an adequate peace-keeping force, it at least has the option of requesting assistance from the United Nations, which has both more experience in peace-keeping operations and greater resources at its disposal."[67] The possibility that he implies in this statement--that the UN would have to intercede at some point during the referendum process--should be obviated by the effective involvement of both the UN and the OAU from the outset. In addition to a larger pool of personnel and equipment that would result, this arrangement is mandated by the shared goals, common efforts, and close collaboration between the two international organizations in this affair. A joint venture will inspire more confidence in the overall integrity of the plebiscite, as well as being legally, politically, and logistically sound.

As for the peace-keeping forces themselves, they should be composed of neutral parties and be stationed in places where the activities of the protagonists can be observed: in and around population centers, border areas, and garrisons. They should, as the OAU and UN plans provide, monitor the confinement to bases of the armed forces of both disputants and ascertain the disposition and location of their weapons.   This will require a large contingent of personnel and equipment, but with extensive and hopefully well-planned joint support from the UN and the OAU, the logistical and "confidence-building" situation, while difficult, falls considerably short of "enormous," much less insuperable.

The issue of interim administration of the Western Sahara during the relevant period, while presenting its own significant logistical problems (party cured by a joint UN-OAU presence), raises other areas of contention.   A prime question will be the disposition of the administrative infrastructure of Morocco and Polisario in the territory during the voting. As stressed previously, Polisario insists upon the pullout by Morocco of its military and administrative presence prior to the plebiscite, a position rejected by Morocco.   Given these firm positions, it is correct to say that any progress in this area is contingent upon the creation of a climate of compromise between the two parties, fostering a middle ground that will satisfy neither side completely but that will ensure the integrity of the voting. It will also guarantee that neither will be able to intimidate or coerce the Sahrawi voters. If the final agreement among the parties does not accomplish this, the referendum process may either break down totally, or its result will be open to substantial question. In either case, the whole endeavor would end in failure.

The demand by Polisario for a full Moroccan withdrawal from the territory is understandable given the nature of Morocco's entrance into the Western Sahara in 1975-76 and its conduct in the territory since that time. However, it is so opposed to Morocco's stance that it could be regarded as an initial negotiating position upon which some compromises can be made when (and if) Morocco finally resumes direct talks with Polisario and is willing to alter its own rigid positions. Whatever the outcome, it is imperative that any interim agreement leave as little room as possible for the intimidation of voters from any quarter or any damaging actions against the Sahrawis, which would at the very least cast aspersion upon the sincerity of the parties and guarantee that a disappointing result will ensue.

A fair arrangement could be along the following lines. A residuum of Moroccan and Polisario administrative presence could remain active in the territory during the referendum. The remainder would be withdrawn or confined to well-monitored areas. The administration left in place would work in concert with the UN-OAU interim regime, and in so doing would lessen the logistical burden on both organizations by performing certain ministerial functions under supervision. This is clearly contemplated by the OAU as reflected by the work of its Implementation Committee. The actual balloting in the referendum, it goes without saying, must be totally in the hands of the neutral interim administration, as must the surveillance of the various military forces.

Realistically, the mutual antagonism that exists between the two parties to the conflict will still necessitate a large number of personnel and high quality of support so as to be able to generate enough "clout" (as Damis terms it)[68] to ensure a good referendum environment. This will, no doubt, stretch the resources of the United Nations and the OAU, but their combined efforts should be adequate if the political will is found. A serious endeavor will also help neutralize any Moroccan tendency to cooperate with the interim administration "only to the degree that [its] work serves Moroccan interests,"[69] and enhance some of the political and logistical advantages that could flow from maintaining Morocco's presence in a small, supervised degree.

The population count in the Western Sahara and the determination of who should be allowed to vote in a plebiscite may present major problems, despite significant progress made so far in outlining the procedures to be used and in preliminary work already done to determine the number of Sahrawis. As discussed earlier, the number of persons who are Sahrawis and who, by definition, should be permitted to vote in a referendum is the subject of much dispute. In 1974, the last Spanish census showed 73,497 Sahrawis in the then-Spanish colony, but this enumeration was fraught with many shortcomings.[70] Therefore, the actual number of Sahrawis either inside or outside the Western Sahara at the present time is much greater than the above figure would suggest. For example, it is estimated that about 165,000 Sahrawis reside in refugee camps in Algeria administered by Polisario.[71] If we assume that many more live (either willingly or unwillingly) in southern Morocco, in Moroccan-held zones of the Sahara, or in other countries, the Spanish census figure becomes less and less credible. It is, however, a good starting point: it is the best effort made to date to count the people of the territory in anything approaching a systematic, disinterested manner. However, due to the dispersal of the population and Polisario's long-standing policy to encourage a high birth rate among Sahrawis to ensure "national survival,"[72] other information will have to be used, perhaps from the United Nations high commissioner for refugees, as envisage by the OAU. In sum, uncritical primary reliance upon the 1974 Spanish census, hinted as being sufficient by Polisario, and its recently expressed belief that a population count would "post no problems"[73] should give rise to some skepticism.

Unfortunately, the foregoing situation will make the task of interim government all the more difficult and longer in duration. A detailed and comprehensive census of the Western Sahara's inhabitants will entail additional manpower, resources, and acumen on the part of those conducting the plebiscite. Add to this the many definitional problems to be faced in terms of voter eligibility, and the matter becomes formidable and at the same time crucial, because it is of great importance in generating acceptance of the referendum's result, whatever it may be. The following assessment by Damis is basically correct, even if somewhat pessimistic:

> The importance of the voter list will guarantee considerable haggling over the criteria used, and the scrutiny applied, in determining the ideally [sic] and potential eligibility of the many thousands of Sahrawis who present themselves. It will require [the] fairness of Solomon on the part of the interim administration. Compromises in this crucial activity will

generate cries of foul from one side or the other--and provide
a basis for rejecting the results of the referendum."[74]

If the adverse circumstances described above actually unfold, it will
prove destructive to any atmosphere of good will that may have been
created between the disputants. It may--if numerous and disinterested
referendum personnel do not exert a firm influence--lead to a breakdown
of the whole voting arrangement, leaving the conflict no closer to
settlement. Without doubt, this aspect of the prospective plebiscite is the
one most likely to generate a good deal of friction.

The remaining points contained in the various referendum blueprints
(for example, those dealing with the restriction of troops to bases, the
exact regulatory structure, the security of the actual polling process, the
precise method of balloting, and other related matters) are clearly
secondary in importance given the above concerns. One basic fact,
however, impacts upon all of those measures: a satisfactory and credible
interim regime in the Western Sahara, enjoying the trust and confidence
of all, can only be emplaced if and when direct negotiations between
Morocco and Polisario are resumed and a climate of safety in the
territory is created. This climate is essential in order for the goals of the
referendum plans of the United Nations and the OAU to be met. Once
this requirement is satisfied, the effort will still falter if comity is not
sustained and cooperation with the interim administration is not
forthcoming. Whatever the agreed-upon disposition of the armed forces
and administration of Morocco and Polisario, it is imperative to ensure--
over the entire period relevant to the vote--that all the troops and
weapons of the combatants be located in areas remote from any balloting
and be effectively supervised by the assigned peace-keeping force.
Polisario has offered, in the event that Morocco withdraws from the
Western Sahara, to disarm its fighters and transport its weapons to a
more distant country such as Senegal, under the supervision of neutral
observers.[75] The goal of all these measure will be to place the
administrative, military, and other structures of Morocco and the
Saharan Arab Democratic Republic in abeyance during the interim
period.

This discussion and analysis of these issues, even in outline, should
illustrate the absolute necessity of devoting sufficient resources,
personnel, and logistic support to any plebiscite. It is necessary to
ensure, by investments in people and equipment, that the power in
administrative control of a given territory does not exercise undue

influence over the referendum process. This could well happen in the Western Sahara if precautions are not taken. No internationally organized sponsorship of a process to facilitate genuine self-determination should be allowed, by accident or design, to become a means by which a state attempts to legitimize its continued military and administrative presence in a territory; and in so doing attempt to place a veneer of legality upon activities that clearly are not countenanced by international law and practice.

What are the prospects for a turn of events that would lead to the establishment of an interim regime and the holding of a referendum? A major theme that emerges from any examination of the Western Sahara problem is that Morocco, by its extensive military and administrative presence in the territory, can effectively block or influence any substantive moves toward the emplacement of an interim administration to conduct a free vote. The enforcement powers of contemporary international law and international organizations are simply not strong enough to overcome this. Regrettably, Moroccan control of the territory, coupled with its refusal to relinquish its hold even temporarily, assumes decisive importance, making a referendum unlikely in the immediate future. And another fact is still more chastening: this situation will persist unless and until Morocco's "no recognition" policy toward the Polisario Front is modified. If and when this occurs, it will remove the largest barrier to the settlement of the dispute, and will facilitate the activation of a process of international conflict resolution so that, at long last, an indigenous people can realize their aspirations.

1990 AND BEYOND

Since the foregoing sections were written, much diplomatic activity regarding the Western Sahara conflict has taken place. The final outcome of this flurry of activity is unclear, for although the pace of settlement efforts by the parties to the dispute and the United Nations has recently increased, many of the same problems and obstacles that were outlined are still present. Namely, there is continuing controversy over direct negotiations between Morocco and Polisario, creation of a climate of security in the Western Sahara to facilitate a fair referendum, questions about the proposed interim administration, and actual referendum modalities. And as if this were not enough to fully engage the attention of observers of the Sahara conflict, there remains to be considered the potential effects of the reordering of the North African political landscape that began to take place in mid-1988.

On May 16, 1988, culminating a process of gradual improvement in relations in prior years, Algeria and Morocco announced that they were resuming diplomatic relations, twelve years after those ties were severed by Morocco following Algerian recognition of the SADR.[76] In the announcement of renewed relations, Algeria and Morocco pledged to facilitate a "self-determination referendum [for the Western Sahara] held with the greatest sincerity and without any constraint."[77] Officially, at least, the desire to implement the expressed will of the United Nations and the Organization of African Unity regarding the proposed plebiscite was guiding the opinions and policies of Algeria and--henceforth--Morocco. But beyond the words of the respective actors themselves, the fact that the two states most intimately involved in the Sahara conflict had chosen to improve the climate between them was cause for considerable commentary, and it focused, not unnaturally, upon the implications of this new state of affairs for the other party to the dispute, the Polisario Front.

Simply stated, some observers could not help but see this restructuring of interstate Maghrebi affairs as a loss, and a rather serious one at that, for Polisario and its efforts to achieve full control over the Western Sahara. Given the fact that Algeria has been Polisario's most important supporter on a consistent basis, the argument went, any improvement in relations with Morocco, the occupier of the Sahara and Polisario's opponent, could portend a softening or even withdrawal of its backing for the Sahrawi organization and the SADR, forcing it to abandon its goal of a fully independent Western Saharan republic.[78] Seemingly implicit in this view was a theory that Morocco and Algeria had struck some sort of behind-the-scenes agreement (tacit or otherwise) at Polisario's expense, and agreed to submerge the dispute. Generally speaking, those who subscribed to this view most strongly were inclined to overlook or downplay the independent role of Polisario in the conflict,[79] while those who were disposed to view the Sahara dispute as one between Morocco on the one hand and Polisario as representatives of the Sahrawis on the other, were more likely to view the renewal of Algerian-Moroccan relations in a more sanguine manner, stressing the new possibilities for a settlement of the conflict, to the inclusion of Polisario, which they believed could result.[80]

Another factor that loomed large in the calculations of the observers of the Maghreb and the Western Sahara was the perceived need to unify the positions of Arab states to give an added measure of support to the Palestinian uprising taking place in the West Bank and Gaza, territories under Israeli occupation since June 1967. An Arab League summit meeting was due to begin in Algiers on June 7, 1988, with the Palestinian issue at the top of the agenda. In these circumstances, it was considered desirable that as many Arab countries as possible should be represented at the Algiers conference. King Hassan reportedly expressed reluctance to attend the summit unless he enjoyed diplomatic relations with Algeria, the venue for the meeting.[81] This gave further impetus to the Moroccan-Algerian rapprochement and made it possible for the summit to go forward as scheduled. Despite some concerns that the interests of the Sahrawis were being "sacrificed on the altar of Arab unity,"[82] and the question posed by one commentator as to whether the "Sahrawis [were] not being sold out in order to win King Hassan's presence at the forthcoming Arab summit,"[83] it is likely that factors not related to the Western Sahara formed a considerable backdrop to the decision by Morocco and Algeria to reestablish diplomatic ties.

The reaction of Polisario to the renewed ties between Morocco and Algeria was the subject of much commentary. According to some reports, the Sahrawi liberation group was greatly concerned and even angry at this turn of events, seeing a possible diminution of support from Algeria.[84] Several days later, however, during the period when the fifteenth anniversary of Polisario's founding was being observed, Polisario officials were making statements that reflected a very cautious optimism about this new set of events.[85] Although the analysis they undertook is not wanting in cogency, it is probably true that the news of restored diplomatic relations was greeted with at least some consternation by Polisario; it is simply unrealistic to suppose that they had not appreciated the possible negative consequences of such a move in the same manner as their supporters and detractors alike.

In rejoinder, Polisario could point to many significant and concrete factors and achievements that indicated a certain solidity in the SADR's position, as well as offer alternative views of Algeria's actions. In the first place, much of this diplomatic activity took place, at least rhetorically, with a view toward using the new situation of amity to solve the Sahara problem within the UN-OAU context. This, of course, dictates that a referendum in the Western Sahara take place "without any administrative or military constraints."[86] Therefore, there was at least the hope on Polisario's part that the restored diplomatic relations could improve the Maghrebi political climate to a degree sufficient to facilitate a settlement taking the Sahrawis fully into account.[87]

Continuing in this vein, Bachir Mustapha Sayed, a high-level Polisario official, pointed out that it was Morocco that had asked Algeria for a resumption of diplomatic relations, hence indicating a possible relaxation of hitherto intransigent Moroccan attitudes regarding negotiations with Polisario, troop withdrawal, plebiscite modalities, and the like.[88] Moreover, Sayed continued, Morocco had accepted relations with a state (Algeria) that not only formally recognized the Saharan Arab Democratic Republic, but had been its most consistent backer for the better part of thirteen years. By extension, Morocco implicitly recognized that the whole Sahara question was one between Morocco and the Sahrawis, thus depriving the kingdom of its oft-employed argument that Polisario's fighters were nothing more than Algerian "mercenaries" and that Polisario was not an independent actor in the dispute. But although the Sahrawis publicly stressed these points, Sayed did state that Polisario was "not more optimistic than necessary," implying an understandable uncertainty about the changed circumstances and Morocco's intentions.[89]

Furthermore, the Sahrawis could also point to their secure diplomatic position in Africa and worldwide. Algerian recognition of the SADR was not an issue, nor was its full membership status at the OAU and its strong standing in the Non-Aligned Movement. The SADR could take comfort in the undeniable fact that seventy-one countries then recognized it diplomatically. In early 1988, the Sahrawi state won recognition from Albania and Barbados, two states with such radically dissimilar political outlooks as to illustrate, if nothing else, the SADR's continued appeal to a world community sensitized to issues of decolonization. So it was not without reason that one commentator stated that "the Sahrawis certainly have grounds for some feeling of security at the diplomatic level."[90]

Lastly, it is almost certain that Algeria's pragmatic self-interest would be harmed if it ceased its support for Polisario. It is believed by many that were Algeria to withdraw its material and diplomatic support for Polisario, it would suffer a massive loss of respect and credibility in Africa and in the rest of the developing world. This possibility may have told heavily against Algeria taking this step, however much it might desire an end to the conflict. Thus, even viewed from a strictly cost-benefit standpoint, the cost to Algeria would outweigh any real benefits it might receive in return. And there was the strong possibility that Algeria was merely seeking new and different means to achieve a

Western Sahara settlement, and do so in a "Greater Maghreb" regional setting, a goal of Algerian diplomacy since at least 1983.[91] For its part, the Algerian government stoutly denied that any diminution of support for the Sahrawi cause was in the offing.

For better or worse, the renewal of Moroccan-Algerian ties is now an accomplished fact. Despite the perception by some that Polisario's explanations and justifications of this step had the appearance of putting the best face possible on an uncertain and still-developing situation, it was one over which the Sahrawi group may have had only a limited degree of control. However, Polisario could still look to its continued firm base of support in the world community, no falling off of Algerian backing in the months following the rapprochement with Morocco, and the prospect, later partly borne out, that the new atmosphere would produce some movement in the endeavors to bring about a cease-fire, interim government, and impartial plebiscite in the Western Sahara. Since the newest peace proposal for the conflict evolves from previous activity detailed earlier in this chapter, and poses some of the same political and practical problems that have troubled prior referendum plans, this plan, and its backdrop, presented to the parties to the dispute in August 1988, deserves significant attention.

Perhaps partly as a result of the improved interstate North African climate, the United Nations' efforts to resolve the Western Sahara question via a referendum gathered momentum during the summer and early fall of 1988. After much preparation, and no doubt drawing upon the findings of the 1987 Technical Mission, UN Secretary-General Pérez de Cuéllar presented to the representatives of Morocco and Polisario a comprehensive settlement proposal on August 11, 1988, in New York.[92] He requested the two parties to respond to the proposal by September 1.[93] Although it was not then made public, it was known that the plan parallelled the previous OAU and UN blueprints in that it provided for a cease-fire, an interim administration of the disputed territory, and a plebiscite under neutral auspices. Reportedly, about 2,000 United Nations personnel would oversee the process, including military, administrative, and referendum-related tasks.[94] In what was, prematurely, hailed as a major breakthrough in the long conflict, both Polisario and Morocco accepted the UN plan in principle on August 30, 1988, opening the door, seemingly, for the imminent implementation of the proposal and the holding of the referendum. However, no timetable with specific dates was written into the text of the peace plan.[95]

One may reasonably ask why the two parties felt constrained to accept the proposal, especially when they had been in bitter conflict for thirteen years and had not publicly altered their basic policy stances in the period leading up to the promulgation of the peace proposal. Specifically, Morocco was still reluctant to consider Polisario an autonomous party to the Sahara dispute, and did not relent from its rigid position against any military or administrative withdrawal from the Western Sahara to aid the process of self-determination. Also, some described as "unimaginable" the possibility that King Hassan would ever withdraw voluntarily from the territory after having expended huge sums in it and having largely staked the prestige of his throne upon the takeover of the "Saharan provinces."[96]

For its part, Polisario still held to a position that demanded a Moroccan withdrawal from the Western Sahara prior to any plebiscite, and also still insisted on direct negotiations between itself and Morocco. It also at no time foreswore the military option against the thinly spread Moroccan armed forces along the "defensive walls" in the territory. In addition, basic differences about the modalities of the prospective referendum continued to divide the parties. For example, Morocco generally adopted a narrower interpretation of voter eligibility than did the Sahrawi organization, which maintained that large numbers of Moroccan settlers had been imported into the Western Sahara in the years since the conflict began. Polisario also wanted the 165,000 or so inhabitants of its refugee camps in the Tindouf region to be counted as Sahrawis for referendum purposes.[97] Given these continued and sharp differences, the key to explaining this about-face lies in the context of the objective positions of Polisario and Morocco and in the manner in which the wider North African and worldwide scene had an impact.

On the Moroccan side, the situation both in the territory itself and in the diplomatic arena could not be called propitious. With up to 150,000 troops manning garrisons in the Western Sahara and constantly subject to surprise attacks by the Sahrawi People's Liberation Army, the war was imposing staggering costs upon the country, with estimates of the cost of the occupation ranging from $1 million to $4 million per day. It was thus to be expected that some observers opined that "the burden was becoming too great for the kingdom."[98] Consequently, some incentive was present for King Hassan to try to find a way out of this debilitating situation. In addition, the series of "defensive walls" in the territory, also constructed at hugh cost, had kept Polisario out of much of the Sahara but had somewhat increased Morocco's exposure to attack.

Politically, the situation for Morocco was stark. Seventy-one countries then recognized the SADR, no nation in the world recognized Morocco's claim to Western Sahara, and the United Nations was showing every sign of formally adopting the OAU-generated peace and referendum blueprints for a resolution of the dispute. And although Morocco and Algeria (Polisario's main benefactor) had resumed diplomatic relations after a twelve-year freeze, the Algerian leadership strongly denied that this meant a change in its overall policy, a denial made more credible with each passing month. Simultaneously, renewed relations with Algeria meant that Morocco's dismissal of Polisario as an Algerian surrogate, never convincing, was now all the more difficult to sustain.

Polisario itself had grounds for feeling relatively secure on the military and diplomatic levels, yet incentives to seriously pursue a negotiated settlement were also present. Although outnumbered at least ten-to-one by the Moroccan armed forces, Polisario had battled the kingdom to a stalemate, with Moroccan soldiers in exposed static positions and indisposed to expand their operations beyond the walls. At the same time, however, the sheer weight of numbers on the Moroccan side, coupled with the barriers, had made all talk of purely military solution by Polisario look unrealistic.[99] Furthermore, the war had failed to either unseat King Hassan or cause the collapse of the Royal Moroccan Armed Forces (FAR) in the Western Sahara as a result of the stresses of the occupation. Lastly, Morocco still enjoyed considerable diplomatic and material support from certain Western and Arab countries in spite of its decided diplomatic isolation.

The improved climate of cooperation in Maghrebi state relations almost certainly played a role in producing the newest spate of diplomatic activity relative to the Western Sahara. One consequence of this, very significantly, was the commencement of direct discussions between Polisario and Morocco.[100] Beginning with secret contacts in Saudi Arabia in mid-1988, and blossoming into a full-scale meeting between King Hassan and three senior Polisario officials in Marrakech, Morocco, in early January 1989, the two parties may now enjoy somewhat better levels of communication than has hitherto been the case. If these meetings continue, it would represent a victory for Polisario, which has consistently called for direct talks with Morocco, and a concession by Morocco, which has always refused to speak with the Sahrawi organization. Although these have not been, to date, the sustained and substantive negotiations that Polisario desires, the

Marrakech meeting is cause for at least some optimism for eventual peace in the Western Sahara. In sum, it is probably not far from the truth to state that neither Polisario nor Morocco could have afforded to give a wholly negative or intransigent response to the undeniably constructive proposal developed and presented by the United Nations, especially when the plan had the prestige of the secretary-general behind it.

This discussion of these political developments is an appropriate prelude to a discussion of the actual modalities for the cessation of hostilities, transitional government, and referendum that form the core of the UN plan. These are of great significance, since it is clear that if the blueprint is to have any chance of success in the territory itself, it must be well-conceived, properly executed, and designed to generate confidence on the part of both disputants. If not, all of the previous diplomatic activity and arduous mediatory efforts will go for naught.

The threshold issue of direct negotiations among the parties to the Western Sahara conflict can be considered preparatory to creating a less hostile climate in the territory and facilitating the resolution of outstanding issues. Not least of these issues is the consummation of an understanding between Morocco and Polisario regarding the behavior of the parties during the period of interim administration and the plebiscite, as well as after the results of the referendum are announced. Another major question to be covered, presumably, will be provisions for the exchange of prisoners of war captured by both sides since the conflict began.

Direct contacts between Polisario and Morocco involving high-level officials on both sides have transpired.[101] If these talks continue productively, a major impasse in the dispute would be at least partly broken, and would mean that Morocco had abandoned one of its most stubborn positions. However, these meetings must be in the nature of comprehensive negotiations covering all issues between the parties if the peace plan is to move forward to its implementation.

Several details have emerged on the withdrawal of the combatants' armed forces in conjunction with the installation of an interim regime to conduct a referendum. According to the plan, Morocco would, subject to verification, withdraw approximately two-thirds of its roughly 150,000 troops from the Western Sahara, at which time Polisario would confine its soldiers to internationally supervised encampments.[102] In the second stage of this process, Morocco will confine its remaining 25,000 or so troops to encampments, again under neutral oversight.[103]

Presumably, these camps would be located within Western Sahara, but would be far from the voting and assembly areas to be used by the Sahrawi population. This is perhaps the most important aspect to any "status of forces" arrangement in any plebiscite scenario, because it will minimize any chance of harmful activity against the Sahrawis during the referendum period and lessen the possibility of psychological intimidation of the voters. It is apparently envisioned that about 2,000 "soldiers and administrators" of the United Nations would carry out the monitoring of the territory and conduct the referendum of self-determination. Not known from published sources is whether an OAU presence would also be included.[104] As to the disposition of the preexisting administrative structures of Morocco and Polisario during the interim period, details remain sketchy. According to one report, the Sahrawis insist upon a near-total Moroccan administrative withdrawal from the Western Sahara, willing only to make an exception for "very low-level administrators, each of which must be accompanied by a Sahrawi with equal powers."[105]

On its face, and keeping in mind the absolute necessity of creating an atmosphere of safety for the voters in the absence of all intimidation, the above blueprint could be an attractive compromise. The acceptance of the plan is some evidence of a softening of the previously rigid positions of the two parties, with Morocco indicating a willingness (yet to be tested in practice) to pull out most of its occupation force from the Sahara and confine the rest to base, and with Polisario not only willing to place its fighters under neutral supervision, but to accept a small-scale and monitored Moroccan presence in the territory during the referendum.[106] Obviously, the willingness of any one of the parties to act upon its undertakings is contingent upon the good faith of the other, but a residual Moroccan and Polisario presence in the Western Sahara during this decisive time would give both the chance to cooperate with the interim administration, perform ministerial tasks, and observe the process to their satisfaction. A small, controlled presence by the parties in the territory during the plebiscite period would thus not be without beneficial psychological consequences.

Mention should also be made of the number of United Nations personnel projected to comprise the interim regime, now placed by one source at two thousand.[107] Given the size of the Western Saharan territory; the number of encampments, polling places, and monitored areas that will surely be necessary; and the many other tasks facing any transitional government, this number seems too small to ensure the effectiveness of the enterprise. It will be necessary to provide for more staff, preferably before the implementation of the peace plan. One obvious source of personnel will be the OAU, which has been heavily involved in cease-fire and referendum efforts almost since the beginning of the dispute.[108]

As might be expected, the issue of voting eligibility and population count continues to be controversial, with differences still present in the positions of the two parties and with advantages and drawbacks apparent in various approaches to the problem. From the incomplete information available thus far, both sides have accepted the 1974 Spanish census as a basis for determining which persons should be allowed to vote in the plebiscite. It will be recalled that this count showed 73,497 Sahrawis in the territory but was attended by many flaws; it was almost certainly a substantial underestimate of the number of inhabitants even at that time. Acceptance and use of this enumeration has both weak and strong points.

Assuming that the 1974 Spanish figure is too low, and given the fact that Polisario claims that over 150,000 Sahrawis live in its refugee camps, reliance on that census, without expansion, has possible severe drawbacks for Polisario. It is conceivable that least some of those Sahrawis counted in 1974 no longer live either in Western Sahara or in the Tindouf region, or are now deceased. If an appreciable number of those persons still alive are now residing in Moroccan-controlled areas of the Sahara, this could constitute a possible advantage for Morocco. It may not be fully in Polisario's interest to accept the restricted population base inherent in the 1974 census, nor could it be in Morocco's interest, since the possibility exists, of course, that a clear majority of those counted reside with Polisario in the Tindouf region. Polisario apparently comprehends the shortcomings in the Spanish census and wants the UN-OAU interim administration to conduct an independent survey of the population once it is installed in the territory. Another tool advocated by the parties in this connection will be to use the knowledge of Sahrawi elders who, it is anticipated, will be able through long experience to identify people so as to ascertain birthplaces, ages, locations of residence, and the like.

Another argument against primary use of the Spanish census is the fact that because the minimum voting age in the plebiscite will be eighteen years, and the census was taken only seventeen years ago, none of those Sahrawis counted in 1974 would have offspring old enough to vote if the plebiscite were held, for instance, in 1991. This would, unavoidably, it seems, deprive the interim administration of having a population group that is more easily traceable than would otherwise be the case and would be another impediment to expanding the voting rolls so as to be reflective of the increased number of Sahrawis.

One aspect of the 1974 census that argues heavily in favor of reliance upon it, however, is its relatively clear-cut nature. Presumably, it is sufficiently well-defined as to eliminate (or at least ameliorate) the many definitional problems that will bedevil a population count carried out entirely by the interim administration. Determining places of birth, residence, and lineage will be difficult and time-consuming, and such a process will, of course, facilitate challenges to the qualifications of the voters. In addition to this less-than-cheerful situation are the charges made by each party that the other is importing non-Sahrawis to the region to influence the outcome of a referendum.[109] These factors make the scenario of taking a new population count assume the dimensions of a potential nightmare. At the very least, it would require an even stronger and more numerous presence by the interim administration, along with an effective dispute-resolution apparatus to decide questions of voter eligibility.

Upon all of the evidence, the problem of determining the population of the Western Sahara and referendum voting qualifications admits of no simple answer. Whatever primary basis is utilized--the less complex but incomplete 1974 census or the involved process of a new and comprehensive count near in time to the plebiscite--there will be an urgent need for a large and astute interim administration that enjoys the complete trust of both protagonists. The transitional regime will have to strike a balance, if the endeavor is to be a serious one, between an oversimplified adherence to Spain's 1974 census and the possibly severe definitional problems of a larger-scale enumeration, with all of the political and logistical difficulties flowing therefrom.

Ideally, the interim administration should adopt a system that will strive to avoid complex or prolonged definitional pitfalls while at the same time attempt in good faith to expand the population base beyond the 1974 figure, even incrementally, in order to achieve at least a measure of fairness to the parties. In the final analysis, however, it may well be necessary for the interim administration to politely but firmly forestall excessive voter qualification disputes, navigate a course that will please neither Morocco nor Polisario completely (yet will not provide grounds for either to abort the process or disown the result), muster the relevant data, and carry out the actual referendum.

A final component of the United Nations plan deserves mention. In keeping with the prior OAU plebiscite proposals discussed earlier in this chapter, the choice offered to the Sahrawi voters by the UN will be one between independence and integration with the Kingdom of Morocco.[110]   A third "option" has been discussed by some commentators: a prospective choice that would mean continued affiliation with Morocco, but under an undefined "federative" or "confederal" arrangement.[111] It is difficult at this time to establish the origin of such proposals, but it should suffice to say that only the two-choice plan (independence or integration) is operative at this time, from what is known of the UN settlement plan.

In reality, the above "federation" scenario stands no chance of acceptance or realization in practice. Aside from the great difficulty in defining the nature and parameters of this disposition to the Sahrawis, the proposal, if executed, would still leave the sovereignty of the Western Sahara in the hands of Morocco.   Morocco would then presumably be free to define for itself over time the precise nature of the territory's status within the kingdom. It would also have the effect of eliminating what international political and legal personality the Western Sahara now possesses and would effectively prejudge the outcome of any referendum.   Too, such a plan is assured of total rejection by Polisario.[112]   Any proposal for Western Saharan autonomy within Morocco of whatever complexion would constitute a distinction without a difference for the Sahrawi population, and substantively would be no different than complete integration with Morocco.

The long-standing cease-fire and referendum plans authored by the United Nations and the Organization of African Unity have had considerable staying power, and have captured the support of most of the world community, as evidenced by the strongly favorable vote taken in the UN General Assembly in October 1989, which manifested a clear consensus that the Sahara problem should be resolved peacefully and democratically. Giving greater weight to this consensus is the example of the ongoing resolution of other conflicts in the developing world and the easing of East-West tensions, enabling the international community to focus more of its attention on the Western Sahara. In mid-1990, moreover, efforts to hold a referendum in the territory took a new turn.

On June 18, 1990, UN Secretary-General Pérez de Cuéllar presented a detailed plan for the actual transition of the Western Sahara either to independence or internationally recognized integration with Morocco. Aside from making public for the first time the plan accepted by Morocco and Polisario in 1988, his report contains an outline for the actual process for the institution of a cease-fire, phased troop withdrawal, the insertion of the UN force necessary to maintain a climate of safety in the territory, and the referendum.[113] In addition, the report also contains a timetable for the process (among other provisions, it calls for the referendum to be held twenty-four weeks after the cessation of hostilities and the return of eligible Sahrawi voters), and mandates that an Identification Commission ascertain voting qualifications under the supervision of a special representative, currently Johannes Manz of Switzerland.[114] The special representative will also exercise extensive powers in the territory if and when an interim regime begins its task.

The following week, a diplomatic watershed in the Sahara dispute was reached. In a brief proceeding on June 27, 1990, the UN Security Council unanimously approved the work of the secretary-general to settle the conflict, called on both Morocco and Polisario to "cooperate fully" with his work, and authorized him to send a second technical mission to the territory as a preparatory step. The Security Council also requested Pérez de Cuéllar to submit a further and even more detailed report on the mission, modalities, and cost of the endeavor, with a view to further Security Council action in the future.[115]

Armed with this mandate, Pérez de Cuéllar immediately traveled to Geneva, where he once again attempted to reconcile the two parties and induce Morocco to engage Polisario face-to-face. Despite personal involvement by the secretary-general, this effort was unsuccessful. Morocco refused to meet and negotiate with Polisario, and so build upon the January 1989 direct meeting with the Sahrawis in Marrakech. On the positive side, efforts to compile a roster of eligible voters continued to bear some fruit; Sahrawi tribal elders from both Morocco and Polisario's refugee camps in the Tindouf region met directly in Geneva in late June 1990 to exchange information as to the whereabouts of those counted in the 1974 Spanish census. However, even this was attended by much controversy, as the parties jockeyed for influence and Morocco raised questions about the legitimacy of the elders.[116] It would be expected, therefore, that some would suspect that Morocco's formal acceptance of the overall UN plan represented only a shift in tactics, with no substantive concessions in the offing. And the prospect of additional military action, which took place most recently in late 1988 and late 1989 with much loss of life, is always fairly close to the surface.[117] What was clear in mid-1991 was that the basic climate of relations between Morocco and Polisario had not yet progressed to a point sufficient to enable solutions to outstanding problems to be reached.

By the middle of 1991, the situation, thus, had changed little in the territory itself, and an array of practical difficulties were still present, but settlement efforts had assumed new dimensions in the form of a United Nations framework (backed by most member-states) that is the most serious attempt to date to resolve one of the longest and most intractable disputes in postcolonial African history. Whether this endeavor will fail as a result of political circumstance, or will open up real possibilities for peace and self-determination, is still beyond the ability of any observer to forecast.

NOTES

1. UN General Assembly, 15th sess., Official Records, supplement 16, resolution 1514 (15), A/4864, 1960, 66-67.
2. Thomas M. Franck, "The Theory and Practice of Decolonization: The Western Sahara Case," in Richard Lawless and Laila Monahan, eds., *War and Refugees: The Western Sahara Conflict* (London and New York: Pinter Publishers, 1987), 11.
3. Ibid., 13.
4. Franck, "The Theory and Practice of Decolonization," in Lawless and Monahan, eds., *War and Refugees*, 11.
5. Tony Hodges, *Western Sahara: The Roots of a Desert War* (Westport, Conn.: Lawrence Hill, 1983), 85-86.
6. See, for example, Appendices 13A through 13C in John Damis, "The O.A.U. and Western Sahara," in Yassin el-Ayouty and I. William Zartman, eds., *The O.A.U. After Twenty Years* (New York: Praeger, 1984), 286-95.
7. UN General Assembly, 20th sess., Official Records, supplement 14, resolution 2072 (20), A/6014, 1965, 59-60.
8. Hodges, *Western Sahara*, 137.
9. Ibid., 104-5. Spain, along with Portugal, a fellow African colonial power with similar attitudes, were the only states voting against the resolution.
10. UN General Assembly, 21st sess., Official Records, supplement 16, resolution 2229 (21), A/6316, 1966, 72-73.

11. Hodges, *Western Sahara*, 105-6, citing UN General Assembly Resolution 2229.

12. Ibid., 106.

13. John Damis, *Conflict in Northwest Africa: The Western Sahara Dispute* (Stanford, Calif.: Hoover Institution Press, 1983), 47.

14. Hodges, *Western Sahara*, 137.

15. Damis, *Conflict in Northwest Africa*, 47.

16. Benyamin Neuberger, *National Self-Determination in Historical Africa* (Boulder, Colo.: Lynne Rienner Publishers, 1986), 115.

17. Hodges, *Western Sahara*, 103. Mauritania, at the United Nations, voted in favor of all the General Assembly resolutions calling upon Spain to allow a referendum to take place.

18. International Court of Justice, *Western Sahara: Advisory Opinion of 16 October 1975* (The Hague: International Court of Justice, 1975), 68.

19. Frente Polisario is the Spanish acronym for the Popular Front for the Liberation of the Saguia el-Hamra and Río de Oro (the two principal component regions of the Western Sahara).

20. Hodges, *Western Sahara*, 131.

21. Ibid.

22. Ibid., 77-82. The joint military campaigns, directed at the resistance shown by Sahrawis against the Spanish and French as embodied by the Moroccan-led Army of Liberation, were named Operation Ouragon ("Hurricane") and Operation Ecouvillon ("Sponge"). They involved the use of thousands of French and Spanish troops and dozens of combat aircraft.

23. Ibid., 132.

24. Ibid., 170.

25. Tony Hodges, *Historical Dictionary of Western Sahara* (Metuchen, New Jersey: Scarecrow Press, 1982), 102-4.

26. Ibid., 278-80.

27. Hodges, *Western Sahara*, 169.

28. Tony Hodges, "The Western Sahara File," *Third World Quarterly* 6, no. 1 (January 1984): 95.

29. Hodges, *Western Sahara*, 238.

30. *The New York Times*, June 18, 1981; March 8, 1982; March 14, 1982; July 25, 1982; July 28, 1982; June 10, 1983.

31. Hodges, "The Western Sahara File," 107. Also see Damis, "The O.A.U. and Western Sahara," in El-Ayouty and Zartman, eds., *The O.A.U. After Twenty Years*, 273-75.

32. Ibid., 263-65.

33. Ibid., 223-24.

34. Ibid., 275-77, 309, citing UN Document A/33/337 of October 31, 1978, regarding the assigned tasks of the committee.

35. Damis., "The O.A.U. and Western Sahara," in El-Ayouty and Zartman, eds., *The O.A.U. After Twenty Years*, 276.

36. Hodges, *Western Sahara*, 310.

37. Ibid.

38. *The New York Times*, June 27, 1981. Also see Hodges, *Western Sahara*, 311.

39. *The New York Times*, June 27, 1981; July 7, 1981.

40. "Everyone will vote to be Moroccan," is how a correspondent for *The Middle East* magazine summarized King Hassan's attitude. *The Middle East*, August 1981, 26.

41. Hodges, *Western Sahara*, 312.

42. The committee was composed of the presidents of Nigeria, Mali Guinea, Sierra Leone, Tanzania, Sudan, and Kenya.

43. See the Nairobi II Decision of the OAU Implementation Committee on Western Sahara, (August 26, 1981), in El-Ayouty and Zartman, eds., *The O.A.U. After Twenty Years*, 286-88.

44. Hodges, *Western Sahara*, 313.

45. *The New York Times*, February 10, 1982. Foreign Minister Boucetta stated:

> For us the Polisario does not exist either legally or internationally. We will never recognize the Polisario. There will be no withdrawal of Moroccan troops from our Saharan province, and there is no way that the Moroccan administration will leave the Western Sahara territory.

46. OAU Charter Article 28, reprinted in Ian Brownlie, ed., *Basic Documents in International Law* (Oxford: Oxford University Press, 1983), 83.

47. See Damis, "The O.A.U. and Western Sahara," in El-Ayouty and Zartman, eds., *The O.A.U. After Twenty Years*, 208.

48. Hodges, "The Western Sahara File," 109.

49. See OAU Charter Articles 2(1)(c), 2(1)(d), 3(3), 3(6), and 4, in Brownlie, ed., *Basic Documents*, 77-78. Also see the resolution of the 1964 OAU Cairo Summit Conference, reprinted in A. Allott, "Boundaries in Africa: A Legal and Historical Survey," in A. Mensah-Brown, ed., *African International Legal History* (New York: United Nations Institution for Training and Research, 1975), 69.

50. See Damis, "The O.A.U. and Western Sahara," in El-Ayouty and Zartman, eds., *The O.A.U. After Twenty Years*, 294-95. This resolution, for the first time, explicitly named Polisario and Morocco as "parties to the conflict."

51. See *West Africa*, November 19, 1984, 3204-5; and *The New York Times*, November 13, 1984.

52. *The New York Times*, November 13, 1984. Only Zaire followed Morocco's lead in absenting itself from OAU proceedings, and then only temporarily.

53. *The New York Times*, November 12, 1984.

54. Tony Hodges, "The Second Decade of War," *Africa Report*, March-April 1986, 77.

55. Ibid.

56. As reaffirmed in UN Fourth (Decolonization) Committee Resolution A/C.4/42/L.5 of October 21, 1987.

57. *West Africa*, October 28, 1985, 2258.

58. *West Africa*, April 14, 1986, 797.

59. *West Africa*, April 21, 1986, 854.

60. UN Secretariat, Secretary-General, 42nd sess., *Question of Western Sahara: Report of the Secretary-General*, A/42/601, 1987, 103.

61. Ibid., 3.

62. Ibid., 5.

63. Ibid., 5-6. In the event, however, the technical mission was received by Polisario during December 1987, and cooperation was forthcoming.

64. *West Africa*, December 28, 1987-January 4, 1988, 2560.

65. *West Africa*, January 11, 1988, 55; and *The New York Times*, December 6, 1987.

66. Damis, "The O.A.U. and Western Sahara," in El-Ayouty and Zartman, eds., *The O.A.U. After Twenty Years*, 282.

67. Ibid.

68. Ibid., 283.

69. Ibid.

70. See Hodges, *Western Sahara*, 77-82, 131-32.

71. See, for example, James Firebrace, "The Sahrawi Refugees: Lessons and Prospects," in Lawless and Monahan, eds., *War and Refugees*, 167-85.

72. Hodges, *Western Sahara*, 344.

73. *West Africa*, December 28, 1987-January 4, 1988, 2560. This statement is qualified by the Polisario leader, Mohamed Abdelaziz, who

said, "Though incomplete, the census conducted by Spain who will have a role to play in the referendum [sic] could give a precise idea of the Sahrawi population."

74. Damis, "The O.A.U. and Western Sahara," in El-Ayouty and Zartman, eds., *The O.A.U. After Twenty Years*, 283.

75. Information from interviews with Polisario Front representatives, January-June 1988.

76. See *The New York Times*, May 17, 1988.

77. Ibid.

78. As examples of this view, expressed by way of analyzing the new situation, see *The New York Times*, May 25, 1988; and *The Middle East*, July 1988, 22-31, especially 22, where it is stated, "The price Polisario will have to pay [relative to the restored diplomatic relations] is as yet unclear . . . but some reduction in assistance seems inevitable."

79. For examples of this view, see *The New York Times*, December 6, 1987, May 17, 1988, and May 25, 1988; in the latter an unnamed American diplomat is quoted as saying, "Although the [Sahara] war issue has been submerged, the reestablishment of ties means that the two countries can now start working on a settlement. The two of them are the key players; the war will end when they are ready to end it."

80. For illustrations of this perspective (which also tends to stress the accomplishments of Polisario and the SADR), see *West Africa*, June 13, 1988, 1060-1; *Africa Events*, June-July 1988, 12-13; and Toby Shelley, "What now for the Polisario Front?" *Middle East International*, June 11, 1988, 12-13. For an article that attempts to strike a balance among the contrasting viewpoints, see *The Middle East*, July 1988, 22-31.

81. *The New York Times*, May 25, 1988.

82. *West Africa*, June 13, 1988, 1060.

83. Shelley, "What now for the Polisario Front?" *Middle East International*, 12.

84. Ibid.

85. See the comments by SADR President Mohamed Abdelaziz as reported in *West Africa*, June 13, 1988, 1060.

86. Ibid.

87. Ibid.

88. Interview with Bachir Mustapha Sayed, Polisario Executive Committee and Political Bureau member, Tindouf region, June 14, 1988.

89. Ibid.

90. Shelly, "What now for the Polisario Front?" *Middle East International*, 12. Another reason for some confidence by Polisario is

its warming relations with the Libyan and Tunisian governments, which in the past had been an uncertain commodity. With reference to Tunisia, see *West Africa*, June 13, 1988, 1060. As to Libya, see *The Middle East*, July 1988, 28. In mid-1989, the SADR was also formally recognized by the conservative governments of El Salvador and Honduras. See *Middle East International*, September 8, 1989, 12-13.

91. See Anne Lippert, *Saharan Peoples Support Committee Letter* 8, no. 4, February-May 1988, 1-2.

92. The Moroccan side was represented by Abdellatif Filali, the foreign minister, while Polisario sent Bachir Mustapha Sayed, a member of its executive committee and political bureau who is considered to be the Front's second-ranking official.

93. As reported in *The Washington Post*, August 12, 1988, and the *Christian Science Monitor*, August 12, 1988.

94. *The New York Times*, August 13, 1988.

95. The acceptance of the UN plan by both parties engendered much press coverage. See *The New York Times*, August 31, 1988; the *Boston Globe*, August 31, 1988; the *International Herald Tribune*, August 31, 1988; *The Times* (U.K.), August 31, 1988; and the *Christian Science Monitor*, August 31, 1988.

96. See *The Middle East*, July 1988, 31; and Shelley, "What Now For the Polisario Front?" *Middle East International*, 12.

97. For recognition of this problem, see the *International Herald Tribune*, August 31, 1988.

98. *The New York Times*, August 14, 1988.

99. See Hodges' comment in *Western Sahara*, 291: "But then, guerrilla warfare had not, in a purely military sense, driven the French from Algeria, the US from Indochina, or the Portuguese from Angola, Mozambique and Guinea-Bissau. The economic, diplomatic, or domestic political repercussions of these wars had been decisive elements too in forcing their eventual withdrawal."

100. See the *Christian Science Monitor*, August 31, 1988; and *The Times* (U.K.), August 31, 1988. See also *West Africa*, August 22, 1988, 1554, where it is stated that the direct negotiations were "a move which would have been unthinkable prior to the rapprochement," referring, of course, to renewed Algerian-Moroccan diplomatic relations. For coverage of the January 1989 Morocco-Polisario meeting in Marrakech, see *The New York Times*, December 28, 1988; January 4, 5, 1989.

101. See the *Christian Science Monitor*, August 31, 1988; and *The Times* (U.K.), August 31, 1988. See also *West Africa*, August 22, 1988,

1554.

102. *The New York Times*, August 31, 1988. It is estimated by the United Nations that Polisario has between 6,000 and 8,000 members of its armed forces.

103. Ibid.

104. *The New York Times*, August 13, 1988.

105. *Christian Science Monitor*, August 31, 1988.

106. In an interview in *The New York Times*, September 18, 1988, SADR President Mohamed Abdelaziz said that a "token" Moroccan troop presence, "separated by the United Nations," would be acceptable. As for civilian administrators, Abdelaziz stated that some of these could remain "so long as they are prevented from trying to influence the referendum."

107. *The New York Times*, August 13, 1988.

108. In an interview with the writer in June 1988, Bachir Mustapha Sayed, a high Polisario official, stated that both the UN and the OAU must be present in the interim administration to be acceptable to the Sahrawis.

109. Regarding these accusations, see *West Africa*, September 12-18, 1988, 1668; and August 22, 1988, 1554, both dealing with reports that Polisario was transporting Tuareg nomads from Mali to the Tindouf region to influence the referendum's voting list. These stories were vigorously denied by Polisario. For accusations of similar Moroccan behavior, see *West Africa*, September 12-18, 1988, 1668.

110. See *The New York Times*, August 14, 1988; and *The Washington Post*, September 25, 1988.

111. *The New York Times*, August 13, 1988; August 31, 1988.

112. *West Africa*, September 12-18, 1988, 1668, in which Lamine Baali, Polisario's representative in Britain, stated that "we utterly reject all formulations of autonomy, federation or confederation."

113. The United Nations force proposed for the interim administration and plebiscite, to be formally set up by the UN Security Council, is known as MINURSO, the French acronym for the United Nations Mission for the Referendum in Western Sahara. It will consist of military, civilian, and security (civil police) units.

114. For the text of the peace proposal accepted by the parties to the conflict in 1988, as well as the secretary-general's detailed outline of the work of MINURSO, see, UN Secretariat, Secretary-General, 43rd sess., *The Situation Concerning Western Sahara: Report of the Secretary-General*, S/21360, 1990. The UN's activities are also

described in *The New York Times*, June 29, 1990; and the *Christian Science Monitor*, July 3, 1990.

115. UN Security Council, 43rd sess., Official Records, resolution 658 (43), S/Res./658, 1990.

116. For coverage of this, see *West Africa*, July 9-15, 1990, 2067; and *The Economist*, July 14, 1990, 41. The latest round of discussions in Geneva, with Pérez de Cuéllar as interlocutor, ended on July 9, 1990.

117. See the *Boston Globe*, September 19, 1988; and *The New York Times*, September 25, 1988, for coverage of a massive engagement near Oum Driega in the central portion of Western Sahara that left scores dead and wounded. Military activity also took place in the fall of 1989, with dozens of skirmishes reported in September, and a large-scale battle on October 7, in which Morocco admitted losing over fifty soldiers (a Polisario communiqué said that over two hundred were lost) in the region of Guelta Zemmour, the scene of much prior military action. See *West Africa*, October 16-22, 1989, 1723.

10

The Western Sahara Conflict in the Post-Cold War Era

Yahia H. Zoubir and Daniel Volman

In August 1991, President George Bush reaffirmed the end of the Cold War by stating, in his preface to the *National Security Strategy of the United States*, that "force cannot be used to settle disputes and that when consensus is broken, the world will respond," with "the United Nations playing the role dreamed of by its founders."[1] According to Bush administration officials, the Allies' response, under the auspices of the UN, to Iraq's invasion of Kuwait, "has truly vindicated and rejuvenated" the role of the United Nations in resolving international conflicts.[2] Now the administration hopes that the world body will be able to play an identical role in settling other regional conflicts, such as those in Afghanistan, Cambodia, Somalia, the Western Sahara, and, more recently, Yugoslavia.

Events in the Western Sahara, however, indicate that this vision is nearly impossible to realize, for it contradicts the Bush administration's principles of realism. It also demonstrates that Bush's embrace of the concept of a "New World Order" is based more on ideological premises than on a political principle.

The conflict in the Western Sahara dates back to 1975 and remains one of the longest-running unsettled regional disputes in Africa, despite the fact that the ingredients necessary to solve it have existed since the beginning of the conflict.[3] These ingredients included King Hassan's ostensible agreement in 1981 to the holding of a referendum in the occupied territory, as well as the emergence of a military stalemate in 1983, which compelled the UN and the Organization of African Unity (OAU) to redouble their efforts to reach a peaceful solution. The latter's efforts were aimed at averting a possible war between Algeria and

Morocco.   In particular, they wished to avoid the outbreak of a confrontation with the potential for the direct involvement of the United States and the Soviet Union.

Notwithstanding the United Nations' objectives, both the United States and the USSR did play an indirect, and at times direct, part in the conflict. Since 1975, the United States has played a significant role by backing King Hassan, although not Morocco's claims to sovereignty over the Western Sahara, by providing vital military equipment and intelligence to the Kingdom of Morocco.[4] On the other hand, the Soviet Union, reflecting its substantial economic ties with Morocco, and in spite of its military and political relationship with Algeria, took a more neutral position on the conflict.[5] Moscow's neutrality, Algeria's policy of non-alignment, and Polisario's nationalism and anti-communism, did not allow the dispute to take an East-West dimension. However, successive American administrations have extended almost unconditional support to Morocco, except for brief intervals. This support derived partly from Morocco's perceived geographic significance as well as King Hassan's conservative and pro-Western attitudes on various regional and international issues.   It was also determined by the existing image of Algeria as a revolutionary power that posed a menace to Washington's friends in the Maghreb, Morocco and Tunisia. Surprisingly enough, U.S. officials seemed oblivious to America's excellent economic ties with Algeria.

The dispute over the Western Sahara generated a number of political alliances in the region.   Nonetheless, due to their pressing social and economic difficulties as well as to the metamorphosis of the international system, the regional players (Algeria, Morocco, Tunisia, Mauritania, and Libya) concluded that regional integration might represent the ideal framework for conflict management and resolution.   Thus, in Spring 1988, the Kingdom of Morocco and Algeria decided to renew their diplomatic relations. As a trade-off for the reestablishment of these ties, Morocco agreed to a joint communiqué calling "for a just and definitive solution to the Western Sahara conflict through a free and regular referendum for self-determination held without any constraints whatsoever and with utmost sincerity."[6] The United States was satisfied with this turn of events, for it was convinced that the reestablishment of diplomatic relations between the two Maghrebi giants would doom the Sahrawi cause.   This perception was based on the somewhat wishful assumption that Algeria would sacrifice Polisario on the altar of Maghrebi unity.[7]

Saudi Arabia played a central role in the rapprochement between Algiers and Rabat and because the government in Riyadh sought to keep up the momentum, it facilitated secret discussions in Taëf in July 1988 between Sahrawi and Moroccan officials. Whereas these talks produced no concrete results, they did create a better atmosphere for further dialogue. In August 1988, the UN secretary-general, Javier Pérez de Cuéllar, submitted a peace plan to Polisario and Morocco that included, inter alia, a cease-fire and a referendum on self-determination. Although they expressed reservations, both parties agreed to this plan. Although the accord did not put an end to the hostilities between the warring factions, it did lead to direct talks between King Hassan and Polisario representatives on January 4-5, 1989.

The overall diffusion of tension in the Maghreb in the late 1980s compelled the Reagan administration to reexamine its policy toward the region. The administration's new approach was also stimulated by American appreciation for what it regarded as Algeria's new pragmatism in international relations, particularly since Algeria's important involvement in helping free the American hostages held in Iran and even more since Algerian President Chadli Bendjedid's official trip to the United States in April 1985. Therefore, in spite of its still ambivalent nature, American policy concerning the conflict in the Western Sahara seemed more even-handed, as demonstrated by public statements by U.S. officials that supported the UN peace process more forcefully.

Even more striking was the fact that when Polisario forces accidentally shot down a U.S. Agency for International Development plane over the war zone in December 1988, at a time when Polisario was seeking to establish good rapport with the United States, this had no negative effect on the U.S. attitude vis-à-vis the Sahrawis as was clearly wished by the Moroccan side. At this time, in fact, America's greatest concern in the region was Libya rather than Polisario. Therefore, by 1988, the United States was more favorable to a diplomatic settlement of the conflict than hitherto. The new American attitude was a reflection of the hopes stated by Reagan administration officials that the end of the Cold War had made it easier to resolve peacefully regional conflicts in Afghanistan, Namibia, Angola, Cambodia, El Salvador, Nicaragua, and elsewhere. Indeed, President Reagan publicly congratulated King Hassan, through the new American ambassador to Morocco, for "seeking a diplomatic solution in Western Sahara."[8]

The process of regional integration resulted in the creation of the

Arab Maghreb Union (UMA) in February 1989, only a month after the meeting between Polisario representatives and King Hassan in Marrakech. Although Washington favored regional integration in general, its reaction to the formation of the UMA was rather negative, because the Union included America's *bête noire*, Qaddafi's Libya.

Despite his pledge, and a series of United Nations General Assembly resolutions urging him to pursue further direct discussions with Polisario, King Hassan refused to hold any more talks with Sahrawi representatives. This compelled Polisario to end the unilateral cease-fire it had observed for the entire month of February. King Hassan's reversal of his promise was predicated upon his belief that he had achieved his goal of seeing the UMA formed without including the Saharan Arab Democratic Republic (SADR) as a member. Moroccan officials hoped--as American officials probably did as well--that the SADR would become such an irrelevant issue in Moroccan-Algerian relations as to die a natural death.[9] Clearly, King Hassan had agreed to the eventual holding of a UN referendum because he was convinced that either it would never take place or that if it did, Morocco would win it because of the votes of the Moroccans induced to settle in the occupied Western Sahara.[10] The severe internal problems faced by the Algerian regime since the October 1988 revolt have reinforced the King's conviction.

Regardless of the type of calculations Morocco had made, the war in the Western Sahara intensified in Fall 1989. In fact, numerous major attacks were mounted by Polisario fighters against Moroccan forces stationed in the Western Sahara.[11] The serious character of these offensives prompted the UN and the OAU to redouble diplomatic actions designed to put an end to the war. Therefore, establishing a cease-fire became one of the United Nations's main objectives.

The UN has displayed greater interest in finding a peaceful solution to what is now the last decolonization problem in Africa, since Namibia's independence in March 1990 in which the UN and, incidentally, the United States played the leading roles. However, insofar as the Western Sahara is concerned, the United States opted for a more passive role. Washington limited itself to backing resolutions adopted by the UN, particularly at the Security Council, for example, UN Security Council Resolution 621 of September 1988, UN Security Council Resolution 658 of June 1990, and UN Security Council Resolution 690 of April 1991. In these resolutions, the Security Council approved the security-general's peace plan and then created a United

Nations force to implement it.

Although the United States has not blocked the actions of the UN, it has not put any pressure on Morocco to cooperate fully with the world body to facilitate the speedy implementation of the peace plan either. In fact, some observers argue that "the United States has shown little inclination to persuade the king [of Morocco] to observe a 1990 peace accord between Morocco and Saharans seeking independence, even when the lives of American citizens [participating in the UN peace force] have been at risk."[12] The reason for the Bush administration's retreat from its ostensible commitment to the UN peace settlement might be that Washington wants to reward Morocco for its participation in the Gulf War.

Iraq's invasion of Kuwait was treated by the United States as a clear violation of international law. The Bush administration, therefore, emphasized the necessity of a forceful UN response with all available means, including military intervention. Furthermore, Morocco was, along with Algeria, one of the first countries in the Arab world to condemn unequivocally the Iraqi invasion of Kuwait. Ironically, King Hassan dispatched to Saudi Arabia 1,700 out of the 120,000 troops that have occupied the Western Sahara to participate in "Operation Desert Shield." This largely symbolic initiative was taken by the king in order to put Washington in his debt. Numerous observers have noted the contradiction between the United States' inflexible position toward Iraq's breach of international legality and its continued reluctance to adopt any firm stance on Morocco's transgression of identical principles.

For example, in a very recent study of the new role of the UN in the emerging world order, William J. Durch, a researcher at the Henry L. Stimson Center, has stated that "Iraq's 1990 invasion of Kuwait was based on historic claims similar to Morocco's, and was rejected by the international community through the actions of the Security Council. In the case of the Western Sahara, 15 years earlier, the Security Council did not act."[13] This highlights once more the fact that U.S. support for international law is selective at best. Only recently, the United States defended its double standards on the application of international rules on the grounds that it was necessary to do so in order to defend its national interest against Soviet global challenges. Today, however, American officials state that the "New World Order" will be based on the strict implementation of international legal principles. But, in the case of the

Western Sahara--as well as in other regions--the Bush administration has clearly continued to apply the double standards of the past.

The Iraqi invasion of Kuwait and the subsequent developments in the Gulf overshadowed the conflict in the Western Sahara. However, once the Gulf War ended, the UN concentrated its attention once again on the Sahrawi issue. Indeed, on April 28, 1991, the UN Security Council passed Resolution 690, in which it decided to set up the United Nations Mission for the Referendum in Western Sahara (MINURSO) and reaffirmed its approval of the secretary-general's peace settlement. The Bush administration's decision to agree to send U.S. military personnel to serve in MINURSO appeared to signal Washington's willingness to make sure that the peace plan is implemented successfully.

Under the provisions of the peace plan, a cease-fire was to take effect on September 6, 1991. In spite of the tacit agreement by both sides not to engage in offensive military operations in the weeks before the cease-fire, the Moroccan Royal Air Force heavily bombed Polisario military positions as well as Sahrawi civilians, without eliciting any strong condemnation of Morocco's actions by the United States or by its Gulf War allies. Although the cease-fire has since been generally observed by the two combatant forces since it came into effect, MINURSO has recorded many violations, largely by Morocco. In February 1992, the UN reported seventy-seven violations, seventy-five of which were committed by Morocco, and between February and May 1992, Morocco was responsible for ninety-seven out of one hundred and two violations of the cease-fire.[14]

In the meantime, the Kingdom of Morocco has also reneged on its commitment to the peace plan by making radical new demands concerning the eligibility of voters. Indeed, Morocco has insisted on the addition of the names of about 120,000 people to the list of eligible voters even though they were not listed on the 1974 Spanish census, which both Morocco and Polisario had accepted as the basis for eligibility. Morocco's intention, obviously, is to determine the outcome of the referendum, if it ever takes place. This question of voter eligibility has been the major obstacle in the path to the holding of a referendum.

When King Hassan visited the United States in September 1991, he did his utmost to win Washington's endorsement of his position. He came to the United States with strong credentials that go far beyond the recent role played by Morocco in the Gulf crisis. American officials continue to perceive the Kingdom of Morocco as one of America's oldest friends. Also, King Hassan's record of support for U.S. policies in the Middle East and Africa is highly valued in Washington. Moreover, he has obtained the support of powerful individuals, such as Henry Kissinger, and of some influential Jewish-American organizations.[15] In addition, before his trip to the United States, he sought to improve Morocco's human rights record by freeing some political prisoners and by destroying the infamous prison of Tazmamart.[16]

Consequently, Hassan had great expectations that his policy would receive backing from the Bush administration. Even though the administration did not publicly endorse his position on the Western Sahara, American officials limited themselves to a passive stance by stating that "it is the responsibility of the UN to make the decisions necessary on this issue."[17] The king correctly interpreted this attitude as a signal by Washington that it will do nothing to prevent him from continuing to obstruct the peace plan, as long as his political maneuvers do not lead to the complete collapse of the peace process.

King Hassan's obstructionist policies and Washington's complacence created grave concern among members of the U.S. Congress, from both political parties, that procrastination over the issue of the Western Sahara would lead to a deterioration of the situation and to the eventual resumption of the war, with unpredictable consequences both for the Maghreb region and for American foreign policy. Thus, in early October 1991, in an attempt to put some pressure on the White House to preserve the dynamics of the peace plan, Representative Mervyn Dymally, chair of the House Africa Subcommittee, submitted a resolution calling for a "free and fair referendum" in the Western Sahara and urging President Bush to "take appropriate steps to ensure that the Security Council takes firm action in the event of any failure to comply with, or attempt to delay, the peace plan which has been adopted."[18] The resolution was adopted by the House and, as of Summer 1992, was being considered by the Senate. Under Congressman Dymally's leadership, the House Africa Subcommittee held a hearing on the Western Sahara in October 1991 in an effort to prevent the UN peace settlement from unravelling.

However, this eventuality almost came true when UN Secretary-General Perez de Cuéllar capitulated to Morocco's persistent demands for changes in the criteria of voting eligibility in his final report to the UN Security Council on December 19, 1991, less than two weeks before his term in office ended. In his report, Pérez de Cuéllar proposed, among other things, new criteria for the eligibility to vote. In particular, he recommended that eligibility be extended to people who can prove that they lived in the Western Sahara continuously for a period of six years or intermittently over a period of twelve years prior to December 1974.[19]   Even though these recommendations on voter eligibility did not meet all of Morocco's demands, they were more favorable to the Kingdom of Morocco than to Polisario and, if implemented, would have guaranteed Morocco's victory in the referendum.

The Polisario, for obvious reasons, found the secretary-general's proposal "unacceptable," and the United States, unlike France (which has recently become more sympathetic to Morocco's claims despite its declarations of neutrality), realized that unless the peace settlement was acceptable to both sides, it would have no chance of being implemented. Therefore, despite France's attempts to win the UN Security Council's endorsement of the secretary-general's proposals, the United States, along with all the other members (with Russia playing only a minor role), did not endorse Perez de Cuéllar's recommendations. Instead, the UN Security Council passed a resolution on December 31, 1991, on Perez de Cuéllar's last days as UN secretary-general, that stated that while it "approves" his efforts, it only "welcomes" his final proposal. Consequently, it was left up to the incoming secretary-general, Boutros Boutros-Ghali, to submit a new proposal on voter eligibility to which both protagonists would agree.[20]

Still dissatisfied with the continued passivity of the White House, Senator Claiborne Pell, chair of the Senate Foreign Relations Committee, decided to conduct his own investigation on the situation in the Western Sahara. In the beginning of January, George A. Pickart, a member of the Committee's staff, visited Morocco and both Moroccan- and Polisario-held portions of the Western Sahara.   Upon his return to Washington, Pickart submitted a detailed report on the evolution of the situation in the region to Senator Pell.

Several key findings were reported by Pickart:

1.   The United Nations peace plan for Western Sahara is in serious jeopardy.
2.   If the peace plan fails, it could have serious consequences for stability in North Africa [and] could lead to renewed fighting between Polisario and Morocco, which could spark the potentially explosive political situation in Algeria.

3. The United Nations' refusal to respond politically to MINURSO's reports of cease-fire violations in the Western Sahara has undermined MINURSO's credibility with both parties.
4. MINURSO's lack of support from the United Nations has been compounded by the government of Morocco's unwillingness to cooperate with MINURSO's operations.
5. If current circumstances are not improved, the United States should anticipate MINURSO's failure.[21]

Pickart's warning that the failure of the peace process would have grave consequences for regional stability should be taken seriously. There have been speculations about Algeria's abandonment of Polisario and the Sahrawi cause, especially since the October 1988 riots in Algeria. However, a closer examination of the facts will demonstrate that such an assessment is deceiving. Material support for Polisario has indeed declined because of Algeria's catastrophic economic situation. But, there is ample evidence to show that the Algerian government, especially the military, has not changed its basic position on the Western Sahara. The Algerian president, Mohamed Boudiaf, made this clear in his statements on the issue after he was named Chief of State in January 1992. The Moroccans were, nonetheless, convinced that he was sympathetic to their position because of the statements he had made in the 1970s while in the Algerian opposition and because of the influence his long exile in the Kingdom of Morocco might have had on his views. Well-informed sources have indicated, however, that Boudiaf was not favorable to Morocco's claims over the Western Sahara, despite appearances.

Ali Kafi, a veteran of the Algerian war of liberation, who succeeded Boudiaf in July 1992 after the latter's assassination, is likely to take a firmer position on the Western Sahara. He, as well as many others in the military and the government, consider the Western Sahara issue a question of Algeria's national security. Lately, Moroccan-Algerian relations have been less warm and promising than they were in the years immediately following the reestablishment of diplomatic ties in May 1988. Therefore, a return to the status quo ante is not unlikely. Furthermore, failure to bring an end to the stalemate will certainly revive tensions in the Maghreb, thus offering Qaddafi a chance to exploit the situation to his advantage. The Pickart report drew the U.S. Congress' attention to the trouble that may arise from complacency toward this conflict and from failure to speed up the peace process. As a result, the House Africa Subcommittee decided to put new pressure on the Bush administration by holding another hearing on the Western Sahara in February 1992.

During this hearing, John Bolton, Assistant Secretary of State for International Organizations, admitted that Morocco's demands for changes in the voter eligibility were a "violation" of the peace plan, but he also insisted that "we take no position" on the issue because, "our interest in resolving the Western Sahara dispute fits into a larger context of developments in the region."[22] This made it clear that the United States' commitment to the peace process is secondary to good relations with Morocco. The Bush administration has said repeatedly that it is grateful to Morocco for its decision to abstain on the vote at the UN Security Council on March 31, 1992, to condemn Libya, a fellow member of the UMA, for its alleged role in the Lockerbie and UTA bombings. Moreover, even though Morocco's role in the Middle East peace process is insignificant, the administration has highlighted Morocco's contribution to this process. Also, the United States acknowledges that it is indebted to Morocco for granting transit rights to U.S. military forces en route to the Middle East in time of crisis.[23] This explains why, more than a year after the Gulf War, Washington is still reluctant even to nudge Morocco to hold a "free and fair" referendum without any delay. And unless the United States takes the lead, there is no reason to expect Secretary-General Boutros-Ghali to make significant progress toward implementing the peace plan in the near future.

NOTES

1. President George Bush, "A New World Order," in *National Security Strategy of the United States* (Washington, D.C.: Government Printing Office, 1991), v.

2. *National Security Strategy of the United States* (Washington, D.C.: Government Printing Office, 1991), 13.

3. See Chapter 1: Yahia H. Zoubir, "Origins and Developments of the Conflict in the Western Sahara." For further details, see Tony Hodges,

Western Sahara: The Roots of a Desert War (Westport, Conn.: Lawrence Hill, 1983), updated version published in French, *Sahara occidental: Origines et enjeux d'une guerre du désert* (Paris: L'Harmattan, 1987); John Damis, *Conflict in Northwest Africa: The Western Sahara Dispute* (Stanford, Calif.: Hoover Institution Press, 1983); and I. William Zartman, *Ripe for Resolution: Conflict and Intervention in Africa* (New York and Oxford: Oxford University Press, 1989), esp. Chapter 2.

4. See Chapters 3 and 7: Stephen Zunes, "The United States in the Saharan War: A Case of Low-Intensity Intervention" and Daniel Volman, "The Role of Foreign Military Assistance in the Western Sahara War." See also Lt. Col. David J. Dean, *The Air Force Role in Low-Intensity Conflict* (Maxwell Air Force Base, Ala.: Air University Press, 1986); and Stephen Zunes, "The United States and Morocco: The Saharan War and Regional Interests," *Arab Studies Quarterly* 9, no. 4 (Fall 1987): 422-41.

5. See Chapter 5: Yahia H. Zoubir, "Moscow, the Maghreb, and Conflict in the Western Sahara." See also Yahia H. Zoubir, "L'URSS dans le Grand Maghreb: une stratégie équilibrée et une approche pragmatique," in Bassma Kodmani-Darwish and May Charouni-Dubarry, eds., *Maghreb: Les Années de Transition* (Paris Institut Français des Relations Internationales/Masson, 1990); and Yahia H. Zoubir, "Soviet Policy Toward the Western Sahara Conflict," *Africa Today* 34, no. 3 (Fall 1987): 17-32.

6. *El-Moudjahid*, May 17, 1988.

7. See Chapter 8: Robert A. Mortimer, "The Greater Maghreb and the Western Sahara." For further details, see Yahia H. Zoubir, "The Western Sahara Conflict: Regional and International Dimensions," *Journal of Modern African Studies* 28, no. 2 (June 1990): 225-43; and Robert A. Mortimer, "Maghreb Matters," *Foreign Policy*, no. 76 (Fall 1987): 160-75.

8. *Maghreb Arab Presse*, January 14, 1989.

9. Yahia H. Zoubir, "The Western Sahara Conflict: Regional and International Dimensions," *Journal of Modern African Studies* 28, no. 2 (June 1990): 238.

10. See Yahia H. Zoubir, "Western Sahara Conflict Impedes Maghreb Unity," *Middle East Report*, no. 163 (March-April 1990): 28-29; and Robert J. Bookmiller, "The Western Sahara: Future Prospects," *American-Arab Affairs*, no. 37 (Summer 1991): 64-76.

11. See Yahia H. Zoubir and Daniel Volman, "Solution Needed for Western Sahara," *New African*, no. 261 (June 1989): 38; and Yahia H. Zoubir and Daniel Volman, "Western Sahara: Back to Battle," *New African*, no. 270 (March 1990): 19.

12. *The Washington Post*, March 14, 1992. See also Daniel Volman, "Bush Abandons Western Sahara," *New African*, no. 299 (August 1992): 19.

13. William J. Durch, "Building on Sand: The UN Experience with Peacekeeping in the Western Sahara" (Paper delivered at the Thirty-third Annual Meeting of the International Studies Association, Atlanta, Georgia, April 3, 1992): 3.

14. UN Security Council, *Report of the Secretary General on the United Nations Mission for the Referendum in Western Sahara*, S/23662, February 28, 1992, 4-5; and UN Security Council, *Report of the Secretary General on the Situation Concerning Western Sahara*, 2/24040, May 29, 1992, 3.

15. *Jeune Afrique*, no. 1607 (October 16-22, 1991): 26-29.

16. *Statement of Amnesty International USA on Human Rights in Morocco and the Western Sahara Before the Subcommittees on African Affairs and Human Rights and International Organizations of the House Foreign Affairs Committee, February 26, 1991*, 2-9.

17. *Statement by Deputy Assistant Secretary of State John S. Wolf Before the Sub-Committee on Africa Regarding the UN Referendum in the Western Sahara, October 8, 1991*, 4.

18. U.S. Congress, House of Representatives, House Concurrent Resolution 214.

19. UN Security Council, *Report of the Secretary General on the United Nations Mission for the Referendum in Western Sahara*, S/23299, December 19, 1992. For further details see John Damis, "The U.N. Settlement Plan for the Western Sahara: Problems and Prospects," *Middle East Policy* 1, no. 2 (1992): 36-46; and U.S. Congress, Senate, Committee on Foreign Relations, *The Western Sahara: The Referendum Process in Danger*, 102d Cong., 2d sess., January 27, 1992, 9.

20. UN Security Council, *Resolution 725 of 31 December 1991*, S/23330.

21. U.S. Congress, Senate, Committee on Foreign Relations, *The Western Sahara: The Referendum Process in Danger*, 102d Cong., 2d sess., January 27, 1992, 4-5.

22. *Statement by Assistant Secretary of State John R. Bolton Before the Sub-Committee on Africa Regarding the UN Referendum in the Western*

Sahara, February 26, 1992, 6.
23. U.S. Department of Defense, Defense Security Assistance Agency
(DSAA), and U.S. Department of State, *Congressional Presentation for
Security Assistance Programs, Fiscal Year 1993* (Washington, D.C.:
DSAA and Department of State, 1992): 245-46.

Glossary

Alawite. Ruling dynasty of the Kingdom of Morocco.

Arab Maghreb Union (UMA). Regional organization formed in 1989 to promote political and economic cooperation among Maghrebi states. Its members are Morocco, Algeria, Mauritania, Tunisia, and Libya.

Djemma. The assembly of Sahrawi notables that acted as a legislative, executive, and judicial body under Spanish supervision. On November 28, 1975, following the signing of the Madrid Agreement, a majority of the members adopted the Proclamation of Guelta Zemmour, dissolving the Djemma and declaring their support for the Polisario Front.

El-Ayoun (variants: El-Aaiun, El-Aioun, Laayoune). The capital of the Western Sahara.

European Community (EC). The collective name of the three organizations (the European Economic Community, the European Coal and Steel Community, and the European Atomic Energy Community) formed in 1951 and 1958 to promote political and economic cooperation among Western European countries. The three organizations were merged to form the EC in 1967.

Euzakadi to Askatasuma (ETA). Basque nationalist organization that seeks to establish an independent state in the predominantly Basque-speaking areas of Spain and France.

Forces Armées Royales (FAR). The Royal Moroccan Armed Forces with 200,000 men under arms. About two-thirds of the FAR are stationed in the Western Sahara or in the southern provinces of Morocco.

FRELIMO. Mozambican nationalist organization formed in 1962 that was supported by the Soviet Union and China. FRELIMO became the governing party when Mozambique gained its independence in 1974.

Frente de Liberación y de las Unidad (FLU). Moroccan-sponsored Sahrawi organization that sought to incorporate the Spanish Sahara into the Kingdom of Morocco.

Government Provisoire de la République Algérienne (GPRA). The Algerian National Liberation Front (FLN) constituted this provisional government on September 28, 1958, to conduct negotiations with France and to obtain international diplomatic recognition.

Green March. The march by 350,000 Moroccan civilians into the Western Sahara that began on November 6, 1975, following the entry of Moroccan troops into the territory, and ended on November 13, 1975. The Green March was the culmination of the Moroccan campaign to prevent Spain from granting independence to the Western Sahara and it led to the signing of the Madrid Agreement.

Hispanidad. Movement and philosophy that promotes the unity of all Spanish-speaking peoples under the leadership of Spain.

Islamic Salvation Front (FIS). Islamic fundamentalist party in Algeria that was formed in 1988 when opposition parties were legalized.

Istiqlal party. Founded in 1943, the Istiqlal (Independence) party was the leading nationalist party in the fight for Morocco's independence from France. Since 1956, the Istiqlal party has advanced Moroccan territorial claims over the Western Sahara as well as over other neighboring countries (including parts of Algeria, Senegal, and Mali, and all of Mauritania).

Madrid (or Tripartite) Agreement or Accords. The tripartite agreement between Morocco, Mauritania, and Spain signed on November 14, 1975. Under the terms of this agreement, the administration of the Western Sahara was transferred by Spain to Morocco and Mauritania, although Spain retained sovereignty over the territory and pledged to respect the right of the Sahrawis to self-determination.

Maghreb. The western part of the Arabic-speaking world (from the Arabic word for west) that includes most of the countries of northern Africa. The Maghreb is generally defined as including Morocco, Algeria, Mauritania, and Tunisia; Libya is also often considered to be a part of the Maghreb.

Moviemento por la Autodeterminación y la Independencia del Archipélago Canario (MPAIAC). Nationalist organization that seeks to establish an independent state in the Canary Islands.

Mozambican National Resistance (MNR). Mozambican insurgent force organized by Rhodesia and South Africa in 1976 to undermine the FRELIMO government of Mozambique and counter FRELIMO support for Zimbabwean nationalist organizations. Since Zimbabwe gained its independence in 1980, South Africa has been the MNR's principal source of support, although South Africa pledged to withdraw its support for the MNR in 1984 and again in 1985.

National Liberation Front (FLN). Algerian nationalist organization created in 1954 to fight for independence from French colonial rule. The FLN became the sole ruling institution in Algeria after independence.

National Union for the Total Independence of Angola (UNITA). Angolan nationalist organization formed in 1964 by Jonas Savimbi after he broke with an earlier nationalist organization (the National Front for the Liberation of Angola). UNITA initially received most of its support from China, but since 1974 it has been supported primarily by South Africa and the United States.

Non-Aligned Movement (NAM). International organization formed in 1961 to represent the interests of countries that were not aligned with either the United States or the Soviet Union and to promote international peace and security.

Organization of African Unity (OAU). Organization formed in 1963 to promote political, economic, and military cooperation among African countries.

Parti du Progrès et du Socialisme (PPS). Moroccan communist party which was originally founded as the PCM in 1943, changed into the PLS in 1968, and then became the PPS in 1974. The PPS has consistently maintained an irredentist position on Moroccan territorial claims regarding not only the Western Sahara, but Algeria, Mauritania, Senegal, and Mali as well.

Partido de la Unión National Saharaui (PUNS). Spanish-sponsored Sahrawi organization that supported continued Spanish rule over the Western Sahara.

Partido Socialista Obrero Español (PSOE). Spanish social-democratic party.

Polisario Front (Frente Popular para la Liberación de Saguia el-Hamra y Río de Oro). Founded in May 1973 by a small group of

Sahrawi nationalists opposed to Spanish colonial rule over the Western Sahara. In 1975, the Polisario Front began receiving Algerian backing and assistance.

Popular Movement for the Liberation of Angola (MPLA). Angolan nationalist organization formed in 1956. It has received support chiefly from the Soviet Union and Cuba. Since Angola gained its independence in 1975, the government established by the MPLA has been recognized as the legitimate government of Angola by most nations and international organizations.

Sahrawi Arab Democratic Republic (SADR). The Sahrawi government established by the Polisario Front in the Western Sahara on February 27, 1975. The SADR has been recognized as an independent state by more than seventy countries and became a full member of the Organization of African Unity in 1982.

Sahrawi Popular Liberation Army (SPLA). Originally formed in 1973 to fight against Spanish colonial rule, the SPLA developed into a strong guerrilla force following the signing of the Madrid Agreement. The SPLA has received most of its military equipment, including sophisticated weaponry, from Libya (until 1983) and from Algeria. The SPLA has an estimated ten thousand to twenty thousand men under arms.

Tindouf. The Algerian town and trade center located in the southwestern part of the country about thirty miles from the borders with Morocco and the Western Sahara. After the Moroccan-Mauritanian occupation of the Western Sahara in 1975, about one hundred thousand Sahrawi refugees settled in camps near Tindouf and the Polisario Front established its political headquarters there.

Treaty of Fraternity and Concord. Agreement on political and economic cooperation signed by Algeria, Tunisia, and Mauritania in 1983. The Treaty of Fraternity and Concord was superseded by the treaty that established the Arab Maghreb Union in 1989.

Treaty of Oujda. Agreement on political and economic cooperation signed in 1984 by Morocco and Libya that provided for the withdrawal of Libyan support for the Polisario Front. The treaty was unilaterally abrogated by Morocco in 1986, but Libya did not resume its support for Polisario.

Unión del Centro Democrático (UCD). Spanish center-right party that won the democratic elections held after the death of Francisco Franco.

Union Socialist des Forces Populaires (USFP). The Moroccan opposition party created in 1972 as a result of the split in the Union Nationale des Forces Populaires. The USFP has consistently supported the annexation of the Western Sahara and has advocated even greater military measures than those taken by the Moroccan government.

Selected Bibliography

DOCUMENTS AND OFFICIAL PUBLICATIONS

International Court of Justice. *Western Sahara: Advisory Opinion of 16 October 1975.* The Hague: International Court of Justice, 1975.

Laipson, Ellen B. *Conflict and Change in North Africa: Emerging Challenges for U.S. Policy.* Washington, D.C.: Library of Congress, 1980.

____. *War in the Western Sahara: Issues for U.S. Policy.* Washington, D.C.: Library of Congress, 1981.

United Nations. "The Question of Western Sahara at the United Nations." *Decolonization,* no. 17 (October 1980).

____. "United Nations Security Council Resolution 658 (1990)," 2929th Meeting, Document S/RES/658. New York: United Nations (June 27, 1990).

United Nations Secretariat. Secretary-General. Forty-Second Session. *Question of Western Sahara: Report of the Secretary-General,* A/42/601. 1987.

____. Forty-Third Session. *The Situation Concerning Western Sahara: Report of the Secretary-General,* S/21360. 1990.

U.S. Congress. House. Committee on Foreign Affairs. *Regional Stability in Northern Africa, Report, July 8, 1980.* 96th Cong., 2d sess., 1980.

____. *U.S. Policy Toward the Conflict in the Western Sahara, Report, August 25-September 6, 1983.* 98th Cong., 1st sess., 1983.

____. *Impact of U.S. Foreign Policy in Seven African Countries, Report, August 1983.* 98th Cong., 1st sess., 1984.

____. Subcommittee on Africa. *Current Situation in the Western Sahara--1980, Hearings, December 4, 1980.* 96th Cong., 2d sess.,1981.

____. Subcommittees on Africa and on International Organizations. *U.S. Policy and the Conflict in the Western Sahara, Hearings, June 23-24, 1979.* 96th Cong., 1st sess., 1979.

____. Subcommittees on Africa and on International Security and Scientific Affairs. *Proposed Arms Sales to Morocco, Hearings, January 24 and 29, 1980.* 96th Cong., 2nd sess., 1980.

____. Subcommittees on Africa and on International Security and Scientific Affairs. *Arms Sales in North Africa and the Conflict in the Western Sahara: An Assessment of U.S. Policy, Hearings, March 25, 1981.* 97th Cong., 1st sess., 1981.

____. Subcommittees on Africa and on International Security and Scientific Affairs. *Hearings on U.S. Policy Toward the Conflict in the Western Sahara, March 15, 1983.* 98th Cong., 1st sess., 1983.

U.S. Congress. House. Committee on International Relations. Subcommittees on Africa and on International Organizations. *The Question of Self-Determination in Western Sahara, Hearings, October 12, 1977.* 95th Cong., 1st sess., 1977.

____. *Arms for Morocco? U.S. Policy Toward the Conflict in the Western Sahara, Report, January 1980.* 96th Cong., 2d sess., 1979.

U.S. Congress. Senate. Committee on Foreign Relations. *Proposed Arms Sales to Morocco, Hearings, January 30, 1980.* 96th Cong., 2d sess., 1980.

U.S. Department of Defense. Defense Intelligence Agency. *Struggle and Stalemate in the Western Sahara.* Washington, D.C.: Government Printing Office, 1979.

ARTICLES AND BOOKS

Aguirre, Jose Ramon Diego. *Historia del Sahara Español: La Verdad de una Traicion.* Madrid: Kaydeda, 1988.

Barbier, Maurice. *Le Conflit du Sahara occidental.* Paris: L'Harmattan, 1982.

Damis, John. "The Moroccan-Algerian Conflict over the Western Sahara." *Maghreb Review* 4 (1979): 49-57.

____. *Conflict in Northwest Africa: The Western Sahara Dispute.* Stanford, Calif.: Hoover Institution Press, 1983.

____. "The O.A.U. and Western Sahara." In *The O.A.U. After Twenty Years*, edited by Yassin El-Ayouty and I. William Zartman. New

York: Praeger, 1984.

___. "United States Relations with North Africa." *Current History* 84, no. 502 (May 1985): 193-96, 232-34.

___. "The Impact of the Saharan Dispute on Moroccan Foreign and Domestic Policy." In *The Political Economy of Morocco*, edited by I. William Zartman. New York: Praeger, 1987.

___. "Morocco and the Western Sahara." *Current History* 89, no. 546 (April 1990): 165-68, 184-86.

Dean, David J. *The Air Force Role in Low-Intensity Conflict*. Maxwell Air Force Base, Ala.: Air University Press, 1986.

De Piniés, Jaime. *La Descolonización del Sahara: Un Tema sin Concluir*. Madrid: Espasa-Calpe, S.A., 1990.

Entelis, John. *Algeria: The Revolution Institutionalized*. Boulder, Colo.: Westview Press, 1986.

Franck, Thomas M. "The Stealing of the Sahara." *American Journal of International Law* 70, no. 4 (October 1976): 694-721.

Friedman, Robert O. *Soviet Foreign Policy Toward the Middle East Since 1970*. 3d ed. New York: Praeger, 1982.

Gaudio, Attilio. *Le dossier du Sahara Occidental*. Paris: Maspéro, 1977.

Grimaud, Nicole. *La politique extérieure de l'Algérie*. Paris: Karthala, 1984.

___. "Sahara occidental: une issue possible?" *Maghreb/Mashrek*, no. 121 (July-September 1988): 89-98.

Harrell-Bond, Barbara. *The Struggle for the Western Sahara*. American Universities Field Staff Reports, no. 37-39 (1981).

Hassan II. *The Memoirs of King Hassan II of Morocco*. London: Macmillan, 1978.

Hodges, Tony. *Historical Dictionary of Western Sahara*. Metuchen, New Jersey: Scarecrow Press, 1982.

___. "The Origins of Sahrawi Nationalism." *Third World Quarterly* 5, no. 1 (January 1983): 28-57.

___. *Western Sahara: The Roots of a Desert War*. Westport, Conn.: Lawrence Hill, 1983.

___. "At Odds with Self-Determination: The United States and Western Sahara." In *African Crisis Areas and U.S. Foreign Policy*, edited by Gerald J. Bender, James S. Coleman, and Richard L. Sklar. Berkeley and Los Angeles, Calif.: University of California Press, 1985.

Hultman, Tami. *Democratic Arab Republic of the Sahara*. Dobbs

Ferry, New York: Oceana Publishers, 1978.

Laipson, Ellen B. "Heating Up the Sahara War." *The Washington Quarterly* (Winter 1982): 199-202.

Lawless, Richard, and Monahan, Laila., eds. *War and Refugees: The Western Sahara Conflict.* London and New York: Pinter Publishers, 1987.

Lewis, William H. "Morocco and the Western Sahara." *Current History* 84, no. 502 (May 1985): 213-16.

____. "War in the Western Sahara." In *The Lesson of Recent Wars in the Third World, Vol. I: Approaches and Case Studies*, edited by Stephanie G. Neumann and Robert E. Harkavy. Lexington, Mass.: Lexington Books, 1985.

Lippert, Anne. "Emergence or Submergence of a Potential State." *Africa Today* 24, no. 1 (Spring 1977): 41-60.

____. "The Human Costs of War in Western Sahara." *Africa Today* 34, no. 3 (Fall 1987): 47-60.

Markham, James M. "King Hassan's Quagmire." *The New York Times Magazine*, April 27, 1980, 116, 118, 120-25.

Mercer, John. *Spanish Sahara.* London: Allen and Unwin, 1976.

____. *The Sahrawis of Western Sahara.* London: Minority Rights Group, 1979.

Miske, Ahmed-Baba. *Front Polisario: l'âme d'un peuple.* Paris: Editions Rupture, 1978.

Mortimer, Robert A. "Western Sahara: The Diplomatic Perspectives." *Africa Report* 23, no. 2 (March-April 1978): 10-14.

____. "The Politics of Reassurance in Algeria." *Current History* 84, no. 502 (May 1985): 201-4, 228-29.

____. "Maghreb Matters." *Foreign Policy*, no. 76 (Fall 1989): 160-75.

____. "Algeria after the Explosion." *Current History* 89, no. 546 (April 1990): 161-64, 180-82.

Naylor, Phillip C. "Spain and France and the Decolonization of Western Sahara: Parity and Paradox, 1975-87." *Africa Today* 34, no. 3 (Fall 1987): 7-16.

Neuberger, Benyamin. *National Self-Determination in Postcolonial Africa.* Boulder, Colo.: Lynne Rienner Publishers, 1986.

Parker, Richard B. *North Africa: Regional Tensions and Strategic Concerns.* New York: Praeger, 1987.

Pazzanita, Anthony G. "Legal Aspects of Membership in the Organization of African Unity: The Case of the Western Sahara." *Case Western Reserve Journal of International Law* 17, no. 1

(Winter 1985): 123-58.

____. "Legal Aspects of the (Western Sahara) Dispute," *Bulletin of the Association of Concerned Africa Scholars*, no. 23 (Spring 1988): 4-5.

Porter, Bruce. *The U.S.S.R. and Third World Conflicts*. New York: Cambridge University Press, 1984.

Price, David Lynn. *The Western Sahara*. Washington Papers, no. 63. Beverly Hills, Calif., and London: Sage Publications, 1979.

Rezette, Robert. *The Western Sahara and the Frontiers of Morocco*. Paris: Nouvelles Editions Latines, 1975.

Romero, Gerardo Mariñas. *El Sahara y la Legion*. Madrid: San Martin, S.L., 1988.

Rothberg, Morris. *The U.S.S.R. and Africa: New Dimensions of Soviet Global Power*. Miami, Fla.: Advanced International Institute-University of Miami, 1980.

Solarz, Stephen J. "Arms for Morocco?" *Foreign Affairs* 58, no. 2. (Winter 1979-1980): 278-99.

Tessler, Mark. *Politics in Morocco: The Monarch, the War, and the Opposition*. American Universities Field Staff Reports, no. 47 (1981).

____. *Continuity and Change in Moroccan Politics*. Universities Field Staff Reports, nos. 1-2 (1984).

____. *Explaining the "Surprises" of King Hassan II: The Linkage Between Domestic and Foreign Policy in Morocco*. Universities Field Staff Reports, nos. 38-40 (1986).

Thompson, Virginia, and Adloff, Richard. *The Western Saharans: Background to Conflict*. London: Croom Helm and Totowa, New Jersey: Barnes and Noble Books, 1980.

Trout, Frank E. *Morocco's Saharan Frontiers*. Geneva: Droz Publishers, 1969.

Villar, Francisco. *El proceso de autodeterminación del Sahara*. Valencia: Torres, 1982.

Volman, Daniel. *A Continent Besieged: Foreign Military Activities in Africa Since 1975*. Washington, D.C.: Institute for Policy Studies, 1980.

____. "Africa's Rising Status in American Defense Policy." *Journal of Modern African Studies* 22, no. 1 (March 1984): 143-51.

Volman, Daniel, and Zoubir, Yahia. "Solution Needed for Western Sahara." *New African*, no. 261 (June 1989): 38.

____. "Back to Battle." *New African*, no. 270 (March 1990): 19.

Ware, Lewis B. *Decolonization and the Global Alliance in the Arab Maghreb: The Case of Spanish Sahara.* Maxwell Air Force Base, Ala.: Air University Institute for Professional Development, 1975.

Wenger, Martha. "Reagan Stakes Morocco in Sahara Struggle." *MERIP Reports*, no. 105 (May 1982): 22-26.

Wilson, Carlos, and Zoubir, Yahia. "Western Sahara: A Foreign Policy Success Waiting to Happen." *TransAfrica Forum* 6, nos. 3 and 4 (Spring-Summer 1989): 27-39.

Wright, Claudia. "Journey to Marrakesh: U.S.-Moroccan Security Relations." *International Security* 7, no. 4 (Spring 1983): 163-79.

Zartman, I. William. *Ripe for Resolution: Conflict and Intervention in Africa.* Oxford and New York: Oxford University Press, 1985.

____. "Foreign Relations of North Africa." In *Annals of the American Academy of Political and Social Science*, edited by Gerald J. Bender. Newbury Park, Calif.: Sage Publications, 1987.

Zoubir, Yahia. "Soviet Policy toward the Western Sahara Conflict." *Africa Today* 34, no. 3 (Fall 1987): 17-32.

____. "Soviet Policy toward the Maghreb." *Arab Studies Quarterly* 9, no. 4 (Fall 1987: 399-421.

____. "L'URSS dans le Grand Maghreb: une stratégie équilibrée et une approche pragmatique." In *Maghreb: Les Années de Transition*, edited by Bassma Kodmani-Darwish and May Chartouni-Dubarry. Paris: Institut Français des Relations Internationales/ Masson, 1990.

____. "The Western Sahara Conflict: Regional and International Dimensions." *Journal of Modern African Studies* 28, no. 2 (June 1990): 225-43.

Zunes, Stephen. "Nationalism and Non-Alignment: The Non-Ideology of the Polisario." *Africa Today* 34, no. 3 (Fall 1987): 33-46.

____. "The United States and Morocco: The Sahara War and Regional Interest." *Arab Studies Quarterly* 9, no. 4 (Fall 1987): 422-41.

Index

About the Contributors

MERVYN M. DYMALLY is former Democratic Congressman from California and chairman of the House Subcommittee on Africa.

ROBERT A. MORTIMER is a professor of Political Science at Haverford College. He is the author of *The Third World Coalition in International Politics* (1984) and the coauthor of *Politics and Society in Contemporary Africa* (1988). He has also written articles for *Foreign Policy* and *Current History*.

PHILLIP C. NAYLOR is an associate professor of History at Merrimack College and a faculty associate at the Center for Middle Eastern Studies at Harvard University. He was previously a research associate at the African Studies Center at Boston University. His published works include articles in *Africa Today* and *Africana Journal*. He is currently preparing the second edition of the *Historical Dictionary of Algeria* for the Scarecrow Press series and a book on the postcolonial relationship between Algeria and France. He is also coediting a book with John Entelis titled *Algeria: State and Society in Transition*.

RICHARD B. PARKER, a retired career Foreign Service Officer, was U.S. ambassador to Algeria, Lebanon, and Morocco in the Ford and Carter administrations. He is currently a fellow at the Woodrow Wilson Center of the Smithsonian Institution, writing a book on miscalculation in the Middle East. His published works include *North Africa: Regional Tensions and Strategic Concerns* (1984 and 1987) and two books on Islamic architecture.

BETH A. PAYNE is an attorney specializing in international law and human rights. She has worked and studied in North Africa and has written extensively on refugee issues, humanitarian law, and the rights of children. She is currently an attorney with the National Center for Prosection of Child Abuse.

ANTHONY G. PAZZANITA received a B.A. degree from Franklin and Marshall College, a J.D. degree from Case Western University, and a M.A. degree in International Relations from the University of Pennsylvania. He is the author of "Legal Aspects of Membership in the Organization of African Unity: The Case of the Western Sahara," which appeared in the *Case Western Reserve Journal of International Law*.

DANIEL VOLMAN received his Ph.D. degree from the University of California, Los Angeles in 1991. His published works include *A Continent Besieged: Foreign Military Activities in Africa Since 1975* (1980) and articles on U.S. military policy in Africa in *The Journal of Modern African Studies*, *New African*, *Newsday*, *The New York Times*, and other publications.

YAHIA H. ZOUBIR was an assistant professor of International Studies in the Washington Semester Program and in the School of International Service at The American University in Washington, D.C. He is the author of numerous articles on Soviet policy in North Africa and the Middle East and on the Western Sahara conflict, which have appeared in the *Arab Studies Quarterly*, *Africa Today*, *The Journal of Modern African Studies*, and as chapters in several books. He is currently teaching at the American Graduate School of Business in Montreux, Switzerland.

STEPHEN ZUNES is executive director of the Institute for a New Middle East Policy. He taught previously at Ithaca College, Cornell University, Temple University, and Whitman College, and received his Ph.D. degree from Cornell University in 1990. His published works include articles on U.S. policy in the Middle East and North Africa in *Africa Today*, *Arab Studies Quarterly*, *The Journal of Palestine Studies*, the *Scandinavian Journal for Development Alternatives*, and *The Christian Science Monitor*. He is currently preparing a book on the